WORK AND ORGANIZATIONAL I
EUROPEAN PERSPECTI

WORK AND ORGANIZATIONAL PSYCHOLOGY

European Perspectives

Selected Papers from the First North-West European
Conference on the Psychology of Work and Organization,
Nijmegen, The Netherlands, March 28-30, 1983

edited by
A.M. Koopman-Iwema and R.A. Roe

 SWETS & ZEITLINGER   LISSE
1984

CIP-GEGEVENS KONINKLIJKE BIBLIOTHEEK, DEN HAAG

Work

Work and organizational psychology : European perspectives
: selected papers from the First North-West European
Conference on the Psychology of Work and Organization,
Nijmegen, the Netherlands, March 28-30, 1983 / ed. by A.M.
Koopman-Iwema and R.A. Roe ; [with contributions by
J.H.T.H. Andriessen ... et al.]. - Lisse : Swets &
Zeitlinger. - Ill. - (Publications of the Netherlands
Institute of Psychologists (NIP) ; 7)
Met lit. opg.
ISBN 90-265-0593-0
SISO 316 UDC 159.9:[331+65.01]
Trefw.: arbeidspsychologie / organisatiepsychologie.

© 1984 Nederlands Instituut van Psychologen, Amsterdam
    and
    Swets & Zeitlinger B.V., Lisse

ISBN 90 265 0593 0

CONTENTS

INTRODUCTION

A.M. Koopman-Iwema and R.A. Roe

The field of work and organization has always been of major concern within European psychology. Starting with scholars like Münsterberg, Lahy, Moede, Heymans, Christiaans, Baumgarten, and Muscio, psychologists from the European continent have studied problems with respect to personnel selection, training, work design, interpersonal relationships, organizational change, etc. and have produced many techniques and practical solutions. Throughout the years they have delivered significant contributions to the discipline (e.g. Baumgarten-Tramer, 1971; Hofstede & Kassem, 1974; De Wolff & Shimmin, 1976; De Wolff et al., 1981).

Seen from an international perspective, the European study of work behaviour and organizational functioning has always shown a more or less distinct character. One of it's features is the tendency to stress fundamental issues in methodology and theory. Much attention is paid to conceptual as well as measurement questions, considerable efforts are spent on the development of comprehensive theoretical systems rather than of isolated hypotheses. And beside aspects of overt behaviour that can be measured by objective techniques, subjective experiences are given due attention too, using introspective verbalization techniques. In these respects, one discerns the roots that European psychology of work and organization has in philosophy as well as in the natural sciences.

Another distinction stems from the societal scene. Both the structure

1

and culture of European society, with its specific history, are reflected in the scientific study of work and organization. The educational
system, structure of industry and business, the role of the government,
the typical labor relations and industrial legislation, the demographical
and economical conditions, they all influence the types of problems that
are studied, as well as the way in which they are approached. Of course,
influences are also visible in the very nature of the positions and
roles that are assigned to work and organization psychologists, both
as researchers and consultants.

Finally, European psychology of work and organization is characterized by a great deal of diversity, so aptly expressed in the title
'Conflicts and contradictions' of the recent book by De Wolff et al.
(1981). Societal differences between the European countries, as well
as distinctions between schools of thought, more or less fostered by
language barriers, underly this phenomenon. It should be noted, however, that the growing interest in the exchange of ideas and in research cooperation among psychologists from the various countries,
may bridge existing gaps and produce more congruence in the future.

The present-day situation in Western Europe's work and organizational
psychology is determined to a large degree by a number of trends that
have become manifest in recent times.

First of all, there is the shift in *labor relations* into the direction of a growing workers' participation and co-determination. All
Western-European countries have established laws that give workers a
say in the determination of company policies, especially in domains
that are of direct consequence for their employment, the nature of
their work, and their safety, health, and well-being. Several forms of
industrial democracy, ranging from job consultation to Works' Councils
and workers' cooperations, have developed and continue to draw a great
deal of attention (e.g. Windmuller, 1977; IDE, 1980).

Secondly, there is the trend towards *humanization* of work, with its
increasing stress on qualitative, immaterial working conditions and outcomes apart from the physical aspects that have been of importance
since the early years of industry. Most countries in Western Europe
have by now replaced their original laws and regulations on safety and

health (covering matters like the use of dangerous materials, standards for technical equipment, etc. on the one hand, and provisions for company health care on the other hand) by new legislation with a much broader scope. The central notion has become that of 'quality of working life' (Davis & Cherns, 1972; Cooper & Mumford, 1979) which encompasses mental health and well-being as well as physical health and safety. Other aspects of the work system are covered now, like 'the organizing of work, the arrangement of work places, and the stipulation of production and work methods' (e.g. ILO, 1979).

Thirdly, there is the rapid introduction of *new technologies* in organizations, raising questions with regard to its effects on employment, qualifications, working conditions, etc., as well as its opportunities for organizational innovation and improvement of the quality of working life (e.g. Lucas et al., 1980). Legislation in this realm is scarce; in some countries employers and unions have set up 'automation contracts' at the company level, garanteeing workers' participation in decision-making, and specifying conditions with respect to employment, job content, remuneration, etc.

Finally, there is, as a result of the *economic recession*, a growing interest in unemployment effects, and in alternative forms of work that may lead to a more even spread of employment throughout the population, and at the same time enhance economic initiative and flexibility. New arrangements for working time and payment are set up, plans to stimulate small enterprises and organizations within the 'informal sector' are heavily discussed, especially in the last few years. All these ideas have important aspects from a psychological point of view.

The kinds of activities that work and organizational psychologists are engaged in, and the questions that are addressed in their research, are exemplified in this book. The 16 chapters that follow are based on selected contributions to the 'First North-West European Conference on the Psychology of Work and Organization', held in Nijmegen, the Netherlands on March, 28-30, 1983. The aim of this conference was to reestablish the tradition of the former Psychotechnical Conferences and to bring psychologists from all European countries together. Several papers from the total number of more than 60 have been (or will be) published independently. It was considered worthwhile to publish a more or less representative collection of papers in one volume, in order to show colleagues and other interested professionals the actual situation within this field of psychology.

Section I of this book has been composed with the objective to supply an overview of both professional and scientific developments in the countries that were involved in the organization of the conference: the United Kingdom, the Federal Republic of Germany, Belgium (Flanders) and the Netherlands. The four chapters were written by leading scholars from each of these countries: *Shimmin, Horney, Selis* and *De Wolff.*

The remainder of the book is devoted to research and consultation projects. *Section II* starts with the domain of 'work and non-work'. *Claes et al.* presents data from an international study on work values, while *Lagrou et al.* deal with the empirical relationship between work values and attitudes towards unemployed people. *Senior* and *Naylor* address unemployment more directly, describing experiences with a cooperative skills exchange network.

Section III contains contributions on the relationship between aspects of the work situation and individual work behaviour and outcomes. *Maasen* shows how in successive automation projects at a bank, the attention has shifted from ergonomic problems in display work towards participative systems development. *Ten Horn* investigates how task characteristics are perceived and reacted to by individual workers, taking into account the possible moderator effect of Maslow-type needs. *Hohner* focusses on room for control in the work situation and on internal-external control expectations of the individual. He considers the implications of research findings for job redesign and personnel selection. In the chapter by *Winnubst et al.* individual reactions to work stressors are studied - here the type A behaviour pattern serves as a moderator variable.

Section IV is devoted to studies on industrial relations. Overview data on workers participation from a multi-national study are presented by *Andriessen* and *Drenth.* Next, *Koopman-Iwema* and *Flechsenberger* compare formal position and perceived influence of the Works' Council in the Netherlands and Western-Germany. A study on organizational preconditions for successful job consultation is described by *Kuipers et al.*

Finally, two contributions on macro-organizational topics are presented in *Section V*. One of these, written by *Nauta*, deals with the concepts of organizational climate and culture, and with cultural differences established among students in two departments of an educational institution. The other, by *Wallis*, describes an organizational development project in psychiatric hospitals.

REFERENCES

Baumgarten-Tramer, F., Chronologie der Entwicklung der Arbeitswissenschaft und der angewandten Psychologie. Zeitschrift für Arbeitswissenschaft, 1971, 8/9, 165-182.

Cooper, C.L. & E. Mumford (Eds.), The quality of working life in Western and Eastern Europe. London: Associated Business Press, 1979.

Davis, L.E. & A.B. Cherns, The quality of working life. New York: The Free Press, 1975.

Hofstede, G. & M.S. Kassem (Eds.), European contributions to organization theory. Assen: Van Gorcum, 1974.

IDE - International Research Group, Industrial democracy in Europe. London: Oxford University Press, 1980.

ILO (International Labor Office), Optimisation of the working environment. Geneva: ILO, 1979. Occupational safety and Health Series No. 43.

Lucas, H.C., F.F. Land & K. Supper (Eds.), The information systems environment. Amsterdam: North-Holland Publ. Co., 1980.

Windmuller, J.P., Industrial democracy in international perspective. Philadelphia: The Annuals of the American Academy of Political and Social Science, 1979.

Wolff, Ch.J. de & S. Shimmin, The psychology of work in Europe: a review of a profession. Personnel Psychology, 1976, 29, 175-195.

Wolff, Ch.J. de, S. Shimmin & M. de Montmollin (Eds.), Conflicts and contradictions: work psychologists in Europe. London: Academic Press, 1981.

I
TRENDS AND PERSPECTIVES

1. THE PSYCHOLOGY OF WORK AND ORGANIZATION IN THE UNITED KINGDOM

S. Shimmin

INTRODUCTION

The psychology of work and organization in the United Kingdom is known generally as 'occupational psychology', an unfamiliar term outside psychological circles in Britain, Australia and New Zealand. It was adopted by the British Psychological Society in place of 'industrial psychology', some forty or so years ago, to show that psychologists plied their trade in non-industrial as well as industrial organizations, and it has persisted ever since. The very ambiguity of the label may account for its continuing use as it embraces academics and practitioners across a wide spectrum whose scientific and professional interests are concerned with the significance of, and the impact on, people of work and organizations. As in other countries, the traditional core of industrial psychology, represented by psychometrics and concentration on selection, training and vocational guidance, has given way to a much wider field which includes the study of organizational structures and processes. 'Occupational psychology', in the United Kingdom thus corresponds broadly with what is known elsewhere as industrial and organizational psychology and it is in this sense that the term is used in this chapter.

What follows are personal impressions, rather than a definitive or historical account of the development of the subject, references to which can be found elsewhere (De Wolff & Shimmin, 1976; De Wolff, Shimmin & De Montmollin, 1981). The issues to be addressed come under three headings: questions of identity, concern for relevance and effectiveness, and constraints and opportunities, together with an assessment of future trends.

First, however, to put these observations in context, some background data are presented on the numbers of psychologists specialising in this area and their fields of employment. Table 1 shows total membership of the British Psychological Society and the proportion belonging to the Occupational Psychology Section and the Division of Occupational Psychology. The difference between these categories of membership is that the Section is open to all with scientific and/or professional interests in the subject, whereas the Division, formed in 1971, has entry requirements signifying professional competence in the practice of Occupational Psychology. It should be noted, however, that neither membership of the Society nor of its Sections and Divisions is mandatory for psychologists, so the figures in Table 1 under-represent the numbers qualified and in practice.

Table 1. Occupational psychologists in the British Psychological Society

Year	B.P.S. Total Membership (excluding student subscribers, foreign affiliates)	Occupational Psychology Section	Division
1941	811	117	-
1965	3,587	381	-
1972	4,555	488	129
1982	8,721	570	267

In comparison with other Sections of the society, the Occupational Psychology Section is now the largest, closely followed by the Education Section with 554 members. The largest of the Divisions, however, is the Division of Clinical Psychology (1,242 members), followed by the Division of Educational and Child Psychology (623 members).

A survey carried out among members of the Division of Occupational

10

Psychology in 1982 showed that they are employed mainly in universities (27%), private commercial firms (19%), departments of central government (16%), or are self-employed (16%). Only a very small proportion work in public corporations (5%) or local government (3%) and, as employers of occupational psychologists, trade unions are conspicuous by their absence. In terms of their activities, teaching, research and consultancy predominate, with a focus increasingly on social and organizational, rather than individual, problems, although occupational guidance and counselling figure among the major sources of income of those in full-time private practice.

QUESTIONS OF IDENTITY

Enlargement of the domain, from the study of individual people and individual jobs, and how to achieve an effective match between them to include group processes, organizational structure and development, the effects of technological change and of legislation governing employment relationships and so on, means that occupational psychology has no clear boundaries. These now overlap with those of other branches of psychology (e.g. social and clinical) and other disciplines (e.g. industrial sociology) and give rise to certain problems of identity.

Within conventional university psychology departments and within the psychology community as a whole, occupational psychology is a minority interest. As perceived by the scientific establishment it tends to have a low status, perhaps more than other areas of application, because the active involvement of occupational psychologists in industry and other organizations is not understood. Within business and management schools and in other multi-disciplinary departments, the subject is often viewed more favourably, precisely because of its applicability. The distinction between occupational psychology, as studied and used by non-psychologists, and as represented by those who are professionally qualified in the subject is further complicated by the absence of a clearly defined career structure for occupational psychologists. Many work as members of cross-disciplinary teams or in positions which could legitimately be filled by people from different backgrounds (e.g. personnel management).

It is therefore an open question as to whether one should define
the field in terms of the qualifications and employment of professional
psychologists or as represented by the wider sphere in which psychological knowledge is put to use by non-specialists. For most of the time
this is not a problem for occupational psychologists, whatever their
job titles, who carry on their work on a day-to-day basis to the best
of their abilities. But it comes to the fore in situations where they
confront members of the scientific establishment who regard them as
less than equals; also when they meet as professionals to consider
matters such as course content, curriculum development and the training
of occupational psychologists.

The British Psychological Society has recently accepted in principle
the necessity of establishing a legal register of psychologists in the
United Kingdom. Questions of definition, such as whether ergonomics is
an integral part of occupational psychology or a separate sub-specialism,
and the extent to which narrow or broad-based training programmes
should be recognized as leading to professional competence in the field
will therefore have to be considered in the context of the registration
issue. In the long-run this may help to establish a stronger identity
among occupational psychologists, but in the short-term it may well
increase personal dilemmas about specialist versus generalist activities.

At present, whether one takes a broad or narrow view of the domain
of occupational psychology, it is still small enough for those at the
centre and at the periphery to be able to envisage it as a whole, i.e.
to know by name and reputation, if not personally, the key figures,
the main centres of teaching and research and the employing organizations where occupational psychologists are to be found in any number,
e.g. the civil service. Although there will not be complete congruence
between individual delineations because of differences in age, experience,
opportunities to meet other professionals and so on, neither will they
diverge completely. Most members of the profession have direct and indirect links with colleagues, who may not share their particular expertise, through attending conferences and through membership of the
Occupational Psychology Division and Section of the B.P.S.

Perhaps the greatest gap is likely to be found between shared perceptions of academics, on the one hand, and groups of practitioners, on the other. The British system of external examinerships, whereby candidates' performances are assessed not only by faculty members of their own institutions but also by an academic specialist in that field from another institution, is one of a number of procedures that create networks through which academics and researchers are continually exchanging information about people and activities. Others in this category include the refereeing of research proposals and articles submitted to professional journals which likewise promote a process of constant definition and re-definition of the domain.

Practitioners in the civil service, industry and private consultancy firms also belong to formal and informal networks which shape their views of the field, but these do not overlap with those of the academics in most instances. Furthermore, as practitioners are thin on the ground in both the public and private sectors they are often working in isolation from fellow psychologists. This can make them feel vulnerable and lacking in support from their academic counterparts, leading them to identify more with their professional roles as, for example, management trainers or organization development specialists than with occupational psychology per se.

CONCERN FOR RELEVANCE AND EFFECTIVENESS

Concern about their professional standing, public image and the relevance of their activities has dominated discussion among British occupational psychologists for several years. Currently, at all points of the employment spectrum they are expressing their desire to participate in, and to be seen as contributing to, the handling of socially relevant problems, such as the impact of the economic recession on individuals and communities. They are also frustrated by their failure to influence policy makers at the highest level, with an increasing awareness that their training as scientists does not prepare them to act politically. Occupational psychologists do undertake research, provide data for, submit evidence to and are consulted by those whose job it is to brief government ministers and chief executives about the context and implementation of policies. They are not, however, among the professionals from whose ranks boards of directors, parliamentary select committees, and even the cabinet itself, seek specialist advisers with whom they will be in regular contact. In other words, the psychologists' contributions are made at least one step removed from the seats of power and, as such, can be discounted by the decision-makers if it suits them.

A related factor is that psychologists are accustomed to operating at a micro-level rather than at a macro-level, which puts them at a disadvantage when seeking to influence those who think and deal in terms of aggregates. This is exemplified by the comments of a professor of industrial relations who stated that psychologists clearly have a contribution to make in explaining why some individuals do not conform to work-place norms (for example in refusing to join a union), but that they have little to offer in the institutional context of collective bargaining or the settlement of industrial disputes. Although some would challenge this assertion, there is no doubt that occupational psychologists are not perceived as front-line candidates in appointing mediators, arbitrators or conciliators, unlike labour lawyers, economists and industrial relations specialists. Thus, while there is an established tradition of industrial relations research by British social and occupational psychologists, they have not become known or experienced as practitioners in this sphere.

To some extent this situation may be attributed to the difficulty of projecting a clear image of a profession whose members engage in diffuse activities that are not exclusive to occupational psychologists. It also reflects the under-representation of occupational psychology in many first degree programmes in psychology. Outside the small number of academic departments which specialise in the subject, those who teach undergraduate students of psychology have usually little first-hand experience of outside organizations and industry and are uneasy about direct involvement in such institutions. Consequently, a lot of students are either unaware of the challenge and possibilities provided by the field of work and organizations or they perceive it as a questionable sphere of activity, on both ideological and scientific grounds.

Efforts to overcome these deficiencies focus at present on proposals to improve professional training. It is recognized that the effectiveness of occupational psychologists cannot be judged by one set of criteria and that it is important to distinguish between effectiveness of research, in terms of contributing to the stock of knowledge, and effectiveness of application, in terms of assistance with practical problems and client's satisfaction. Training, therefore, cannot be confined to what is learned in academic settings.

The Training Committee of the Division of Occupational Psychology, membership of which signifies professional competence as a practitioner, has identified three stages in the development of this competence:
- the first subject-based, the second problem-based and the third concerned with the management of application. An undergraduate course in psychology is the usual education for the first stage. Problem-based learning, i.e. the second stage of development, is seen as essentially post-graduate, involving working on problems in the real world under the supervision of an experienced mentor. Key features of this stage are learning to identify problems, to compromise, to interpret inadequate data and to work in multi-disciplinary teams. The third stage, concerned with management aspects, is expected to take place in the work situation where, through experience of working with others, occupational psychologists will develop social and negotiating skills, learn how to compete for scarce resources, direct expert effort and so on. To improve the quality and extent of professional training in the second and third stages, the Committee proposes that candidates for Divisional membership must be registered for at least three years as a 'probationer', attached to a mentor or adviser appointed by the Division (preferably an employee of the same organization), and must demonstrate that they have had experience of, and acquired the requisite problem-solving skills in at least three areas of professional activity. To this end, they must attend a professional interview conducted by two members of the Division.

These proposals are still under discussion, but they constitute an advance on present practice in which the entry requirements for the Division do not specify sufficiently the range of practical experience and skills expected of members. They also show the increased emphasis which is being placed on working with and learning from other people, and the need to diagnose and seek to solve problems rather than to present packaged solutions. In one of the many discussion papers designed to stimulate debate on the future of the subject, Ian Howarth and Wendy Pritchard (1981) endorsed George Miller's (1969) plea to 'give psychology away' as a means of reducing the political problems inherent in collaborative ventures. They point out that, in so doing, occupational psychologists become less threatening to non-psychologists than they might otherwise appear, an aspect of professional practice which is apt to be overlooked. One of the disadvantages of psychology, in comparison with other social sciences, is that many lay people associate it with clinical assessment and treatment and fear that, in any encounter with a psychologist, they will be subject to probing assessment. For this reason, some occupational psychologists prefer to work under more functional titles, e.g. management consultant, research officer, training and development adviser.

CONSTRAINTS AND OPPORTUNITIES

The consequences of the economic depression for occupational psychologists are many and varied. For those who teach it, there is the problem of making occupational psychology credible and relevant. As Brotherton (1982) observed: 'It is not easy for students to be taught theories of organizational development at times when they see around them organizations contracting unevenly and often without rationality. It is not easy to present theories of job satisfaction when students know that there are over 3 million people officially without work in the country. It is not easy to lecture on selection when they have evidence that for every job vacancy there are at least likely to be 90 potential applicants.' Furthermore, in some institutions, the teachers themselves may be anxious about their own continued employment in the face of reduced expenditure on higher education by central and local government.

Academics and researchers in the United Kingdom are now painfully aware of their dependence upon governmental policy and funding. Research in occupational psychology is largely financed, directly or indirectly, by central government and its agencies. Late in 1981, the Secretary of State for Education and Science queried the need for the Social Science

Research Council, which has been the major source of financial support for psychological research, and ordered an independent review of its activities by Lord Rothschild. Although reprieved by the latter's report, the S.S.R.C. has subsequently had its budget reduced to a level which limits severely the amount of research it can support and the number of studentships available for postgraduate training.

Financial constraints of this kind and resulting retrenchment have created an academic crisis, of varying degrees of severity in different centres, which is not conducive to new developments. There have never been many career posts in research in occupational psychology and, in in present circumstances, those that do exist (e.g. in the Social and Applied Psychology Unit at Sheffield) become all the more valuable and important.

On the other hand, there are also opportunities arising directly from the recession. The Government is introducing a Youth Training Scheme for unemployed school leavers, more comprehensive than previous schemes, in the design and monitoring of which occupational psychologists are active. Research on the effects of unemployment continues, as well as counselling and short courses for those who lose their jobs. Occupational psychologists are also engaged in examining the demands made on people by new technologies, in job design projects in this sphere and in related research on training procedures. Linked with this is an increased interest in vocational guidance and preparation in the context of technological and social change and greater involvement in the training of student counsellors and careers officers.

Some professional activities of occupational psychologists are affected, directly or indirectly, by a proliferation of legislation relating to employment in recent years, e.g. concerning health and safety at work, race relations, sex discrimination, trade union and labour relations, to which must be added the effect of E.E.C. directives. It has been left to individuals to alert the profession to the consequences of, for example, the Employment Agencies Act, intended to prevent the unauthorized recruitment of nationals for overseas service, which requires that occupational psychologists are licensed by the Department of Employment if they operate any kind of service for placing people with employers. Likewise, the intricacies of unlawful indirect discrimination on the grounds of race or sex have been drawn to the attention of other occupational psychologists by those who have been used as expert witnesses in such cases. Comparatively little has been done by psychologists in the area of equal opportunities, but the British Psychological Society has now established a standing committee to look at the implications of the legislation for professional practice and research.

The position of women in employment, their career aspirations and opportunities and, more fundamentally, the underlying social values and attitudes which shape their domestic and employment roles, education and achievement, is a live issue, quite apart from its legal aspect. So too is stress, although with rising levels of unemployment it is the absence or loss of work rather than the stressful characteristics of occupations which is becoming the focus of attention.

In short, despite the limits on resources, occupational psychologists are making a contribution to contemporary social problems, albeit on a small-scale. Fundamental and innovative action research is being conducted largely by individuals or small groups of perhaps only two or three people who, together, are not sufficient to form a 'critical mass' that will impinge on public awareness. How to achieve the latter is now regarded as of prime importance by many members of the profession.

WHAT OF THE FUTURE?

The directions in which both occupational psychology and occupational psychologists will move in the future are not easy to discern. For some time the domain has been in a state of flux and it is likely to remain so for the next few years. The current social and intellectual climate is one in which many, formerly unquestioned, assumptions are being challenged, e.g. the notion that science is value-free. There is a significant body of opinion that attaches more importance to the exploration and study of meaning than to ever more refined methodology and measurement. In the context of discussions about the social responsibilities of scientists, linked with questions of on whose behalf they are working and to what end, many occupational psychologists experience conflict. They subscribe to humanitarian values and wish to use their skills and knowledge to promote the well-being of others, but feel trapped by working in an environment in which the state of the pound is taken as a more important indicator than the state of the people.

If occupational psychologists are to contribute to a more humane and less economic view of work and organizations, they cannot act in isolation, but will have to establish effective communications and exchange with economists, politicians, managers, accountants, engineers and technologists, and participate in design and policy formulations. Now that many of these other specialists are recognizing the psychological dimensions of their activities, opportunities for such interactions are on the increase. New developments like information technology that cut across the conventional boundaries of academic disciplines also highlight the need to learn how to collaborate effectively with others. This has implications for professional training. It is important that occupational psychologists have the confidence and competence in their knowledge and skills to feel at ease in a multi-disciplinary context and to appreciate what and how to contribute to it. Furthermore, that they acquire the political sophistication to maintain their positions and promote their aims and ideals in the face of power struggles and competing and conflicting loyalties.

Although the trends outlined in this chapter indicate some tensions and uncertainties within the profession, as well as reflect the long-standing debate about science and application found in all branches of psychology, occupational psychologists are showing a sense of realism which augures well for the future. Emphasis is being placed on learning to collaborate with other people in joint approaches to the diagnosis and solution of problems. To the extent that occupational psychologists are developing the ability and the will to do this, the long-term prospects are hopeful.

REFERENCES

Brotherton, C., Occupational Psychology at Nottingham. B.P.S. Occupational Psychology Newsletter, 1982, 9, 6-7.

Howarth, I. & W. Pritchard, Development of Occupational Psychology. B.P.S. Occupational Psychology Newsletter, 1981, 7, 22-24.

Miller, G.A., Psychology as a means of promoting human welfare. American Psychologist, 1969, 24, 1063-1075.

Wolff, C.J. de & C. Shimmin, The psychology of work in Europe: A review of a profession. Personnel Psychology, 1976, 29, 175-195.

Wolff, C.J. de, S. Shimmin & M. de Montmollin, Conflicts and contradictions: Work psychologists in Europe. London: Academic Press, 1981.

2. THE PSYCHOLOGY OF WORK AND ORGANIZATION IN THE FEDERAL REPUBLIC OF GERMANY

H.-L. Horney

INTRODUCTION

Let us start with a glimpse at two simple but revealing as well as informative figures: in January 1983 H. Heckhausen, former President of
the German Society of Psychology, published two statements in which he
mentioned clinical psychology 21 times, and work and organizational
psychology 14 times (Heckhausen, 1983a, 1983b). This ratio of 21 to 14
is astonishing: never before did work and organizational psychology
attain such a level of importance. Hence, one might wonder what kind of
reasons are at the bottom of it.

Before supplying answers to this question, a general remark ought to
be given. Perspectives - as mentioned in the title of this chapter -
need a definite position, a point of view from which those perspectives
unfold. This chapter then, is based on personal impressions stemming
from experiences in teaching, acting as an industrial psychologist, and
being a member of the Board of the Section of Work and Organizational
Psychology within the Professional Association of German Psychologists
(Berufsverband Deutscher Psychologen BDP).

Three major subjects relating to West German work and organizational
psychology will be mentioned in detail:
1. professional position, legal aspects, and perspectives;
2. education and research;
3. current trends and perspectives.
General facts and figures will not be presented here. They have been

summarized elsewhere (Horney, 1980, 1981; also Heckhausen, 1983a).

PROFESSIONAL POSITION, LEGAL ASPECTS, AND PERSPECTIVES

The professional position of work and organizational psychology and its perspectives are characterized by complexity and tension. Some selected actual problems may exemplify this.

Since 35 years German psychologists are asking for statutory protection governing the practice of psychology. Although psychologists in Germany are examined by Official (State) Boards of Examiners and the title 'Diplom-Psychologe' is protected by law (since 1941), their position is rather weak. Especially clinical psychologists are forced to fight with medical practitioners, compulsory sick funds, etc. for official recognition, adequate fees, etc. According to a decision of the Supreme Court of Social Affairs, that has been published in 1983, clinical psychologists may not treat patients with medical cards unless there is permanent superintendence from physicians.

The Professional Association of German Psychologists has recently made proposals for solving this problem. One of them aims at Federal Regulations for Psychologists, which would assign a legal status to psychologists similar to that of medical practitioners, lawyers, etc. Another proposal concerns the recognition of psychology as 'Heilkunde' (incompletely translated as 'Medical Science' or 'therapeutics'), as a result of which all psychologists would be licensed or qualified as 'clinical' psychologists, and have a position equal to that of physicians. This raises several questions, like: will the legislator establish public institutions for official recognition, and under which conditions could the title Clinical Psychologist be bestowed?

As the existence of two types of professional psychologists - officially recognized ones and all others - would split up the Professional Association, and threaten the unity of the profession itself, work and organizational psychologists opt for (a similar or equal) recognition also. But there is no consensus about the conditions. E.g. what about the protection of private ownership that experienced

colleagues have obtained during many years of independent and successful working? Besides, the general idea that all psychological professions would necessarily belong to the 'Heilberufe' may be a doubtful
one as far as work and organizational psychologists are concerned.
Until now, the German Society of Psychology (the association of academics in psychology) has not accepted this application.

Another current and future trend is that work and organizational
psychologists are entering other domains, without using the title
'Diplom-Psychologe' or without even evidencing their professional
identity as psychologists. Such fields are personnel management, work
safety, professional training, etc. Such developments are well known
in the USA for a long time, in Europe they constitute a new trend however. This trend will lead to both advantages and disadvantages. There
is the positive aspect of the good reputation that work and organizational psychologists were evidently able to obtain in the past. Negative
aspects are that professional identity may be weakened in general, and
that work and organizational psychologists will not enter or even leave
the Professional Association, the Section of Work and Organizational
Psychology included.

A very acute problem arose from the growing number of students in
psychology, as well as unemployed post-graduates. Unfortunately, there
are no exact figures which show the composition of the group of unemployed psychologists.
As a matter of fact the German Civil Service no longer offers new
positions for psychologists, positions that were mainly preferred by
clinical psychologists in the past. One consequence will certainly show
up: the industry will be asked for positions by unemployed psychologists,
inclusive those who specialized in clinical psychology during their
education (about 80% of students). Apart from the fact that these
applicants may have a different way of thinking, they have had no
training in work and organizational psychology. Employers as well as
those beginners will sooner or later experience frustration. In addition
to this, the present recession in industry and trade does certainly not
induce companies to hire more psychologists. The earlier aversion to

industrial work from the side of many young students may have stopped, it does not mean that companies are ready to act as stopgaps.

Finally there is an urgent need for continuous education, both for experienced work and organizational psychologists and for beginners in this field. The Section of Work and Organizational Psychology installed a task force which is working at programs to be offered to interested colleagues concerning e.g.
- the field of work and organizational psychology in general;
- job analysis and job design;
- organizations in industry and their problems;
- professional training in industry and administration;
- safety at work;
- industrial law;
- electronic data processing and its effects;
- federations and unions in industry;
- basic economics.
The first proposals show a program of at least 30 days, exercises included. Unemployed psychologists may participate with grants from the unemployment insurance. The Board of the Section will offer this program in collaboration with the Working Group on Work, Industrial and Organizational Psychology of the German Society of Psychology, hoping that there will arise an active demand for this project.

EDUCATION AND RESEARCH

The first point worth to be mentioned is the fact that the homogeneity of the education in psychology that has existed since 1941, seems to be disturbed now by some universities. Therefore, a proposal has been made, very recently, towards a compulsory degree examination in three fields of psychology at all universities: work and organizational psychology, clinical psychology, and educational psychology. Work and organizational psychology will be revalued as soon as this proposal will come into operation. This might be another reason for mentioning work and organizational psychology more frequently nowadays.

With respect to the education in work and organizational psychology
an interesting investigation must be mentioned. Thomas (1982) reports
on results which have been obtained from a survey among work and organizational psychologists with some years of experience in industry:
- young work and organizational psychologists became more self-confident
  during the last decade, due to better, i.e. practically based education;
- the transition from university to industry went without any problems
  as the beginners had some earlier practical experience in industry;
- learning in engineering and economy is more important and useful than
  in - strictly speaking - 'academic' psychology;
- beginners are disappointed because they lack direct help from scientific research which is said to work in an ivory tower;
- as a result Thomas asks for more specialized research in work and
  organizational psychology which should give aid in special subjects
  by practically based theories.
These results, based on interviews, show the urgent and problematic
situation, worth to be discussed by professors as well as by students
just now.

A survey of the most outstanding fields of research was given by
papers on the 1982 Conference of the Section of Work and Organizational
Psychology (Fischer et al., 1982). Some of the major fields cover the
ones mentioned in this book. It is unnecessary to mention that research
lacks money.

Within this context, another subject is of importance: the cooperation of work and organizational psychologists with professionals from
neighbouring fields, like medicine, engineering, law, education, etc.
Work and organizational psychologists must be aware that definitions,
ways of thinking, targets, methods, and concepts differ from field to
field. Some of them are important for work and organizational psychologists also, but others are not; a fact to be taken into consideration
very carefully.

How professionals from different fields may learn from each other is demonstrated by working committees that try to formulate standards in ergonomics. By the way, there also is an opportunity to inform other people about the value of work and organizational psychology via examples. The results of discussions will necessarily be compromises, but the learning that takes place during the discussions is usually very fruitful for all participants.

Psychologists must learn about technical conditions, physical axioms, legal aspects, etc. Therefore teamwork, both in field work and in research is recommendable. If psychologists don't understand the language of engineers, medical practitioners, lawyers or even members of the works' councils, or if they don't succeed in making themselves understood, their position will become a very weak one.

Who is going to teach these important facts to students? Only very few experienced work and organizational psychologists are appointed as lecturers in universities, though - as experts stated - many full professors are hardly acquainted with factories from inside, and base their experiences on writing or reading theoretical books. This happens to be in clear contrast to the period of some 30-60 years ago.

For instance: questionnaires that have been developed for measuring well-being of workers, theoretically based intrinsic and extrinsic factors of motivation and satisfaction - mostly of them directly translated from abroad - don't give a sufficient basic knowledge for proper training and research in modern work and organizational psychology; who uses these instruments or puts them into practice?

Some research work seems to be directed at better work conditions and job design, but often the employees concerned dislike the final report with its results because it tries to tell them whether and when their working conditions are better or worse. They may disagree with prescriptions from outside, and offer excellent arguments in reverse. Research work often lacks feedback from the persons concerned. Also it has been stated that particular findings of industrial psychologists, e.g. from USA, are taken over and applied without discrimination. Their one-sidedness is often not noticed by professors or work and organizational psychologists, though there evidently are cultural, educational, technical, social, and linguistic differences, and a diversity of politically, legally, and historically based effects.

To sum up: education in work and organizational psychology must learn from the results published by Thomas about the ways to more effective teaching, and from other fields by means of close cooperation in research and practice. Work and organizational psychology departments should give aid on special subjects by practical theories and results from research that considers domestic conditions, and in close cooperation with the persons in question. In West Germany, university research work in work and organizational psychology is somewhat underdeveloped, mainly because of a shortage of money.

CURRENT TRENDS AND PERSPECTIVES

This topic covers a lot of open questions. What the future will bring for work and organizational psychologists, is unknown. But there is definitely a need for helping people in the context of organizations. A question of importance is whose servant work and organizational psychology should be. According to our view, the objective must be: to create better conditions of work in the broadest sense. The problem of values should be solved individually by work and organizational psychologists themselves.

Some more specific remarks are the following:

Work and organizational psychologists in Germany should publish about their activities and results to avoid people to rely on popular and often misunderstood or one-sided publications. At the same time editors should accept the manuscripts.

There is a need for work and organizational psychologists in organizations to become members of working groups with different objectives, e.g. selection, training, safety at work, job design, alcoholism at work, foreign workers, disabled and unemployed people. Very often managers and works' councils are asking questions about how to deal with those problems effectively. This gives opportunities to show other people in which way work and organizational psychology is able to solve such problems.

27

There is a demand for long range research programs in collaboration with universities and practitioners, trying to answer important questions concerning actual situations and future trends in industry. Examples are

- psychological aspects of multiple stress that sense organs are faced with;
- job analysis with categories suitable for work evaluation;
- conditions for decision making which avoids conflicts;
- general trends towards work places of higher quality versus reduction of work places, unemployment and early retirement, and the consequences which will arise from this dilemma;
- effects of modern technology on qualification, selection, education, retraining, number of work places, working time, social effects, etc.;
- safety at work and occupational diseases; especially influences of technical and organizational conditions in relation to human behaviour, and possibilities to influence people towards more care and safety by the way of better job design, managerial behaviour, and training;
- needs for support of small enterprises in several fields of work and organizational psychology;
- last not least, the design of work places, equipment, and training in order to avoid mistakes.

CONCLUSION

As pointed out, there are professional and legal problems, developments in education and research, and a lot of open questions. All aspects should be taken into consideration against the background of changing economic conditions, and of a rising figure of newcomers who, without sufficient education and being faced with unemployment, look for positions in work and organizational psychology. Many young colleagues need help now, asking for solidarity. What must be done?

One possible answer may be: enlargement of the field and enrichment of the application of work and organizational psychology. For this purpose there is an urgent need for more European cooperation. A common development of research programs and an exchange of know-how, might be fruitful for education in universities, application in industry, and employment opportunities for newcomers.

REFERENCES

Fischer, H., H.L. Horney, C. Lippmann, H. Methner & U. Winterfeld (Eds.)
Bericht über die 24. Fachtagung der Sektion Arbeits- und Betriebspsychologie zur arbeits- und betriebspsychologischen Fortbildung
in der Bundesrepublik Deutschland, 17.-19.5.1982, München. Duisburg: Sektion A & B Psychologie, 1982, 545-558.

Heckhausen, H., Zur Lage der Psychologie. Psychologische Rundschau,
1983a, 34, 1-20.

Heckhausen, H., Rechenschaftsbericht des Präsidenten der Deutschen
Gesellschaft für Psychologie am 28.9.1982 in Mainz.
Psychologische Rundschau, 1983b, 34, 47-52.

Horney, H.L., Arbeits- und Betriebspsychologie in der Bundesrepublik
Deutschland - ein Überblick. In: X. Zamek-Gliszcýnska (Ed.),
Work Psychology in Europe. Warszawa: Polish Scientific Publishers,
1980, 49-64.

Horney, H.L., Work Psychology in West Germany. In: Ch. de Wolff, S.
Shimmin & M. De Montmollin (Eds.), Conflicts and contradictions:
Work psychologists in Europe. London: Academic Press, 1981, 59-67.

Thomas, A., Probleme der Anwendung wissenschaftlicher Ergebnisse der
Psychologie in der arbeits- und betriebspsychologischen Praxis.
In: H. Fischer, H.L. Horney, C. Lippmann, H. Methner & U. Winterfeld
(Eds.), Bericht über die 24. Fachtagung der Sektion Arbeits- und
Betriebspsychologie zur arbeits- und betriebspsychologischen Fort-
bildung in der Bundesrepublik Deutschland, 17-19.5, 1982, München.
Duisburg: Sektion A & B Psychologie, 1982, 545-558.

BIBLIOGRAPHY

Hoyos, C. Graf, Arbeitspsychologie. Stuttgart: Kohlhammer, 1974.

Liebel, H. et al. (Eds.), Führungspsychologie. Goettingen: Hogrefe
Verlag für Psychologie, 1978.

Mayer, A. & B. Herwig (Eds.), Betriebspsychologie. (Handbuch der
Psychologie, Band 9; 2. edition). Goettingen: Hogrefe Verlag für
Psychologie, 1970.

Mayer, A., Organisationspsychologie. Stuttgart: Poeschel, 1978.

Schmidtke, H., Lehrbuch der Ergonomie (2. edition). München: Hanser, 1981.

Seiffert, K.H., Handbuch der Berufspsychologie. Goettingen: Hogrefe Verlag für Psychologie, 1977.

Weinert, A.B., Lehrbuch der Organisationspsychologie. München: Urban und Schwarzenberg, 1981.

3. THE PSYCHOLOGY OF WORK AND ORGANIZATION IN BELGIUM (FLANDERS)

R. Selis

INTRODUCTION

In this chapter we will present the psychologists working in Belgium's
northern part, the universities where they got their education and the
fields they are working in. Next we will briefly give an overview of
the organizations they are employed by and the pressures they are ex-
posed to. Finally we will discuss the kind of activities that psychologists are involved in and the way in which these activities have developed
and most likely will evolue in the future.

THE PSYCHOLOGISTS WE ARE TALKING ABOUT

Work and organizational psychologists form a very young profession. Few
psychologists worked in this field before 1960. Since then the studies
of psychology became more popular - they were even booming in the seventies - and many mainly new organizations needed a professional staff in
the human resources management field. This led to an employment today
of some 200 to 350 work and organizational psychologists. They are young
($\pm$ 32 years in average) at least 80% are men, one out of two graduated
at the University of Leuven, then followed by Ghent and then Brussels,
and most of them work in their field in industrial organizations or in
consultancy business. Very few work in the public or town administra-
tions (except a large group of $\pm$ 40 in the State unemployment services),
because the job of psychologist is not yet statutorally defined.

The same is true for hospitals because the rules for subsidizing do not take into account the position of psychologists in the work and organizational field. As far as we know no work and organizational psychologist is directly employed by union organizations.

We have already stated that they graduated at one of the three universities, Leuven, Ghent or Brussels. Students graduated in Ghent after 5 years, and from this year on this will also be the case in Leuven. Brussels is still at 4 years. To illustrate the program, we have taken the one of Leuven. The three 'licentie' years consist of 37 semester hours of general courses and 31 semester hours of specialized courses in work, community and organizational psychology. The third year the student has to spend 7 months training in organizations and at the end he has also to present a thesis. At the three Universities twenty people obtained their Ph.D. in this field.

The 'industrial psychology' section has never been the most populated one. In the 1960-1970's the lead was taken by the 'vocational guidance and school psychology' section. Many guidance centres were set up and had to be staffed. In the 1970's the section suffered from identification with service to capitalistic institutions. Today the 'clinical psychology' section has taken over the earlier popularity of the vocational guidance section. Over the last five years at the Leuven University 10% in average of the students followed the vocational guidance and school psychology section, 18% the industrial and 72% the clinical section.

The university is also a research institute. More than 20 professors, assistants and graduates are involved in this activity. The topics are very diversified, the largest group focusing on the issue of task oriented discussions in groups, and another one on the meaning of work. Only two people are involved in ergonomics research (road safety). Some other topics include organization-identity - use of time of top managers - work ethics etc.

Most of the professors teaching in the work and organizational field are also teaching at other faculties, mainly to business graduates and post-graduates. The importance of this may not be underestimated. That a large group of businessmen today is familiar with concepts on organization development, quality of work life, just to name two, is indeed very important. In daily practice we see that top management is the driving force behind organizational changes and they are the ones who invite the work and organizational psychologists on their firm or a consultant to help them make the changes.

To close this paragraph we like to mention especially the activities of the 'Hoger Instituut van de Arbeid' (Leuven) - the Higher Institute of Work. The Board of this Institute is formed by 7 Heads of Faculties and by 7 representatives from different institutes of the Social-Democratic workers organization. It concentrates mostly on workers issues. The 15 researchers, under the direction of a professor on Community Psychology, concentrate their research on working conditions (mainly work in shifts) - unemployment - income (re)distribution - attitudes of employees about the union organization they belong to. Much of the research work, especially about unemployment and income distribution, is used at the Government level to evaluate and inspire some initiatives.

WHO EMPLOYS THESE WORK AND ORGANIZATIONAL PSYCHOLOGISTS?

Like we have already said, the majority of them is working in the industry and more and more also in industry-related consultant firms.

After the second world war Belgium was very successful in attracting foreign companies. A skilled and hard working labour force, competitive wages, the international city of Brussels, the infrastructure, and attractive investment subsidies brought to Belgium many foreign companies. In some business segments they employ today even more than 50% of all the employees working in that segment. Many of these new firms wanted also a more professional staff in their personnel departments and this created many job opportunities for work and organizational psychologists.

Traditionally the personnel department job was more an administrative job where knowledge of labour law was very important. Most of the energy was indeed spend on administrative tasks and on industrial relations. Needless to say that many personnel directors had a background in law or were lawyers. Today our best guess is that one out of six personnel directors has a university degree in behavioural sciences or social sciences. In large firms like Philips or Agfa-Gevaert psychologists for the first time have acceded to the position of personnel director.

The interesting point about this invasion of foreign companies was that their personnel staff in Belgium got familiarized with concepts, ideas and techniques already more developed in the country of origin of the firm. So was the concept of 'work enrichment' (werk-structurering) mainly spread around through experiments in several factories of Philips in Belgium, and morale surveys as a tool for action research got introduced through IBM. How many young professionals got not familiarized with 'Blake's grid' by working in a subsidiary of an American company like Procter & Gamble.

Today the picture has changed and most work and organizational psychologists are working in firms which fight for survival. Compared to a few years ago firms react differently to the crisis; instead of reducing costs, (manpower) overall, they invest and disvest at the same time, strengthening their particular assets and getting rid of those things they are not good at. As a result a lot of energy is spend in many companies on re-organization.

To fight the very high level of unemployment (now 12% of the active population) the strategy of the Belgian Government has been first of all to strengthen the financial situation of the firms by devaluating the Belgian franc and by imposing a wage and salary moderation, part of which was a disconnection of the automatic link to the evolution of consumer prices. On the other side the Government stimulated firms to reduce working time and compensate it by adding people. It is important to note also that personal taxation has now become the highest in Europe and has reached now a point that it leads to less job mobility (affects recruitment), reduces work motivation and even worse, leads to emigration of our most valuable asset.

ROLE AND ACTIVITIES OF THE WORK AND ORGANIZATIONAL PSYCHOLOGIST

We have presented briefly the work and organizational psychologist, the university where he was trained and the organization which is employing him. Let us now discuss his role and activities, using the following simple model of human resources management (Figure 1).

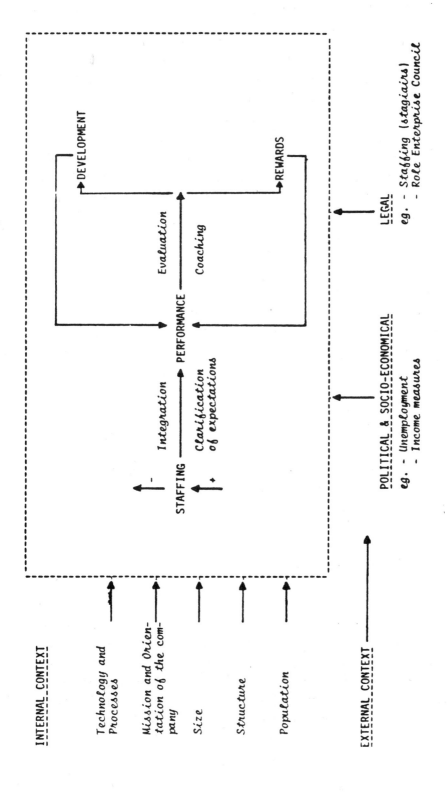

Figure 1. Human resources management model

Staffing

Twenty years ago the main duty of the work and organizational psychologist was to recruit large groups of workers and clerks and some junior professional staff members. He was expected to do an effective job by using professional selection tools. With the numbers involved the job was a boring one and seen by many as a good start for a career by demonstrating practical effectiveness. Selection tools flourished, and many will remember us asking workers to make nice sketches of trees or to rank order coloured cards.

In the crisis situation the key-word was not anymore to recruit and select people but to reduce the working force. Again in some companies the job was given to personnel departments to execute top decisions and the work and organizational psychologists in the worst case had to fire people. Today the focus is less on the execution of selection or firing, but more on the help management needs to define its staffing strategy. Management expects many more things than selecting the right candidates or firing those who do not fit or are superfluous:

- What kind of people do we need, in which kind of positions, to fulfill our mission?
- How can we attract these people, switch people in the organization so that we achieve these goals?
- How can we disinvest in one kind of operations and strengthen at the same time other ones?
- How can we continue to keep people to stay with us in a motivated way till their own activity is stopped and the department, plant etc. is closed down?
- What is the right job for this person at this stage of his/her career to fully use his talents?

Looking at selection tools, we get the impression that the interview and practical job-oriented tests are becoming again the main selection tools. Psychological testing has become inpopular due to the impersonal way of practizing them (certainly amongst professional employees), companies are less interested in lengthy sophisticated reports but are much more looking at effectiveness in finding the right people.

Personality factors are taken much more in consideration ('the chemistry') than before as well as capability for further learning.

Influence on the performance of employees in organizations

Twenty years ago, after having selected the right people, the work and organizational psychologists concentrated most on helping supervisors to effectively manage their resources. The psychologist was somewhat familiar with sensitivity training which was introduced in Europe in the late fifties, early sixties, so he was the best man to teach social skills, like he also was the best man to teach factory supervisors about 'the psychology of the working female'.

Later on with better educated workers on the shop floor and the growing influence of data processing on work organization he was dealing with 'job design' and 'workers participation'. Automation and availability of information is now rapidly changing the basic nature of jobs at all levels in the organization: the operator on the shop floor becomes a technician, the office clerk an information processor, the executive a change agent.

On the other hand people are expecting to get more freedom and prefer more individual solutions. The demand for flex-time, free choice of vacation periods, part-time jobs is an indication for this. Management in his strive for survival is finding that one of the few ways to compete on world markets is to produce high performance quality products and to give the customer the best services. This creates a demand for well functioning, effective organizations, fast responding to changing market needs. Effective cooperation, creativity and initiative are needed to get to the new products and the fast market response.

Needless to say that again the work and organizational psychologist's role is changing. He is not only dealing with individual or group problems but more with organization-wide problems. Where previously he was asked to help change people and work, he is asked now to help change organizations. Also his involvement is changing. Where he was before a not-integrated adviser, or a coach at the side-line, he is expected to intervene as a partner who has to play an effective role and help produce results.

In the past also his interventions were much more fragmented; now they have to be part of an overall strategy. For instance, 'job evaluation and function classification' were subjects he would deal with apart. Now there will be a concern to see them as an element of the strategy of rewarding people, which cannot be disconnected from questions like: to make these kind of products, to fulfill this mission, what kind of people do we need, what kind of environment do we have to create to help them to be effective, and how do we have to reward these different people to have them motivated. Management is less impressed by fancy techniques but much more by mature help at the strategic level.

It is clear that not all work and organizational psychologists have the capability to function at that level. This leads to a rapidly growing demand for help from outside consultants.

Let us close this part by mentioning that the demand for ergonomical advises and action research inspired implementation is rapidly growing especially in the process industry, in power plants, and in organizations where the clerical work is rapidly and fundamentally influenced by computer technology (banks, insurance companies etc.).

Training and development

It is obvious with what was mentioned before that what people expect from training is also different today. Training has to help to create a learning environment and has also to prove to be effective. Therefore it is much more integrated than before. The work and organizational psychologist has less to be a teacher on 'coaching skills' or to select people who could most benefit from a 'presentation skill course', but is expected to help management find out what, for example, the causes are that people in the organization use their time so little effectively and help design the company or departments a learning intervention which can be re-inforced in the daily practice. Needless to say that from a content point of view information processing is a main subject of teaching these days.

We also see a real concern for career development aspects, as a reaction to the question of how to keep employees motivated and creative in a non-growing environment. Systematic career coaching, more frequent

job changes, and also taking more risks in assigning people to tasks
they are less familiar with, are indications to support this.

Reward systems

Most of the reward systems in use lead to 'average attitudes about work
involvement', and emphasize 'conformity to rules' and 'seniority'. We
have got a lot of peace, but no stimuli anymore for extra effort, involvement, creativity, risk taking, entrepreneurial attitudes and aiming
high at all levels in the organization.

Government income and tax policies have re-inforced the former by
reducing substantially the distance between different income levels.
Today industry in his strive for survival on the world markets needs
mostly entrepreneurs, and this at all levels in the organization. And
if and where people could be stimulated by redistributing part of the
profit or the growth they helped create, in general there is not much
profit left today. And even in cases where there is, the profit sharing
is taxed so highly that it is experienced as ridiculous; it can even
have an adverse effect.

The subject of reward systems is a very little studied one in Belgium.
Lately we heard that in some companies people were interested to try
out systems which would more reward individual learning results (skill
block system) than positions. At the professional level U.S. research
about determinants of professional income could bring us to much more
individualized, but also more transparent salary systems.

CONCLUSIONS

Today, management in industry cannot just talk anymore about people.
The time of slogans like 'On n'a besoin que des hommes' lies behind us.
To survive management has to capitalize on their most valuable asset,
it has to get the highest return on its investment. You do this very
simply by getting people with you instead of against you.

Managers are looking for help, for effective help. Therefore there
are still opportunities for well trained work and organizational psychologists. The demands and expectations are even much higher than in

general we can provide for. We are still part of a very young profession. We may feel optimistic about employment opportunities and impact in a wide variety, although still mostly industrial, organizations.

Further we see a tendency that the lip service paid to people and the dual morale of former days is coming down and realistic, mature and adult dealings with people are growing. This creates a better environment for psychologists.

But, the quality of the people going in this field has to be high, they have not only to be effective social technocrats but also mature individuals, with good presentation, and process intervention skills, and being able to deal with people at different levels in the organization, with different specialities.

And therefore, the education at the University has to stay in close touch with the best research work and their own research has to find a ground in the needs of the organizations in their environment.

In preparing this paper I appreciated very much the information provided to me by colleagues, H. Awouters, N. Derdaele, K. de Witte, L. Janssens & L. Hoebeke, M. van den Noortgate and the Professors J. Borgers, P. Coetsier, G. de Cock and L. Lagrou.

40

4. THE PSYCHOLOGY OF WORK AND ORGANIZATION IN THE NETHERLANDS

Ch.J. de Wolff

INTRODUCTION

During the past decade I have had many conversations with colleagues
from Europe and the United States regarding the status of work and
organizational psychology in our respective countries. These discussions
have left me with the impression that the status of the field in the
Netherlands compares quite favourably to that in most other countries.
This favourable status can be characterized as follows. Most generally,
the title of 'psychologist' is recognized by the Dutch state which, at
least in Europe, is somewhat of an exception. More specifically, the
academic standing of the subject is good and psychologists are well
regarded professionally. As well, almost all universities have a chair
in work and organizational psychology and there are many other chairs
in technical universities and schools of economics. Finally, the acceptance of the discipline in industrial and other organizations is good.
Many organizations employ psychologists or make use of the services of
consulting agencies. In elaborating on the current status of work and
organizational psychology in the Netherlands, I will try to provide an
answer as to why and how this present state of affairs came to exist.

FROM 1920 TO 1940

It is of course a matter of some speculation, but it nonetheless seems
to be the case that the current favourable status of the field has its
roots in the earliest period of psychology as a discipline in the

Netherlands. We are here interested in the period from 1920 to about 1940. Of course, at that time work and organizational psychology was not a separate field as it is today. Psychology was itself a part of philosophy and there was usually only one chairholder. The psychologists in that period were generalists, and the chair included responsibility for a variety of topics, including work and organizational psychology. Moreover, almost all psychologists in this period not only had a very strong interest in applied psychology, but were also actively engaged in practical work (Ter Meulen & Van Hoorn, 1981; Eisenga, 1981).

In this period several large organizations in the Netherlands, such as Philips, the Dutch Postal Service, the Dutch State Mines, the City of Amsterdam, and Rotterdam Harbour, began establishing psychological services departments. These involved one or more psychologists who were active primarily in personnel selection. In addition, a number of consulting agencies were established in this period, usually by professors from the universities (Roe, 1982).

One can see, then, that the first generation of psychologists had a very strong external orientation. This means that they had many contacts with society and in particular with industry. In fact, if one notes that prior to 1940 only 51 individuals graduated from psychology, it is surprising to see that a large number of these were active in the applied field. One person became a prime minister, another became a minister of education, another a director of a large company, while others held positions in political parties, were advisers to the royal family, and so forth.

There is another factor in this first phase of the relation between psychology and industry which may have had some effect on the current state of affairs. In the twenties and thirties the ideas of Taylor were introduced to Dutch industry. Stated briefly, Taylor's ideas concentrated on scientific management in industry. For example, by studying the movements required to perform a given task, performance and thus productivity could be increased. Production engineers would then design work systems within which workers would have a strictly prescribed task. Another way of stimulating production was by linking pay to productivity through the use of a bonus system. A worker's pay might be rather low

unless he attained a given level of productivity, at which point he
would receive a pay bonus.

In this period there was a great deal of public discussion on the
merits of such a system. For example, Roels, appointed to a chair in
Utrecht in 1922, lectured widely, not only in university but also to
groups of employers, or to groups of union leaders. He condemned the
Taylorian approach as a "ruthless utilarism" which views man simply as
a component in a machine. Although Roels recognized the need for im-
proving productivity, he argued for a positive reconstruction of
Taylor's system based on a more idealistic and humanitarian view of the
worker as an individual. Roels believed that applied psychology could
provide the required scientific knowledge to improve systems and organizations along these lines. Finally, he expressed the idea that psychologists should be leaders of multidisciplinarian teams, including
managers and production engineers, which would engage in solving the
complex moral and social problems inherent in existing organizational
schemes (Ter Meulen & Van Hoorn, 1981).

It is worth noting how the concerns of Roels anticipate later developments during the late sixties. One can see, however, that his orientation was still towards industry, with the goal being to modify it. This
is in sharp contrast to the next phase where psychology is much more
inner directed, concentrating on developing methods for increasing knowledge.

THE POST-WAR PERIOD TO THE SIXTIES

After the war there was a period of rebuilding. This was a period where
separate study programs in psychology were beginning to be established
in universities. This trend continued through the fifties and sixties,
and coincided with an important period of growth of the universities,
both in terms of student enrollment and in the resources allocated in
universities by the government. As an illustration, there were 49 psychologists employed in programs in 1963. This number increased to 290
by 1972. In the same period the number of psychologists employed in the
universities as a whole increased from 94 to 595 (Krijnen, 1975, 1976).
It was during the sixties that separate chairs in work and organizational

psychology within psychological subfaculties were first established.

During this period we can see a clear reorientation in the interests of work and organizational psychologists in universities, generally towards an emphasis on research and methodology (Roe, 1982). It was believed that psychology should concentrate on statistical, scientific methods and that much more had to be known before it could be applied effectively to a work situation. With respect to topics such as personnel selection, this statistical approach became dominant (e.g. Van der Giessen, 1957).

Part of the reason for this shift in emphasis may be due to the fact that in this period we are dealing with a new generation of psychologists, trained in the post-war period and influenced by American psychology. Concurrent with this trend there occured in the Netherlands a debate between clinicians and other psychologists regarding the validity of methods then used in for example, evaluation procedures. Impressionistic methods predominated, including projective tests and interviews, where the observations of the psychologist constituted the main part of the evaluation. Based on such observations a clinical assessment would be made regarding the ability of a person under consideration. During the fifties there were many theses, lectures, and discussions devoted to the validity of such methods for personnel selection and assessment. The general conclusion was that these methods had low validity or even no validity at all. As a consequence there was a shift in universities towards the adoption of statistical methods. Such a statistical approach is very much a prescriptive one, and in a book such as Thorndike's Personnel Selection (1949) one can see that the method involved the strict application of a specific number of steps.

There was also an expansion of work and organizational psychology programs during this period. The subject of personnel selection remained dominant, but there was an increased interest in such topics as ergonomics (human factors) and social-industrial psychology, which later came to be termed organizational psychology.

This reorientation was only partly successful with psychologists working in industry and other organizations in this period as many continued to rely on the use of impressionistic methods (De Wolff & Van den Bosch, 1980). There was a number of reasons for this. First of all,

44

there were some who were not convinced that the statistical methods were better. Second, there were difficulties in applying a statistical approach in industry. On the one hand it took a lot of time and research in universities before tests were available for use in the industrial sector. On the other hand, there were not always the appropriate opportunities or resources available for psychological services in organizations to develop their own tests and validate their programs. Finally, there was the problem that there would be a large number of specific jobs with only a small number of people being selected per year. Such a situation precluded the possibility of developing adequate testing programs (De Wolff & Van den Bosch, 1980).

THE LATE SIXTIES

At the end of the sixties there was another reorientation in the area of work and organizational psychology. This was inspired by the enormous shifts in values in society at that time, expressed by student unrests which in turn led to the restructuring of universities. These shifts in values were towards ideas of participation and democratization as well as worker emancipation in social institutions. Another trend visible in this period was towards the idea that universities should concentrate on subjects which had social relevance and should not engage for its own sake. Furthermore, there was the idea that the pursuits of science are not value free in that they can have an enormous impact on the lives of people. These value implications should always be assessed in research activity.

Such events had a great impact on work and organizational psychologists. They had traditionally identified with management which was seen as the client. In this new atmosphere it was stressed that psychologists should identify with the workers. This had consequences for the kind of work which was pursued in universities. The topic of 'selection' was no longer well-regarded as the selection process was seen as biased in favour of management interests. Topics which received more attention included organizational development, workers' councils, and participation. There was also a change in the name of the field. It was no longer referred to as Industrial Psychology but as Work and Organizational

Psychology. This was motivated partly out of a desire to eliminate the negative connotations which came to be associated with the term 'industry'. On the other hand the new name expresses real changes in the domain of study of the area, which was not simply industry but of organizations in general (De Wolff, Shimmin & De Montmollin, 1981).

One other trend in universities to be noted is that student enrollment continued to increase but interest in work and organizational psychology decreased. In this period, the number of graduates in psychology increased exponentially. For example, in 1950 there were 100 graduates; this number increased to 600 in 1960 and to 2000 in 1970 (Krijnen, 1975, 1976). However, the number of graduates in work and organizational psychology was only increasing linearly in this period. This means that student interest in the area was decreasing relative to other areas, particularly the areas of clinical and social psychology.

One can see a similar situation with the practising psychologists. They were confronted with a prevalence of hostile attitudes towards management. It was felt that management abused workers, and that they emphasized economic factors over social considerations in their decision making. Psychologists found themselves needing to reassess their position towards management, with which they traditionally identified.

Other developments fostered a shift in subjects on which the psychologists focused. There was a shift in government policy from acting on the basis of consensus to taking initiative in interventions, such as passing a new law giving more influence to workers' councils. Also in this period the unions tried to change the balance of power, in the sense that workers would have more influence on organizational activities. With companies now trying to cope with changes in the work environment, psychologists became increasingly interested in subjects such as organizational development and worker participation programs. And of course, as with the situation in universities, there was a de-emphasis on selection procedures which were viewed by union officials and others as biased against the employee.

The attitudes of managers towards psychologists were ambivalent.

On the one hand they generally demonstrated willingness to see if it would be possible to modify organizational structure to be more in line with the needs of employees. On the other hand, there was some mistrust of the loyalties of the psychologists whose help was required to effect such changes. The psychologists were now seen as being inclined to identify with the workers and to hold utopian and unrealistic views on how management was to be restructured.

These trends had some implications for the status of the area of work and organizational psychology generally which are worth noting. In the earlier periods the departments of psychological services in organizations and counselling agencies were very important, and graduating work and organizational psychologists would typically start their first jobs there. Such a situation supported a unity of the field. However, in the present period there was an increased tendency for psychologists to enter a variety of departments in organizations, such as training or personnel departments. The effect was that they had less contact with colleagues with a concommitant weakening of the ties within profession. In addition, once work and organizational psychologists began leaving their traditionally defined field and take up new subjects, there was an increasing overlap with other disciplines such as sociology or business science which also worked in these new areas. This would also have the effect of weakening the unity within the area of work and organizational psychology (De Wolff, 1983).

THE TREND OF THE LATE SEVENTIES

By the end of the seventies one can detect the start of a third reorientation within work and organizational psychology. This comes as a consequence of the economic recession which began at that time. Many companies were required to lay off workers, government deficits increased and this in turn forced the adoption of economizing measures. There was also a clear change in public attitudes towards industry. In witnessing the increases in unemployment, people began to realize that economic growth was essential to reduce that problem.

Within universities there are now increased government interventions aimed at reducing costs and increasing governmental control over university programs. In the Netherlands three important interventions can be noted. First, starting in 1982, university study programs are reduced from five-to-six years to four years in psychology. A limited number of students can attend a professional training cycle in universities. It seems unlikely, however, that work and organizational psychologists will be among those admitted.

Second, there is a change in the funding of research programs. Until now the state paid universities on the basis of number of students and staff employed. Since 1982 a distinction is made between teaching programs and research programs. The intention is that only programs of a certain size, which have obtained external approval will be recognized, and will receive funding.

Finally, staff reductions will occur as a consequence of a general funding decrease of about 8%.

There is also a sharp increase in the number of unemployed psychologists in this period, as can be seen in Figure 1 (De Wolff, 1983).

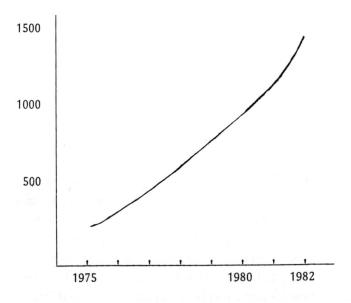

Figure 1. Number of unemployed psychologists (as registered by employment offices)

This can be attributed mainly to the large number of students entering universities during the seventies. Until recently the labour market
was able to absorb the large number of graduates from university programs. By the eighties, however, approximately a thousand graduates
were entering the labour market each year and there were simply not
enough positions available. Unemployment among work and organizational
psychologists comprised about one percent of this total. This increased
to two percent by 1982, due partly to other psychologists (such as
clinial psychologists) who were now applying for positions usually
restricted to work and organizational psychologists in the past.

Predictions for the next few years present an agonizing picture.
Ritzen (1982) who is an economist at Nijmegen university, examined the
unemployment patterns of university graduates in general. According to
his figures, there were 7.000 unemployed in 1982. This number will grow
to 35.000 in 1984 and to 69.000 in 1986, which represents approximately
20% of the total graduates in that year. We can thus expect that the
question of employment within psychology will become a dominant issue.
There will be fewer positions available in the universities and when
work and organizational psychologists seek positions in other sectors,
such as industry, there will be strong competition from other disciplines. This in turn might continue the trend towards fragmentation of
the area of work and organizational psychology which we noted in the
previous period. Graduating work and organizational psychologists will
be forced to accept positions outside the present domain and this will
lead to fewer ties within the profession. Also, since graduates from
other disciplines will apply for jobs within the domain, the amount of
overlap with other disciplines will increase.

IMPLICATIONS FOR THE FUTURE OF WORK PSYCHOLOGY

Given this situation, a number of actions are possible. It is now important that the profession should concentrate on areas where there are
still employment opportunities. The expectation is that a number of
traditional subjects will do quite well. There will be an increased
need for effective selection procedures since the number of job applicants

is high. Job training will also be important not only for the number of new types of jobs which are created but also for the retraining of individuals within organizations. In addition, a number of new areas should receive greater attention, such as health, personnel policy, and new technologies.

It is becoming apparent that within organizations there are increasing problems which can be related to matters of mental and physical health. There are a number of indicators of this trend. We can see that the incidence of work disability has grown immensely in the Netherlands over the past ten years. For example, in 1968 the WAO (Law on Disability Benefits) was adopted which gave workers who had been ill for over a year certain social benefits. Initially, there were about 150.000 recipients of these benefits; by 1982 this number has grown to about 700.000 (GMD, 1983). To appreciate the magnitude of this figure, one may compare it to the number of individuals employed in industry in the same period, which was about 844.000. In considering the kinds of diagnoses which are made it turns out that psycho-social disorders are prominant. Second, absenteeism has increased rapidly, particularly during the seventies, from about 4% in 1950 to around 10% by 1982. This number has subsequently dropped to 8%, which is still a high figure if one considers the current rate of unemployment. Thirdly, company physicians indicate that about 50% of the workers paying them a visit do not have problems which can be attributed to somatic factors, but which are related to psycho-social causes. To deal effectively with these problems one has to examine health-psychological issues. It would be best to focus on prevention which in turn is related to personnel policies, which is a second new area open to examination.

At present, there is what can be called a 'turbulent environment' in organizations. This is due to a variety of factors, including government interventions, the introduction of new technologies, and discussions between management and unions. This means that personnel policies have to adapt to these changes. For example, if it is decided that there will be shorter working hours, an organization must decide on how this is to be implemented. Some problems which this situation might raise include how one is to handle shift workers or how to deal with special staff positions. What is required, then, is a group within personnel departments which is responsible for working out new personnel policies as required. However, what we learn from research on this matter is that personnel officers have difficulties in dealing with the problems related to introducing change in organizations. The reason for this is simply that, at least in the Netherlands, there are no university training programs for this kind of work. It seems possible, then, that this is an area into which graduates in work and organizational psychology might move.

The third new area for study is the effect of new technologies on organizations. An example here is the use of computers in the banking industry. The use of computers makes possible a constant interaction between a small corner bank and a head office. This in turn means that one has to rethink the nature of the organizational structure, not simply in terms of a local variation where the technology was introduced but in terms of the entire organization. The general problem of work structuring now becomes very important. Expertise will be required on the subject of the kinds of abilities which people have and how these are to be integrated into new technological systems. Moreover, there is a need for the use of multiple criteria in planning changes which will satisfy both organizational objectives and employee needs.

Another general area of concern for the field of work psychology is the training of graduates and the relation of the profession to graduates who have just entered the job market. One should realize that graduates are rather vulnerable, particularly in the first period of employment. This is particularly true where the graduate accepts a job outside of his professional domein. Under these circumstances he is isolated from colleagues who might otherwise offer support during the initial period of employment. For example, an individual is typically trained to deal with the needs of the client, but little attention is given to how one is to interact with one's managers or with professionals from other disciplines such as medical officers or sociologists. What I would advocate is that the profession and the universities can cooperate both in the training and the support of the graduate during the early and vulnerable period of employment.

It might also be a good idea to give support to those who are searching for jobs. This is always a difficult task and is even more difficult if one is isolated from colleagues. Under these circumstances a graduate might end up in a job which is unrelated to his profession, or he might not find a job at all. What I would advocate in these circumstances is a joint program between the professional organizations and the universities which could be combined with post-doctoral courses to assist graduates through this transition period.

There is also the opportunity to restructure the relationship between universities and work and organizational psychologists in organizations. It might be appropriate if these first line service providers can fall back on a second line of service providers in universities. In this way they can gain access to expertise for problems which are too difficult to handle at the first line level.

Further there is a need within the area of work and organizational psychology to focus on matters of development. In universities, there are many programs doing research which aims at providing new knowledge, for example on the topic of stress. What you find, however, is that when people start to work on this problem within organizations, they are faced with a new range of difficulties which have to do not so much with the initial studies on stress but which have to do with effectively applying this knowledge in the organizations. It is this latter problem of application - or development - which requires more attention.

Finally, there is a need for more international collaboration. Within work and organizational psychology there are a large number of specific subjects which have to be covered. However, it is usually the case that a given university can concentrate on only a small number of subjects. What is needed is an effective and cooperative division of labour, where one university will work on a number of specific problems and another university will focus on other problems. Particularly with the universities within Europe this exchange of information will of necessity have to occur on an international level.

REFERENCES

Eisenga, L.K.A., De ontwikkeling van de A- en O-psychologie in Neder-
land. In: Drenth, P.J.D. e.a. (Eds.), Handboek Arbeids- en Organisati
psychologie. Deventer: Van Loghum Slaterus, 1980.

Giessen, R. W. van der, Enkele aspecten van het probleem der predictie
in de psychologie. Amsterdam, 1957.

Jaarverslagen van de Gemeenschappelijke Medische Dienst, Amsterdam, 1983.

Krijnen, G., Ontwikkeling functievervulling van psychologen. Deel I.
Nijmegen: Instituut voor toegepaste sociologie, 1975.

Krijnen, G., Ontwikkeling functievervulling van psychologen. Deel II.
Nijmegen: Instituut voor toegepaste sociologie, 1976.

Meulen, R. ter & W. van Hoorn, Psychotechniek en menselijke verhoudin-
gen. Grafiet, 1981, 1, 106-155.

Ritzen, J.M.M., Hoger opgeleiden in de knel. Economisch Instituut,
Katholieke Universiteit Nijmegen, 1982.

Roe, R.A., Korte geschiedenis van de personeelsselektie. Delft: Delft
University of Technology, Onderafdeling W&M, 1982.

Thorndike, L.J., Personnel selection; test and measurement technique.
New York: Wiley, 1949.

Wolff, Ch.J. de, De rol van de A&O-psycholoog. In: Drenth, P.J.D. e.a.
(Eds.), Handboek arbeids- en organisatiepsychologie. Deventer: Van
Loghum Slaterus, 1983.

Wolff, Ch.J. de & G. van den Bosch, Personeelsaanname. In: Drenth, P.J.D
e.a. (Eds.), Handboek Arbeids- en Organisatiepsychologie.
Deventer: Van Loghum Slaterus, 1980.

Wolff, Ch.J. de, S. Shimmin & M. de Montmollin, Conflicts and contradictions. London: Academic Press, 1981.

II
WORK AND NON-WORK

5. MEANING OF WORKING: A COMPARISON BETWEEN FLANDERS, GERMANY AND THE NETHERLANDS

R. Claes, P. Coetsier, A. Ruiz Quintanilla, B. Wilpert,
J.H.T.H. Andriessen, P.J.D. Drenth & R.N. van der Kooy

INTRODUCTION

In 1978 research teams from Belgium, Israel, Japan, the Netherlands, United Kingdom, United States, West Germany and Yugoslavia, initiated the 'Meaning of Working (MOW)'-project.

The objectives of the MOW-study (MOW-International Research Team, 1981) are fourfold:
- identifying and understanding the major patterns of meanings individuals and significant groups (target groups) attach to working in industrial societies;
- understanding how these meanings develop within and across national/ cultural systems;
- understanding the consequences of different work meanings to individuals, organizations and societies;
- providing policy suggestions and implications from the findings.
The approach of the MOW-project fits into the new directions of motivation studies, since it uses not only the individual's past work experience, his current work situation and his future perspectives on work but also macro socio-economical explanations of work motivation and an occupational frame of reference on the meaning of working through a target group approach.

Although we refer to an earlier publication (MOW-International Research Team, 1981) for the background and the description of the total MOW-project, we present in Figure 1 the heuristic research model which specifies the major variable sets used and the relationships analyzed in this study.

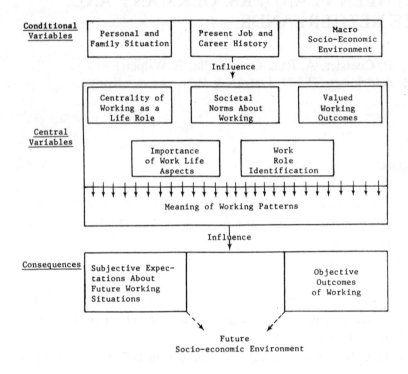

Figure 1. MOW heuristic research model

For the collection of data carefully designed questionnaires and scales have been used for the measurement of the sets of variables indicated in Figure 1. Data were collected from two sample-sets: a national representative sample (N=1000) and a set of 10 common target groups in each country (N target group approx. 90). This chapter is based on target group data. In the present chapter we will report and discuss some findings of the MOW-project in a few countries which could be referred to as the Germanic country cluster: Flanders, the Federal Republic of Germany, and the Netherlands.

The results to be presented are based on target group data (see below) and include: the definition of work; the central MOW-variables (centre boxes in Figure 1) and the relationships between central MOW-variables and both antecedents and consequences.

The findings will be analyzed from two main angles: diversity and similarity between the three countries on the one hand and specific meanings attached to working by the target groups on the other.

SAMPLE AND METHODOLOGY

The target groups were selected because of their critical importance to policy concerns, expected difference in work patterns, representation of career developmental stages, their different skill level and occupation and international homogeneity. The defining characteristics of the target groups are:

Unemployed: 50% males and 50% females of medium to low skill levels, all having been unemployed for at least the past six months. (Physically handicapped individuals or seasonal workers were not included).

Retired: 50% males and 50% females of normal retirement age and not presently working. If possible they were selected from among teachers, low skilled white collar workers and chemical engineers.

Chemical Engineers: All males of higher professional training (till 21 years) or university level training and currently doing professional chemical work (not managers) in companies of more than 200 employees (not food companies or pharmaceutical companies).

Teachers: All females teaching 9-10 year-old students and in situations where they have the main teaching assignment for a whole class as opposed to teaching only one subject to many classes. Teachers were selected from both private and public schools in approximate proportion to their relative frequency in the area from which data were collected.

Self-employed Businessmen: All males with less than eight employees, to be selected from among commercial, service and crafts type businesses. Professionals such as lawyers, physicians or dentists were not included. The intent was to take 'small shopkeepers'.

Tool and die makers: All males of high skill level selected from the automobile industry or related industries.

White collar employees: 50% males and 50% females. The intent was to select low to semi-skilled, or lower service function employees, whose occupations are being influenced by automation and technology. They were selected from the banking and insurance industry.

Textile workers: 66% males and 34% females of low or semi-skilled job level such as 'weaver'.

Temporary workers: All females doing clerical work, non-skilled to low skill levels. They work for and are assigned to temporary work by either private or governmental employment agencies; no students but rather individuals whose present occupation is temporary clerical work through an agency.

Students: 50% males studying mechanical or machine trades or equivalent in vocational-technical schools, 50% females studying for clerical-secretarial occupations in full-time schools. These individuals may be employed part time but are primarily students who will go directly into employment after their vocational-technical training.

Table 1 shows the sample composition for Flanders, Germany and the Netherlands per country, per target group, combined over the three countries and combined over the ten target groups.

	FLANDERS	GERMANY	NETHERLANDS	TOTAL
UNEMPLOYED	100	91	90	281
RETIRED	90	92	86	268
CHEMICAL ENGINEERS	90	not available	90	180
TEACHERS	90	103	90	283
SELF EMPLOYED BUSINESS	90	99	103	292
TOOL & DIE MAKERS	83	51	98	232
WHITE COLLAR EMPLOYEES	92	102	88	282
TEXTILE WORKERS	90	33	84	207
TEMPORARY WORKERS	82	14	88	184
STUDENTS	90	114	90	294
TOTAL	897	699	907	2.503

Table 1. Sample composition

The data were gathered through individual interviews using a questionary of about 80 items (MOW-International Research Team, 1981), covering the three levels in Figure 1.

Statistical procedures included: analysis of frequency distributions, ranking, t-test comparison of means, correlational analysis (Kendall, Pearson, multiple R), analysis of variance, multiple classification analysis and chisquare. Most statistical analyses were performed four times: once on the total Germanic cluster (sum of the three countries, N=2503) and once per country.

SOME RESULTS

Work definitions

How do the various groups in our study define working? In order to answer this question the respondents have been asked to choose from the list below four statements which to their opinion best define when an activity is 'working':

A —— if you do it in a working place;
B —— if someone tells you what to do;
C —— if it is physically strenuous;
D —— if it belongs to your task;
E —— if you do it to contribute to society;
F —— if, by doing it, you get the feeling of belonging;
G —— if you do it at a certain time (e.g. from 8 until 5);
I —— if it adds value to something;
J —— if it is not pleasant;
K —— if you get money for doing it;
L —— if you have to account for it;
M —— if you have to do it;
N —— if others profit by it.

For the total Germanic cluster, the statements most frequently chosen are of four different content areas: financial reward (K), accountability (D), feelings of belonging (F) and purpose of the activity (I).

As can be seen from Figure 2 the same four content areas appear in the definition of working in Flanders while in Germany the accountability aspect and in the Netherlands the functional aspect is more frequently used to define an activity as working.

Flanders, Germany and the Netherlands in a similar way define an

activity as working in so far that the areas of 'reward' and 'accountability' are included in the work definition of each country.

Flanders shares with Germany the 'belonging' aspect (F) and with
the Netherlands the purpose-item I 'if it adds value to something' as
important in the definition of work.

Characteristic for Germany is including statement L 'if you have to
account for it' in the work definition which neither of the two other
countries do so frequently.

The specificity of the Dutch work definition lies in the frequent
choice (more than in the two other countries) of statement E 'if you
do it to contribute to society'.

GERMANIC CLUSTER	FLANDERS	GERMANY	NETHERLANDS
REWARD (K 58 %)	ACCOUNTABILITY (D 61 %)	REWARD (K 59 %)	REWARD (K 60 %)
ACCOUNTABILITY (D 48 %)	REWARD (K 54 %)	ACCOUNTABILITY (L 47 %)	PURPOSE (I 51 %)
BELONGING (F 41 %)	BELONGING (F 50 %)	ACCOUNTABILITY (D 40 %)	PURPOSE (E 49 %)
PURPOSE (I 41 %)	PURPOSE (I 42 %)	BELONGING (F 34 %)	ACCOUNTABILITY (D 41 %)

Figure 2. Content areas most frequently chosen to define an activity
as 'working' per country

Chemical engineers, tool & die makers and teachers do not include
all four content areas in their definition of an activity as working,
the other seven target groups do.

Chemical engineers define an activity as 'working' by chosing the
following statements most frequently:

. if it adds value to something (purpose);
. if you get money for doing it (reward);
. it it belongs to your task (accountability);
. if you have to account for it (accountability).

Their definition of working in general corresponds very well with their present job (research for new products, highly paid job, in which they have a high degree of responsibility).

In their definition of an activity as 'working' tool & die makers choose the following statements most frequently:

. if you get money for doing it (reward);
. if it belongs to your task (accountability);
. if you have to account for it (accountability);
. if, by doing it, you get the feeling of belonging (belonging).

This definition of working, again, reflects the responsible key-function of the tool & die makers within the production process.

Finally, teachers have the most specific definition of an activity as working choosing the following statements most frequently:

. if it belongs to your task (accountability);
. if it adds value to something (purpose);
. if you do it to contribute to society (purpose);
. if you have to account for it (accountability).

It is striking that teachers are the only target group which does not include the reward aspect of working in its definition. The statements selected to define an activity as working correspond with the role one expects from teachers: educating the children in our society (item E).

Central MOW variables

Operationalization

Meaning of working is defined conceptually in terms of five major domains (see Figure 1). These core variables were operationalized as follows:

Centrality of working as a life role
Respondents rated on a 7-point scale how important and significant working is in their total life.

Societal norms about working
An original set of 42 societal norm statements about work and working in terms of what should be expected from working (entitlements) and what should be expected from the worker (obligation) was reduced through international pilot-testing to ten statements. The respondents expressed their disagreement/agreement with the statements on a 4-point scale. An internationally pooled factor analysis on these ten items revealed the two dimensions for each of which an index was created.

The opportunity (or entitlement) index takes into account the statements:

A. If a worker's skills become outdated, his employer should be responsible for retraining and reemployment.

E. When a change in work methods must be made, a supervisor should be required to ask workers for their suggestions before deciding what to do.

G. Every person in our society should be entitled to interesting and meaningful work.

I. A job should be provided to every individual who desires to work.

The obligation index is formed by the statements:

D. Persons in our society should allocate a large portion of their regular income toward savings for their future.

J. A worker should value the work he or she does even if it is boring, dirty or unskilled.

Valued working outcomes
Respondents assigned a total of 100 points, to the following six statements:

A1 Working gives you status and prestige.
A2 Working provides you with an income that is needed.
A3 Working keeps you occupied.
A4 Working permits you to have interesting contacts with other people.
A5 Working is a useful way to serve society.
A6 Working itself is basically interesting and satisfying to you.

Work role identification

Respondents ranked the following aspects of working according to their significance and importance:

A The tasks I do while working.
B My company or organization.
C The product or service I provide.
D The type of people with whom I work.
E The type of occupation or profession I am in.
F The money I receive for my work.

Importance of work aspects

A combined ranking-rating method of facet appraisal was utilized to get to know the relative importance of the following aspects of working for the individual:

A A lot of opportunity to LEARN new things.
B Good INTERPERSONAL relations (supervisors, co-workers).
C Good opportunity for upgrading or PROMOTION.
D CONVENIENT work hours.
E A lot of VARIETY.
F INTERESTING work (work that you really like).
G Good job SECURITY.
H A good MATCH between your job requirements and your abilities and experience.
I Good PAY.
J Good physical working CONDITIONS (such as light, temperature, cleanliness, low noise level).
K A lot of AUTONOMY (you decide how to do your work).

Relations within central MOW

A first screening of the data per above described question, leads to the conclusion that in three domains of meaning of working (valued working outcomes, importance of work aspects and work role identification) the same aspects of working appear as most important in each country: pay, work itself and people (see Figure 3). A slight diversity between countries occurs in the rank ordering of identifications with work roles, although roughly the three similar content areas appear as most important. Here again - as with the work definition - Flanders stands a little apart from the two other countries that share the same work role identification rankorder.

It is clear that the respondents in the three countries don't make the distinction between the conceptually different dimensions. For them, primarily the content of the work aspects counts, not so much the modality under which they appear.

CENTRALITY OF WORKING	SOCIETAL NORMS ABOUT WORKING	VALUED WORKING OUTCOMES
RATHER HIGH	FLANDERS MORE OBLIGATION ORIENTED, GERMANY & NETHERLANDS MORE OPPORTUNITY ORIENTED	1ST INCOME 2ND WORK ITSELF 3RD CONTACTS
SIMILARITY OF COUNTRIES DIVERSITY OF TARGET GROUPS	DIVERSITY OF COUNTRIES DIVERSITY OF TARGET GROUPS	SIMILARITY OF COUNTRIES DIVERSITY OF TARGET GROUPS

IMPORTANCE OF WORK LIFE ASPECTS	WORK ROLE IDENTIFICATION	
	FLANDERS	GERM.+ NETHERL.
1ST INTERESTING WORK 2ND GOOD PAY 3RD INTERPERSONAL RELATIONS	1ST MONEY 2ND OCCUPATION 3RD PEOPLE	1ST PEOPLE 2ND MONEY/TASKS
SIMILARITY OF COUNTRIES DIVERSITY OF TARGET GROUPS	DIVERSITY OF COUNTRIES DIVERSITY OF TARGET GROUPS	

Figure 3. Summary findings for central MOW

The following five central MOW dimensions are taken into account in this chapter[*]:
. social norms about working with two subdimensions: obligations and opportunities (obligation index and opportunity index);
. work centrality (absolute measure);
. instrumental dimension pay (valued working outcomes A2);
. expressive dimension work itself (valued working outcomes A6);
. social dimension (valued working outcomes A4).

The following significant relationships between the five MOW dimensions are found in each country separately and in the total Germanic cluster:
. the higher work centrality, the higher the agreement with obligatory societal norms about working. If one feels that work is very central

---

[*] In view of possible statistical analyses we operationalize these dimensions by indices or questions on interval level of measuerment.

in life, one has strong feelings of obligation towards society;
. the more important the financial incentive, the less important the
  intrinsic value of work itself;
. the more important the financial incentive, the lower work centrality;
. the more important the financial incentive, the lower the social
  dimension.
If money is very important, working is considered only as a means to
provide it. Work does not occupy a central place in life and neither
the nature of the work nor the social contacts through work are considered important.

In our discussion of the relationships of antecedents and consequences
with the central MOW variables - societal norms, centrality, pay, work
itself, contacts - the findings will be arranged according to the above
reported relations within these central MOW dimensions.

Relationships of antecedents and consequences with central MOW variables

The relationships of central MOW - societal norms, centrality, pay, work
itself, contacts - with antecedents were tested through multiple classification analyses with the central MOW variables as dependent variables
(one by one) and a number of antecedents as independent variables or
predictors. Antecedents covering the boxes 'personal and family situation'
and 'present job and career history' and 'macro socio-economic environment (country)' from Figure 1 were included.
    As criterium for a significant influence on central MOW an eta or
beta > .20[*] was used. Some antecedents show few or no significant relationships with central MOW: urban/rural upbringing, religious upbringing,
ups/downs in work history, aggravating work conditions. They will not
be discussed any further.
    From the multiple classification analyses on the Germanic cluster
(sum of three countries) the variable 'country' has only an important
influence in predicting the obligatory societal norms. Therefore only

---

[*] Due to the large N in our samples the R had usually a significance
  level < .05.

that central MOW dimension will be treated per country.

The antecedents to be discussed are:
. country;
. target group membership;
. sex;
. educational level;
. quality of work (an index which combines the amount of variety, participation, learning, skill utilization and the impact of mistakes).
The relationships of central MOW variables with some consequences were
tested with chi square, t-test comparison of means and Pearson correlation coefficients, according to the measurement level of the respective variables.

For a number of consequences no significant relationships with central
MOW variables have been established: months of unemployment in past
five years, promotion orientation, importance of work in future, life
satisfaction. These will not be discussed any further.

The consequences to be dicussed are:
. time commitment to work (average hours work per week including over-
  time);
. lottery question (reaction on the question "imagine you won a lottery
  or inherited a large sum of money and could live comfortable for the
  rest of your life without working, what would you do: stop working or
  continue to work");
. occupational satisfaction;
. mobility intention (willingness to be retrained for a different job
  and the intention to actually change jobs in the near future);
. choice for high expressive jobs versus the choice for high instrumental jobs: an index derived from a series of choices between jobs
  having various levels of expressive characteristics such as high participation, skill utilization, pleasantness versus various nodes of
  increase or decrease of pay;
. willingness to give up working hours and money.

Societal norms about working reflect cultural values. It is, therefore, no surprise that the three countries under study differ in this respect. Figure 4 locates each country in a two-dimensional space using their scores on the opportunity and the obligation index. In Figure 5 the same has been done for the ten target groups.

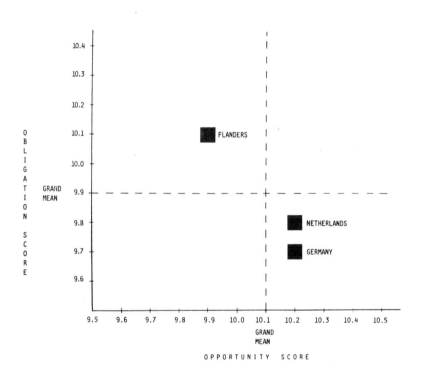

Figure 4. Societal norms about working - country picture

As can be seen in Figure 4, Flanders is more obligation-oriented while Germany and the Netherlands are more opportunity-oriented.

A closer look to the mean degree of agreement of each country with single items of the societal norms question will clarify this finding.

All three countries 'agree' with the opportunity item A on the employer's responsibility to retrain and reemploy workers whose skills become outdated. Flemish, Dutch and German respondents 'strongly agree' with the individual right to work (I).

High opportunity scores for Germany and the Netherlands arise respectively from a strong agreement with item G 'entitlement to interesting and meaningful work' and from a strong agreement with item E 'right to direct participation, werkoverleg'.

Low obligation score for Germany and the Netherlands is caused by disagreement in these two countries with both obligation items (D and J) that form the obligation index. In Flanders on the average respondents agree with these statements.

Figure 5 illustrates that German target groups have a more varied opinion about societal norms than their Flemish and Dutch colleagues. Moreover, four clusters of target groups with an rather extreme score on either obligation or opportunity dimension can be identified:
. high obligation and low entitlement is found in Flanders for self employed, textile workers and retired;
. high obligation and entitlement exists in the Netherlands for retired and textile workers;
. low obligation and entitlement appears with the Dutch students;
. low obligation and high entitlement is found with the Dutch teachers and the German unemployed, temporary workers, students and techers.

With respect to societal norms, it can be concluded from our data that a higher obligation orientation is found with the lower level jobs and the lower level of education; it is also associated with higher satisfaction and motivation and a weaker intention to change the work (situation).

The opportunity orientation, which is lowest among the self employed and highest among the school teachers, is negatively related with time commitment and satisfaction with one's career and positively with intention to change.

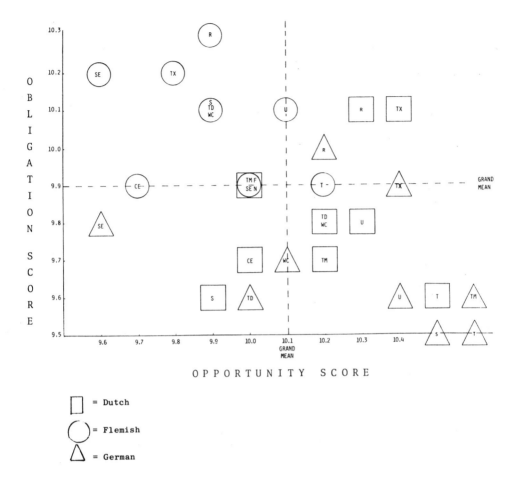

Figure 5. Societal norms about working - target group picture

Work centrality

Generally speaking the absolute degree of work centrality is rather
high (mean = 5 on 7 point scale) for the Germanic cluster. The multiple
classification analysis shows no significant influence for 'country'
although Flanders has a slightly higher work centrality than Germany

and the Netherlands. The positive relationship found between obligation and work centrality may account for that. Figure 6 summarizes the relationships of antecedents and consequences with work centrality for the total cluster.

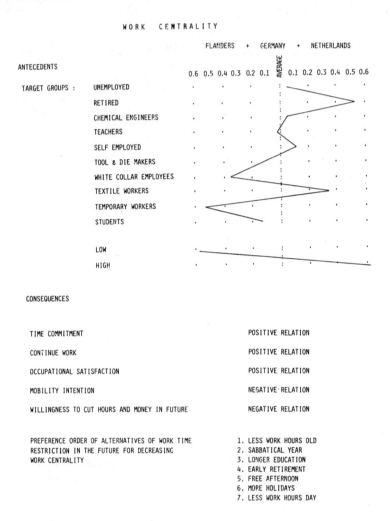

Figure 6. Antecedents and consequences of work centrality

Especially for retired and textile workers working was and is very central in their life. Temporary workers illustrate their somewhat alternative view on working by a lower centrality of work. Again looking to Figure 5 we see retired and textile workers have on the whole a higher obligation score than temporary workers so that here again the positive relationship between obligation and work centrality is illustrated.

It is further apparent that for those who occupy a job of high quality, working takes a high central place in their lives.

Some significant relationships of consequences with work centrality are logically consistent: there is a positive relationship with time commitment, with continuation of work even when having enough money available, with satisfaction with work career, and a low intention to future work changes.

When working takes a central place in life, people are less willing to give up part of their working hours (and payment) and if they are forced to work less they prefer to postpone it to the later part of their life and not to be restricted in their immediate work time.

Pay, work itself, contacts

Flanders, Germany and the Netherlands are equal in the importance evaluations of these three MOW dimensions.

On all three dimensions - pay, work itself, contacts - target groups can be divided into low scoring (far below the grand mean) and high scoring (far above the grand mean) groups.

Figure 7 shows the position of each target group in the three dimensional model.

The antecedents sex and educational level show overall significant relationships with the value attached to contacts and to work itself. Women value the social dimension of working higher than men; respondents of higher educational level attach higher importance to work itself. In Figure 7 these relationships are illustrated by the position of temporary workers and teachers (exclusively female respondents) versus chemical engineers, tool & die makers and self employed (exclusively male respondents) on the contact-dimension, and by the position of especially teachers and chemical engineers (high educational level) versus most of the other target groups on the expressive dimension.

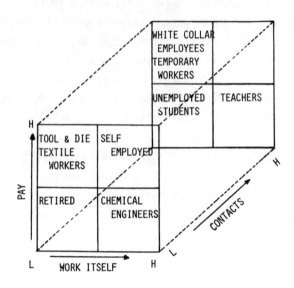

Figure 7. Position of target groups on three
MOW dimensions

Furthermore, some country-specific effects of sex and educational
level could be observed: Flemish and Dutch men value pay more than
women; the higher the educational level op Flemish and Germans the less
importance is attached to pay; the higher the educational level of
Germans the higher contacts are being valued.

Respondents who have an intrinsic valuable job at present, evaluate
the expressive dimension of working as very important. In Flanders and
Germany there is a negative relationship between quality of work and the
importance of pay.

Looking at the consequences of the value attached to the three MOW
dimensions, almost the same relationships appear for pay, work itself and
contacts but in the reversed direction for the instrumental as opposed
to both the expressive and social dimension.

Low value attached to pay and high value to work itself and/or contacts correspond with extreme low and extreme high time commitment to
work respectively (see Figure 7 unemployed and students versus chemical

engineers and teachers). High importance of pay and low value for the expressive and the social dimension correspond with normal time commitment to work (36 to 42 h/w) (see Figure 7 tool & die makers and textile workers who have strictly defined work hours).

Respondents who value pay high as opposed to those who attach great importance to work itself and/or contacts:

. would stop working earlier if ever they had enough money available;
. are less satisfied with their occupation (only in Flanders a positive relationship between contacts and occupational satisfaction);
. have low willingness to cut hours and especially money in future;
. choose for jobs with very poor intrinsic value but which pay well (only positive relationship between job choice and work itself, not with contacts);
. have different preferences for work time restriction options.

Finally only the respondents who attach great importance to the interpersonal contacts at work express intentions for future change concerning work.

CONCLUSIONS

From the comparison of MOW target group data of Flanders, Germany and the Netherlands, a greater similarity between countries than between target groups can be concluded.

Asked to describe the term 'working' respondents in Germany especially stress the accountability aspect and the Dutch respondents are more functional in their definition.

When it comes to agreement with societal norms about working, Flanders seems to be more obligation-oriented than the two other countries while Germany and the Netherlands share the same (stronger) degree of opportunity-orientation.

In spite of the above mentioned differences, the three countries agree on a rather high degree of work centrality. In addition, the Flemish, Germans and Dutch appreciate the same working outcomes namely: income, work itself and contacts.

Looking at three major MOW dimensions - pay, work itself and contacts - it appears that blue collar workers, textile workers and tool & die makers, in spite of their different skill level, group together sharing a high importance attached to pay and a low importance to the intrinsic and the social dimension of working. Clerical workers (white collar employees and temporary workers) attach high value to pay and contacts and low value to work itself. Unemployed and students, both non-working groups, show a high importance attached to contacts and a low importance to both pay and work itself. Two rather individualistic target groups, self employed and chemical engineers, attach high importance to the content of their work. The former are very much concerned with pay, the latter very little. Retired score low on each of the three dimensions (instrumental, intrinsic and social). Teachers attach a very low value to pay but work itself and interpersonal relationships are appreciated very highly.

The impact of the developmental variables - educational level, sex, quality of present job - upon the major constitutive dimensions of the meaning of work: societal norms, centrality, pay, work itself and contacts can be summarized as follows:

. the higher the educational level, the lower agreement with obligatory societal norms, the lower value attached to pay and the higher the importance of both work itself and contacts;

. women emphasize the social dimension of working and the interpersonal relationships stronger than men;

. the higher the quality of the present job in terms of intrinsic value, the higher the importance attached to work itself and the higher work centrality.

The major dimensions of work meanings have a significant influence on time commitment to work, intended continuation of work, occupational satisfaction, mobility intention, willingness to give up hours and money in the future.

REFERENCES

MOW-International Research Team, The meaning of working. In: G. Dlugos & K. Weierman (Eds.), Management under differing value systems. Political, social and economical perspectives in a changing world. Berlin/New York: Walter De Gruyter, 1981, 565-630.

6. THE OBLIGATION TO WORK AND THE RIGHT TO WORK AS DETERMINANTS OF THE ATTITUDE TOWARDS THE UNEMPLOYED

L. Lagrou, H. de Witte & J. van Rensbergen

INTRODUCTION

In psychological research, less attention is given to the study of attitudes toward the unemployed in psychological research than to the study of the psycho-social consequences of unemployment (Fraser, 1980, 183-184). It should be noted here that attention has been given to the attitude of the employed and the unemployed toward unemployment in recent opinion polls: N.O.S., 1975, U.N.I.O.P. 1977, The European Omnibus 1978, (Cegos) Makro-test 1981. Such opinion research, however, does not provide a theoretical framework to structure the diversity of opinions and to interpret or explain the sometimes divergent results. This is also the case with the already existing image studies about the unemployed, which are rather exploratory in nature (De Goede & Maassen, 1979; Vanderleyden, 1981). Therefore, in the present study, a theoretical model has been worked out that is closely linked to the social problem of structural unemployment. This model, which is also tested empirically, differentiates both within the group of the employed and within the group of the unemployed: the attitude differs in function of the social position that one occupies as an employed individual or as unemployed. We will now further clarify this model.

Stereotypes held by the employed about the unemployed contain a striking paradox: the unemployed are reproached for not being willing to work and also for taking jobs away from others who have more right to it. The reproach that the unemployed are not willing to work is expressed in opinions such as these: they are lazy; they live at the cost of the community. On the other hand, the unemployed are reproached for actually being willing to work: the unemployed may not perform any productive or useful work; they must be stringently controlled and harshly punished for working on the black market.

This contradiction is a result of the combination of two principles or value judgments: the principle of the obligation to work and the principle of the right to work. According to the *obligation* to work or the work ethic, adults must provide for their own living and for that of their dependent family members by working. This principle is propagated by employers who want to stimulate their employees to give their full efforts (Anthony, 1978). The achievement motivation also implies that the individual be motivated to develop and surpass himself and others by his performances (McClelland, 1961). The work ethic is profoundly rooted in the value pattern of our industrialized society, and particularly in the Protestant countries where children are or were imbued with the value of achievement, autonomy, and self-reliance (Weber, 1930). This ideology formed the basis for achievement motivation that stimulated hard work, which in turn resulted in rapid economic growth (Brown, 1965, p. 452).

Whoever believes in the obligation to work will tend to judge the unemployed negatively. This connection is confirmed by a recent study on the relationship between the Protestant work ethic and attitudes toward unemployment (Furnham, 1982).

The principle of the *right* to work, on the contrary, does not have this long tradition, but has only recently arisen out of the present state of massive and long-term unemployment, long-term because this unemployment is structural. The right to work implies access to the labor market. For work satisfies not only the need for income, but also a number of other needs that Marie Jahoda calls latent functions (Jahoda, 1979, p. 313): the need for time structure, for social contact, for wider goals, for personal status and identity, and for activity and self-realization. Now the unemployed are demanding replacement work in compensation for these latent functions. Indeed, in our countries the unemployment benefits compensate to a certain extent for the loss of income.

The principle of the right to work interferes with that of the obligation to work. It now becomes very difficult or extremely unrealistic to attribute the responsibility for unemployment to the unemployed themselves. Due to the massive shortage of jobs, the labor market mechanism comes too obviously to the fore. This does not alter the fact that the obligation to work is still experienced as an important principle. We are thus in a transition phase where the obligation and the right are being affirmed simultaneously.

THE SOCIAL POSITION AS A VARIABLE

In our study attention is given primarily to a differentiation of the attitude toward unemployment in function of the *social position* that is occupied by the employed and by the unemployed. Our research hypotheses rest on the assumption that the favorableness of unfavorableness of the attitude toward unemployment is determined by:
1) the social position of the unemployed individual who is evaluated;
2) the social position of the subject.
The social positions are associated with more positive or more negative attitudes toward unemployment by the obligation to work and the right to work. These determinants are thus intermediate variables in our model. The social position of the unemployed individual determines the basic pattern. The subject can reinforce or weaken the impact of the social position of the unemployed on the evaluation of the obligation

and the right to work in function of his own position. For example, a working woman will not contest the right to work of married women, while her male working colleagues will. This theory is presented schematically in Figure 1.

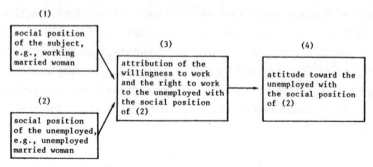

Figure 1. Hypothetical relationship between the social position of the
subject (1), the social position of the unemployed (2) and the
attitudes toward the unemployed (4), with willingness to work
and the right to work (3) as intermediate variables

As regards the social position of the unemployed (cf. position 2 in Fig. 1), four positions are distinguished:
1. the structurally unemployed,
2. the younger unemployed (less than 25 years of age),
3. the unemployed married woman, and
4. the unemployed immigrant.

These categories are taken into account in discussions about measures to reduce unemployment. Depending on the individual's political convictions and/or his social position, priority is given to one or more of these categories and other categories are excluded or are given fewer opportunities. Factor analysis of the answers to three successive surveys among employed people about their attitude toward the unemployed confirms this distinction.

The first survey was made in 1979 as an exploratory study. The analysis was carried out for a list of 39 statements about the unemployed. These statements were derived from content analysis of interviews and from an analysis of the content of articles about the unemployed in popular newspapers and magazines. This survey was conducted with 97 subjects (Simons, 1980).

The second survey with an adapted series of 36 statements was taken of 80 subjects (Van Hemelrijck, 1981).

Finally, factor analysis of the data of the study presented here also confirmed the distinction between the four social positions. In these three studies, however, there was a fifth factor alongside the four categories, namely, the abuse of unemployment, which we will not discuss in this paper.

GENERAL RESEARCH HYPOTHESES

Our research hypotheses are related to these social positions. We limit ourselves, however, to the prediction of tendencies, for the attitude toward unemployment is also influenced by other variables such as religious conviction that do not necessarily coincide with the social position. Moreover, we did not measure the importance that our subjects attach to the obligation to work and the right to work, nor did we study the variables that influence these value judgments.

Hypothesis 1

The employed rate the structurally unemployed very favorably and the young employed less but still predominantly favorably. Their judgment on unemployed immigrants is rather unfavorable and that about unemployed married women is clarly unfavorable or negative.

This general hypothesis about tendencies in the evaluation of unemployment was derived from a cognitive analysis of the degree unemployment seems to be justified with respect to the two principles mentioned above. First, the question is whether the unemployed of each category in general fulfill their obligation to work. In other words, are they in general willing to work or is this not the case? Then we investigate whether the unemployed of each of the categories should be granted general priority in the assignment of jobs. In other words, do they have the right to work, or does the opposite apply? We wish to stress that we are not concerned here with the justifiability of the opinions. We contend only that an analysis of the argumentation (the cognitive aspect of the attitude) allows a prediction of tendencies toward a position for the unemployed or against the unemployed (the affective aspect of the attitude). Figure 2 gives an overview of the attribution of the determinants to the four categories of the unemployed.

	structural unemployed	young unemployed	unemployed immigrants	unemployed (married) women
obligation to work (willingness)	+	−	+/−	−
right to work (priority in job allocation)	+	+	−	−

Figure 2. Degree to which, according to public opinion, willingness to work and job allocation priorities are attributed to social categories of unemployed

The signs in Figure 2 justify the predictions of the first hypothesis concerning the more favorable or more unfavorable tendency in the attitude toward the categories of the unemployed.

The argumentation for the attribution of a plus or a minus sign in the various categories of the unemployed is as follows:

The structurally unemployed are judged favorably, for they satisfy the requirement of willingness to work and must be given priority for employment. They are heads of families, almost exclusively men with work experience. They are, in our opinion, perceived as predominantly willing to work for the following reasons:

1. They are unemployed involuntarily as a result of external circumstances such as plant closures or company reorganizations.
2. Remaining unemployed is unattractive to them; they are bored since they are oriented to an active professional life.
3. They are oriented to work because they were raised that way (the work ethic was central in their socialization).

These structurally unemployed people enjoy priority in public opinion as regards employment and this primarily for the following reasons:

1. As breadwinners, they have to support their families.
2. The community must reward them for the many years they have already worked (recognition of seniority).
3. Their skills and professional experience must be made use of.

The younger unemployed generate ambivalent reactions: on the one hand, the seriousness of the high percentage of unemployment among young people is stressed (in Belgium, one third of the school-leavers between 16 and 25 years old are unemployed). On the other hand, the willingness of many young people to work is often questioned. There is the conviction that it is easier for young people than for older people to find work but that they make less effort to do so.

The willingness to work of young people is judged rather negatively, and that primarily for the following reasons:

1. Many young people do not get work because they do not really look for it or because they are too choosy.
2. For many young people, being unemployed is rather attractive: they enjoy a free and easy life without worry because the compensation suffices for someone without a family to support.
3. Many young people are influenced by alternative values that would rate the enjoyment of life higher than the work ethic. This is also regarded as a consequence of a more permissive upbringing.

The attributuion of an ambiguous willingness to work to young people is compensated for by giving them job priority. The main arguments for this are the following:

1. The continuity of employment must be assured: young people are the future breadwinners.
2. Employment promotes the integration of young people in the society and thus prevents anarchy and deviance.
3. The quality of the committment must be assured by the introduction of new, youthful energy and of newly acquired, up-to-date expertise.

In the context of the present economic crisis, there are many reasons why the employed react negatively to unemployed immigrants. Nevertheless, the appreciation here, too, is somewhat ambivalent. This ambivalence concerns primarily their willingness to work. There are arguments for and against.

Pro:

1. Immigrants are willing to work because they have left their countries to look for work.
2. Immigrants are prepared to do the undesirable and low-paid work that the natives reject.

Con:

1. Being unemployed is attractive for immigrants because they still
   have a higher income with unemployment compensation than what they
   could earn in their country, even if they could find work there.

   As regards the right to work, however, the position of the immigrants
is weak. There are some strong arguments against it:

1. They take the places of the natives.
2. They profit from our system of unemployment compensation.
3. They belong to another labor market, namely, that of their own country.

   Finally, the most disputed seems to us to be the position of the
unemployed married woman. The economic crisis is thus undermining the
progress women have made in the last decade toward more professional
equivalence with men. First of all, her willingness to work is contes-
ted with the following arguments:

1. Many unemployed women voluntarily quit or provoke dismissal.
2. For many of them, a period of unemployment is attractive because
   they can then take care of their small children.
3. Married women are supposed to fulfill caring functions and not to
   work outside of the home (the 'old' ideology of sex-specific roles).

   These arguments clearly imply the negation of the arguments pro-
willingness to work of the structurally unemployed. This applies also
for the principle of the right to work. Married women (whose husbands
work) do not have the right to work because:

1. They take jobs away from male breadwinners.
2. They unjustifiably increase their family income, because many women
   do housework without being compensated for it (Francken, 1981;
   Francken & Lagrou, 1983).
3. They are better qualified than anyone else for housekeeping tasks.

   With this explanation, we have attempted to demonstrate that the
classic negative stereotypes of the unemployed fit very well into the
attribution model of Figure 2. Trends in the attitude toward the unemployed, however, are influenced not only by the social position of

the unemployed individual (see Fig. 1: (2)), but also by that of the subject (see Fig. 1: (1)).

Our second general hypothesis, therefore, concerns the influence of the social position of the subject on the attitude toward the unemployed. The second hypothesis is associated with the first in the sense that the basic pattern is formed by the rank ordering we have just described of the four social positions of the unemployed on a scale varying from favorable to unfavorable judgments. The second hypothesis describes when and how the social position of the subject alters this basic pattern.

When is the basic pattern altered or adapted?

The subject will tend to alter the basic pattern in function of his own position in two cases, which are not necessarily mutually exclusive:

1. The subject alters the basic pattern when he identifies more strongly with one of the positions of the unemployed than with another. For example, a 40-year old section chief who has been working for 20 years in the same company identifies strongly with the category of the structurally unemployed. If his company should close down, he would be in this category himself.
2. The subject alters the basic pattern when he experiences one category of the unemployed more as a threat to his own job than another category, principally by black-market labor, or as competition on the labor market. For example: the housewife of a low-level employee will feel threatened by the competition of younger unemployed female employees.

How is the basic pattern altered or adapted?

1. The subject will tend to consider more favorably the category of the unemployed with which he identifies from his own position than is the case in the basic pattern. For example, a student (applicant employee or applicant unemployed) will indignantly reject the negative stereotypes about unwillingness to work of the unemployed who have just finished school. He will evaluate this group on the same level as that of the structurally unemployed.

2. The subject will tend to consider more unfavorably the category of
the unemployed that is experienced as a threat to his own interest
or to the interests of the group with which he identifies than the
other categories for which this is not the case. For example, an
unskilled laborer may feel that his job is threatened by immigrants.
He evaluates them even lower than the unemployed women because the
latter do not compete for jobs in his sector. He denies immigrants
the right to work (as potential employees) and accuses them of living
at his expense.

These two general hypotheses will be further concretized in specific
working hypotheses adapted to the limitations of our sample and of our
research instrument.

DESCRIPTION OF THE STUDY

The sample

During the months of October and November of 1981, the first-year students of a faculty of economics were asked to participate in a study
of the psychological aspects of the economic crisis. The students who
were willing to participate on a voluntary basis (about 60% of the
group) filled in a questionnaire and asked their parents to do the same.

In this way, 263 useable questionnaires were provided. Since the 59
male students and the 34 female students had virtually all involved
their parents in the study, the group of respondents was heterogeneous
as regards age and sex. The four subgroups: fathers, mothers, and male
and female students were, however, equivalent as regards family background, for the families of our samples were represented in the sub-
groups by both parents and by a son or daughter. The two groups of
young people were also homogeneous as regards age (18-19 years old),
activity pattern (students), and professional interest (economy). For
the group of the fathers (N = 89), the average age was 50.5 y. (SD =
4.89). With the exception of 5 who had retired, all were professionally
active. The mothers (N = 81) were an average of 47.7 years old (SD =
4.98). One third (N = 27) of them were professionally active and two-thirds

(N = 54) were housewives.

For that reason the position of married women has been divided into housewives and employed women. The hypotheses then are specifically related to the five following positions:

1. Professionally active heads of families. This is the largest group, and it can be further divided according to professional status. This social position is henceforth indicated as the employed.
2. Professionally active married women, henceforth indicated as working women.
3. Married women who stay at home, henceforth indicated as housewives.
4. Young male applicant employees or unemployed, further indicated as male students.
5. Young female applicant employees or unemployed, further indicated as female students.

For the division according to social status, use was made of the professional prestige classification system of Van Heek (Van Tulder, 1978) combined with the level of education. This leads to a division whereby the highest status level has a slight predominance: 36% (N = 95) as opposed to 27% (N = 71) for the low status level and 29% (N = 76) for the middle. To the low professional status category belong workers and lower-level white-collar workers, and to the high status level belong the higher-level white-collar workers, management staff, and members of the liberal professions. The married women were assigned the status of the husband unless the woman herself was professionally active on a higher level than her husband. The students were also assigned the professional status of the head of the family. Globally, therefore, the socio-economic status of our sample is rather high. Moreover, our sample is more homogeneous than the data would lead us to suppose. Indeed, all the parents in this sample have children attending university, from which we may conclude an upward social mobility for the low and middle categories.

The instrument

The study was presented as an opinion poll. A three-part questionnaire was given to each subject. Only the first part has been used for this study. This first part consists of opinions about unemployment and the unemployed: an attitude scale consisting of 36 items with answers on a 5-point agree/not agree scale. We had designed this scale ourselves and had tested it in two exploratory studies (Simons, 1979; Van Hemelrijck, 1981). The two other parts were related to the judgment of payments and measures to reduce unemployment, and to attitudes towards abuses of unemployment. The answering of the questionnaire took 20 to 30 minutes.

The 36-item attitude scale was transformed into a series of five sub-scales. A factor analysis with varimax rotation of the answers of the 263 subjects yielded five factors of which four were clearly related to the social position of the unemployed. On the basis of the results of this factor analysis and with account being taken of the results of a cluster analysis of the 36 items, four sub-scales were formed, each grouping a number of items. The answers of a subject to the items of a sub-scale then reflect his or her attitude toward the group of the unemployed concerned. Thirty of the 36 items were retained in this way. Six items were eliminated because they had no loading on any of the five factors of more than .30 and also did not appear in any of the clusters.

We describe the content of the four sub-scales by one item that refers to the willingness to work and one that refers to the right to work, adding the factor loadings.

Sub-scale 1: The structurally unemployed

This scale consists of 6 items.

Willingness to work: Most of the unemployed would immediately accept work under their level just in order to be able to work (.53).

Right to work: If there isn't work for everyone, the work must be redistributed, and therefore one should shorten the work week (.46).

The factor of this sub-scale accounts for 12.7% of the common variance of the 36-item scale. The reliability of the scale is rather low: .535.

Sub-scale 2: unemployed young people

This scale consists of 7 items.

Willingness to work: A great deal of unemployed young people would

rather live off the society than look for work (.73). None of the 7
items, however, implied the right to work. The factor of this scale
accounts for 22.8% of the common variance: .785.

Sub-scale 3: unemployed immigrants

A short scale of 4 items.
Willingness to work: Unemployed foreign workers do not look for work
(.60). Right to work: The foreign workers take work away from Belgians
(.50). The scale factor accounts for 17.9% of the common variance and
seems to be very reliable: .804.

Sub-scale 4: unemployed women

The scale consists of 6 items.
Willingness to work: Most women who sign up for unemployment benefits
do not want to work (.50). Right to work: In times of crisis, women
should be laid off first (.80). The factor of this scale accounts for
a significantly larger part of the variance than the others, namely,
27.8%. The scale is reliable: .838.

RESULTS

The data are analyzed in two phases: first, the general pattern that
follows from Hypothesis I is tested and then the modifications of the
general pattern that follow from the Hypothesis II. Where necessary,
the general hypotheses are specified in function of the sample and the
instrument.

First hypothesis

Public opinion judges rather favorably the structurally unemployed
and less favorably unemployed young people. It judges rather unfavorably unemployed immigrants and extremely unfavorably unemployed married
women (for the argumentation, see above).

The basic profile of Figure 3 (see page 92) shows that the locali-
zation of the sub-groups on the scale corresponds to the sequence
predicted by the first hypothesis. The observation that all of the sub-
groups are situated in the unfavorable half of the scale does not
confirm the hypothesis. The most favorably judged sub-group, the struc-

turally unemployed, is situated next to the theoretically neutral 3 value with 2.93. The structurally unemployed and the unemployed young people are situated close together toward the favorable pole, while the immigrants and the women are close to each other toward the unfavorable pole. Both pairs, however, differ significantly from each other (p < .01).

Second hypothesis

According to the second hypothesis, the basic pattern is altered under the influence of identification and/or conflicts of interest of the evaluating subject with one or more sub-groups of the unemployed. When we now differentiate this hypothesis for the five social positions that are represented in our sample, this results in an extended number of sub-hypotheses. We specify the sub-hypotheses by social category of the respondents.

1.   Sub-hypotheses regarding the position of *working married men:*

1.1. They will differentiate the basic pattern. For they are the typical representatives of the traditional work ethic, and they are also vulnerable to competition on the labor market.

1.2. They will rate the position of the structurally unemployed higher because they will identify more with this position than with the others.

1.3. Working men with a low professional status will rate unemployed women and particularly unemployed immigrants lower. For them, these groups are a threat (competition on the labor market), while this is not the case for respondents with a higher professional status.

2.   Sub-hypotheses concerning the position of *housewives.*

2.1. They will differentiate the basic pattern further, more than assumed in 1.1., because they attach more importance to the obligation to work and the right to work than their husbands on whose employment they are completely dependent.

2.2. They will rate the structurally unemployed higher because of their importance as breadwinners for the family.

2.3. They will rate the unemployed married women who receive unemployment compensation very low because they, in their perception, receive extra payment for keeping house, while housewives do not receive any pay for doing the same work.

3.   Sub-hypotheses concerning the position of *employed married women*:

3.1.   They will differentiate the basic pattern in the same way as the working married men do (cf. 1.1.).

3.2.   They will rate unemployed married women higher because they identify strongly with this position.

4.   Sub-hypotheses concerning the position of the *male students*:

4.1.   They will globally rate all the groups of the unemployed more favorably because they identify with the unemployed in general more than the older subjects. They still have to find a job in a period of structural unemployment and of increasing unemployment among young people.

4.2.   They will rate unemployed young people higher. They identify with this position and reject the attribution of a lack of willingness to work.

5.   Sub-hypotheses concerning the position of *female students*:

5.1. and 5.2., cf. 4.1. and 4.2. As college students, they are in many respects in a similar situation.

5.3.   They will rate the position of unemployed married women much higher. As intellectual young women in a period of economic crisis, they identify strongly with that position.

Figure 3 shows the degree to which the results conform to the tendencies formulated by the hypotheses. A rather favorable or a rather unfavorable judgment of a particular category of unemployed can be deduced from a higher(favorable) or lower (unfavorable) location on the vertical line. This line represents a scale with a theoretical range of 1 to 5.

The first vertical line on the left, presents the results for the group as a whole (the basic pattern, see the first hypothesis). The other vertical lines represent the results for specific groups: I: the working married men, I bis: the working married men with lower professional status, II: the housewives, III: the working married women, IV: the male students, and V: the female students.

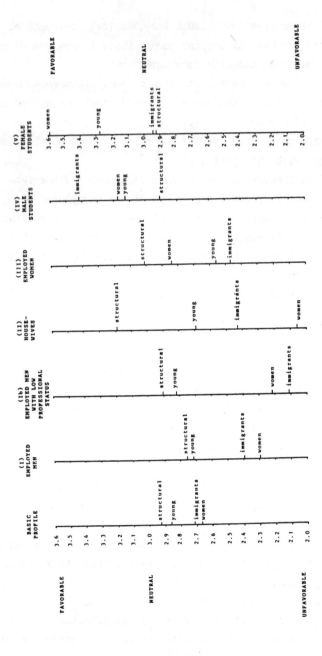

Figure 3. Location of the means of the subscales (related to subgroups of unemployed) on seven 5-point scales: basic profile, (I) employed men, (Ib) employed men with low professional status, (II) housewives, (III) employed women, (IV) male students and, (V) female students

The basic pattern has been discussed above (hypothesis 1). We will now discuss the results per sub-group of subjects.

1. How do the *working married men* judge the four sub-groups of the unemployed? (see vertical line I).

Sub-hypothesis 1.1, which states that this group will differentiate the basic pattern is confirmed. The two pairs: structurally unemployed and unemployed young people and immigrants and women, are situated further from each other than in the basic pattern.

Sub-hypothesis 1.2, which states that the structurally unemployed will be rated higher is not confirmed. They are not judged significantly more favorably than the young unemployed.

Sub-hypothesis 1.3 states that men with a low professional status (cf. line Ib) will rate unemployed women and particularly unemployed immigrant workers and also slightly for the women.

2. How do *housewives* rate the four sub-groups of the unemployed (cf. vertical line II).

The profile of this group confirms all of the sub-hypotheses:

Sub-hypothesis 2.1 states that they will differentiate the basic pattern further than the working married men, and this seems to be the case: the sub-scale results lie farther apart.

Sub-hypothesis 2.2: As assumed by this sub-hypothesis, this group gives the structurally unemployed a high score. The average is even slightly positive.

Sub-hypothesis 2.3: As this sub-hypothesis assumes, the unemployed married woman is treated by them very negatively.

3. How do the *working married women* rate the groups of the unemployed? (cf. line III).

3.1. The sub-hypothesis that they would differentiate the basic pattern as do the working married men (line I) is not confirmed. The pattern of this group conforms better to that of the housewives (line II).

3.2. The sub-hypothesis that they would rate the unemployed married woman higher is confirmed. In comparison with the sister profile of housewives, this shift is even striking.

4. The rating of the position of the unemployed by the *male students:*

4.1. The sub-hypothesis that they would rate all positions more favorably is confirmed. While the sub-groups in the basic pattern are all situated in the unfavorable half of the scale, here they are mostly situated in the favorable half.

4.2. A higher rating of young people is also noted, at least in comparison with the profiles of the three sub-groups discussed. Noteworthy and unexpected is the reversal by this group of the rank order of the basic pattern. Particularly the very high score of the unemployed immigrant is surprising. We interpret this as resulting from ideological influences: in student circles at that time there were demonstrations in favor of the immigrants. Opponents of equal treatment of immigrants were then labeled racists and fascists.

5. Rating of the position of the unemployed by the *female students*:

5.1. and 5.2. are confirmed in the sense that the female students have the same answer pattern as the male students.

5.3. is emphatically confirmed: the unemployed married women here receive a very high favorable score.

Here, too, the sequence of the basic pattern is reversed. The foreign worker is here placed on the level of the structurally unemployed and not above it as the male students placed them.

DISCUSSION

The results demonstrate, in our opinion, the validity of the theoretical model, in the social positions of the evaluating subject and of the evaluated unemployed function as central variables. By identification and by the positionally determined perception of conflicts of interest, the unemployed are evaluated according to their willingness to work and their right to job assignment when jobs are scarce.

An initial empirical testing of this model was done in an exploratory way. Our sample was limited and certainly not representative for the population (public opinion). Representativity was, however, not required to test the model, and, in this respect, the homogeneity of our sample had advantages. Nevertheless, testing of the model on a representative sample is indicated. In this case, the influence of age and socio-economic status have to be studied in particular.

The research instrument that is used in this study was not appropriate to test the model completely. Indeed, it was not constructed as a systematic operationalization of the theory. Chronologically, the model was only completely worked out after the instrument had already been tested for consistency and reliability in two preliminary studies.

Moreover, in this paper we have not reported all of the research data. We limited ourselves to the reactions of the subjects to the subscales that concerned the social positions of the unemployed. In another paper, we will discuss the results obtained with regard to the rating of abuses, of the compensation payments, and of governmental measures to reduce unemployment. For these variables, too, our model provides testable hypotheses.

This exploratory study has confirmed most of the specific hypotheses. However, there were also tendencies that did not correspond to our hypotheses, and there were results that could not have been predicted or explained on the basis of our model. Thus further research must take into account additional variables. Ideological conviction seems to be important in this regard, for it can generate answer trends. The very favorable rating of unemployed immigrants by the students was interpreted as a result of the influence of this variable, but this assumption was not tested.

Finally, it must also be stressed that the obligation to work and the right to work, which function in our model as intermediate variables, are only assumed in this study but not operationalized or measured. The measurement of these variables is also a task for further research.

REFERENCES

Anthony, P.D., The ideology of work. London: Tavistock Publications, 1978.

Brown, R., Social psychology. New York: McMillan, 1965.

Dixon, W.J. (Ed.), BMDP statistical software 1981. London: University of California Press, 1981.

Fabrimetal, Werkloosheid en werktijden. Beschouwingen naar aanleiding van een onderzoek. Fabrimetal, march, 199, p. 13.

Francken, L., <u>Beoordeling van werklozensteun aan gehuwde vrouwen met kinderen</u>. Niet gepubliceerde licentiaatsverhandeling. Leuven: K.U. Leuven, 1981.

Francken, L. & L. Lagrou, <u>Beoordeling van werklozensteun aan gehuwde vrouwen met kinderen</u>. Publikatie in voorbereiding, 1983.

Fraser, C., The Social Psychology of Unemployment. In: M. Jeeves (Ed.), <u>Psychology Survey no. 3</u>. London: G.Allen & Unwin, 1980.

Furnham, A., The Protestant work ethic and attitudes towards unemployment. <u>Journal of Occupational Psychology</u>, 1982, <u>55</u>, 277-285.

Goede, M.P.M. de & G.H. Maassen, <u>De publieke opinie over niet-werken. Analyse van een onderzoek naar de beeldvorming over werklozen en arbeidsongeschikten</u>. Lisse: Swets & Zeitlinger, 1979.

Hemelrijck, B. van, <u>De houding van werkenden t.a.v. werklozen in functie van socio-economische status en geslacht</u>. Niet gepubliceerde licentiaatsverhandeling. Leuven: K.U. Leuven, 1981.

Jahoda, M., The impact of unemployment in the 1930s and the 1970s. <u>Bulletin of the British Psychological Society</u>, 1979, <u>32</u>, 309-314.

Lagrou, L., Weerslag van de economische crisis op het individu: de werkloosheid. <u>Leuvens Bulletin L.A.P.P.</u>, 1982, <u>31</u>, 6, 385-397.

<u>Makrotest</u> (GEGOS), Hoe denkt de Belg over de werkloosheid. Brussel, 1981.

McClelland, D.C., <u>The achieving society</u>. Princeton: Van Nostrand, 1961.

Simons, M., <u>Houding van werkenden tegenover werklozen</u>. Niet gepubliceerde licentiaatsverhandeling. Leuven: K.U. Leuven, 1980.

The European Omnibus, <u>Chômage et recherche d'un emploi: attitudes et opinions des publics Européens</u>. Etude no. 78/31. Brussel, 1978.

Tulder, J.M.M. van, Een onderzoek naar beroepsprestige-stratificatie en beroepsmobiliteit van 1945-1980. In: J.L. Peschar & W.C. Ultee (Red.), <u>Sociale stratificatie. Op weg naar empirisch-theoretisch stratificatie-onderzoek in Nederland</u>. Deventer: Van Loghum Slaterus, 1978.

Vanderleyden, L., Werkloosheid. In: G. Dooghe, L. vanderleyden, L. vanden Boer & F. van Loon, <u>Feiten en meningen over aktuele problemen</u>. Brussel: C.B.G.S., 1981, Studies en documenten 15, 59-99.

Weber, M., <u>The Protestant ethic and the spirit of capitalism</u>. (1st. ed., 1904). Transl. by T. Parsons. New York: Scribner, 1930.

X.X., Meningen over werken en werkloosheid. Kijk- en Luisteronderzoek NOS. Intern rapport nr. B75-22, code TE/R, voor: Dingen van de Dag, 28 april, 1975.

X.X., Sondage exclusief: 90 p.c. des Belges pour le contrôle des abus du chômage. Le Soir, 22/10/1977, p. 2.

7. A SKILLS EXCHANGE FOR UNEMPLOYED PEOPLE

B. Senior & J.B. Naylor

INTRODUCTION

Many projects have been set up in recent years in an attempt to amelio-
rate the effects of unemployment upon individuals. In addition studies
have begun to identify with greater precision what these effects might
be. Jahoda (1979) discusses the impact of unemployment in terms of the
loss of those latent consequences of employment (time structuring,
sharing and widening experience, a sense of usefulness, personal status,
enforcing activity) which meet the more enduring human needs, whilst
Hill (1978) describes, in terms of psychological impact, the phases
individuals go through as the length of unemployment increases. Morley-
Bunker (1982) confirms a Department of Health and Social Security survey
that activities outside the home are the first ones to be given up when
people become unemployed, and Banks et al. (1980) found positive correlations between unemployment and lowered mental well-being in unemployed school leavers and adults. If the distinction is made between
employment as an economic relationship (Hartley, 1980) and work as
structured activity (Shepherd, 1981), the conclusion emerges that effective initiatives for unemployed people must fulfill functions similar
to those offered by work and potentially satisfy members' practical,
social and psychological needs. A skills exchange is one such initiative
through which a person may obtain all the satisfactions of working with
the exception of monetary payment.

98

This chapter describes a skills exchange, called 'Network', which has been running since 1979. It presents the results of an interdisciplinary research activity which has been carried out concentrating on data collected from the middle of 1979 up until the Autumn of 1982.

Network is a resource exchange organization accommodated in the centre of Liverpool sponsored by a charitable trust. Facilities include a small office with telephone, a workshop and lounge. Any person, employed or unemployed, can become a member by signifying some 'offer' of skill or time and some 'want' to be satisfied. There is no payment in money, exchanges do not necessarily take place reciprocally and the basis of all transactions is reasonable give and take. The group who established Network in 1979 expressed its aims in terms of a need "to find practical solutions to the problems of rewarding work"(MCVS, 1980). They felt that a resource exchange had the potential to provide the non-economic functions of employment and that successful operation would lead to changed attitudes, in the wider society, towards work, the unemployed and welfare benefits. The 12 founder members originally hoped for a large scale operation in an area where the number of registered unemployed is around 100.000. They saw the key operational problems mainly in terms of coping with a large membership. Instead of this extensive impact, however, a smaller organization with average membership of 130 has emerged. The total number of jobs (exchanges) done by 191 members in the three years to June 1982 was 469. Appendix 1 gives examples of jobs done and illustrates the range of activities undertaken.

The decision-making body is the weekly members' meeting which has a rotating chairman and minutes secretary. Day to day running of the organization is carried out by a paid coordinator who was appointed after $1\frac{1}{2}$ years of operation, to supplement and partially replace a members' rota.

Network members have, in addition to exchange, been involved in group projects, workshops and social events.

THE RESEARCH PROGRAMME

The research programme is action orientated in that it collects data
about the organization and its members and feeds this back to the
members meeting at regular intervals. The aim of the research has been
to document the development of the organization, its structure and
processes together with an assessment of the satisfactions gained by
the members.

Method

Activities at the group level have been studied by participant observation backed up by reference to the registers and records maintained
by Network. Detailed notes have been kept of all meetings of the decision-
making body and there have been ad hoc observations of administrative
work, general discussions and social events.

Content analysis, based on the number of times issues have been
mentioned, length and frequency of contributions, incidents giving rise
to conflict and decisions made together with observation of dominant
persons has allowed the examination of the causes and management of
conflict, power, control, goals and implementation of decisions.

Following a 10-interview pilot study, all available past and present
members have been interviewed using a schedule including socio-economic
data, open-ended questions and specially developed questionnaires.

The 21 statement *personal needs satisfaction* scale required subjects
to report both the importance of and satisfaction with various aspects
of involvement in Network. Similar reports were required in relation to
importance of the same aspects applied to employment (a scale asking
for degree of satisfaction actually obtained from employment was omitted
after the pilot study, it made the interview overlong, respondents
showing signs of boredom and restlessness).

Subjects were asked to respond to the questions "How important to
you is/was (satisfied or dissatisfied are/were you with) this aspect
of being a member of Network?" and "How important to you is/was this
aspect of doing a job?" Examples of statements in the scale are:

- the opportunity to do something;
- being able to organize your own time;
- feeling a sense of belonging;
- having the opportunity to learn new things.

Responses were chosen from a 7-point scale with point 1 being 'not at all important' (extremely dissatisfied) and point 7 being 'extremely important' (extremely satisfied). Rotated factor analysis of all the responses suggested six factors and these appear in Table 2. Factor scores are an unweighted mean of the related responses.

Nineteen statements on *attitudes* to Network as an organization with questions and response scales related to importance and satisfaction as described above, led to the identification of six factors and these appear in Table 3.

Examples of statements in this scale are:
- having an experienced full-time organizer;
- regular contact with members;
- the development of other Network centres;
- advertising for members with particular skills;
- making members welcome even if they contribute little.

Eight statements measuring *commitment* to Network yielded three factors shown in Table 4. These statements required responses ranging from 'strongly disagree' (point 1) to 'strongly agree' (point 7) to the question "Would you please indicate how much you agree or disagree with the following statements?" Examples of statements are:
- I feel myself to be part of the Network organization.
- I don't take the Network organization too seriously.
- I would not recommend a close friend to join the Network.

The *open-ended questions*, which were subjected to content analysis for frequency of mention of relevant items or opinions, are presented in Appendix 2.

Sample

Every attempt was made to interview, in their own homes or the Network office, as many members past and present as possible. The samples represent all those available and willing to be interviewed.

Differences in sample size, according to response, occur because (a) relatively new members and those having little contact with Network were unable to express attitudes of satisfaction (or dissatisfaction), (b) some members had never been employed or had forgotten what it was like so couldn't respond to the 'employment' orientated questions.

Socio-economic data for the samples are presented in Table 1.

Sample size	60 (refer tables 2, 3, 4)	46 (refer tables 2, 3)	51 (refer table 2)
employment status			
unemployed	40	30	35
employed	17	13	14
retired	3	3	2
sex			
men	33	22	26
women	27	24	25
marital status			
married	18	16	16
single	42	30	35
age			
under 21	6	5	5
22-40	28	22	25
41-60	20	14	17
over 60	6	5	4
qualifications			
no qualifications	40	28	32
some '0' levels	2	2	2
above '0' levels	18	16	17
time unemployed			
up to 6 months	7	4	7
7-12 months	11	9	11
over 12 months	22	17	17

Table 1. Composition of samples

Results and discussion

The results are presented and discussed according to the following key areas:
- recruitment and retention of members;
- resource exchange activity;
- decision-making and administration;
- satisfaction of members' practical, social and psychological needs.

Shortage of space has meant that the data from the observations, record analyses and open-ended questions have not been presented separately in detail, but have been incorporated in the discussion.*

Tables 2 to 4 summarize the responses to the attitude scales and Figure 1 is a sociogram of a sample of 125 of the tasks done by all members during the period September 1981 to May 1982.

| Subscale | No. of items | NETWORK | | EMPLOYMENT |
		Importance response	Satisfaction response	Importance response
Activity needs	4	5.5 (1.29)	4.8 (1.48)	6.0 (1.14)
Social needs	4	5.2 (1.32)	5.1 (1.33)	5.6 (0.95)
Autonomy needs	3	5.2 (1.26)	5.14 (1.04)	5.7 (1.05)
Achievement and recognition needs	3	4.8 (1.41)	4.0 (0.85)	5.4 (1.00)
Learning and know-ledge needs	3	5.6 (1.09)	4.8 (1.46)	6.0 (0.92)
Self-esteem needs	3	4.9 (1.11)	5.1 (1.05)	5.8 (2.32)
Sample size		60	46	51

Table 2. Summary of responses to items in the scale 'Personal Need Satisfaction' (mean scores; s.d. between brackets)

---

* These detailed analyses are obtainable from the authors.

Subscale	No. of items	Importance response	Satisfaction response
Aspects of management	4	5.4 (1.07)	4.3 (1.07)
Organizational growth and development	3	5.8 (1.04)	3.9 (1.18)
Contact with and care of members	4	5.8 (0.81)	4.3 (1.20)
Supervision and control of activities	3	4.5 (1.56)	4.1 (1.10)
Response to members	2	5.7 (1.25)	4.9 (1.32)
Office situation	3	5.1 (1.26)	4.3 (1.12)
Sample size		60	46

Table 3. Summary of responses to items in the scale 'Network Structure and Procedures' (mean scores; s.d. between brackets)

Subscale	No. of items	
Organizational loyalty and identification	4	5.0 (1.43)
Organizational involvement	2	6.1 (1.12)
Commitment to organizational aims	2	5.1 (2.29)
Sample size		60

Table 4. Summary of responses to items in the scale 'Organizational Commitment' (mean scores; s.d. between brackets)

Recruitment and retention of members

In the responses to open-ended questions, 50% of the members mentioned "something to do" and support for the idea of mutuality as the reasons for joining whereas only 6% expressed a belief in alternatives to employment. The promotion of interest in Network was initially seen as a problem of media access yet it has emerged that personal contact is the more successful means of recruitment. These findings match the results of Snow et al. (1980) who show how relatively unimportant ideology is in recruitment whereas they say that "links to one or more members through a pre-existing or emergent interpersonal tie" coupled with the absence of "countervailing personal networks" (p. 798) dominate. The need for something to do matches one of Jahoda's (1979) latent functions of work and also Hepworth's (1980) findings that "the best single predictor of mental health during unemployment was whether or not a man felt his time was occupied" (p. 139).

The impression that many of Network members had limited pre-existing social ties poses a problem in recruitment strategy. Such people are less likely to resist joining an organization yet are more difficult to reach by personal contact. Stark and Bainbridge (1980) stress the importance of the early development of interpersonal bonds in the induction process into organizations requiring membership commitments. However, reference to Table 3 shows that although "contact with and care of members" was felt to be very important, satisfaction with this aspect of Network administration was not high. Until the appointment of the full-time coordinator, induction procedures were very haphazard, with the organization failing to satisfy two of the latent functions of work (Jahoda, 1979): maintaining contact outside the family and linking the individual to wider goals and purposes.

Kanter (1968) proposed that the retention of members has three aspects - continuance, cohesion and control. Firstly, continuance is sustained when members see profit in remaining as members. Network members build up a stake in the organization's success, by investing time in group activities and routine duties such as office work and leaflet distribution. Secondly, cohesion comes from participation in decision-making, group activities such as gardening, and social rituals including parties and outings. Thirdly, control requires a commitment to the norms of the group and is expressed through a constant appeal to ideology and, for new members, a developing mystique and reference to the "old days".

Both Knoke (1981) and Etzioni (1975) show how normative control requires an intense flow of positive communication. Network records, observations and interviews (Table 3) show that for the majority of members this is lacking.

Only 12% of those interviewed mentioned "wanting a job done" as a reason for joining. Together with the responses to the subscale 'organizational involvement' in Table 4, this indicates that involvement is not instrumental and therefore continuance depends on the satisfaction of personal needs.

Resource exchange activity

An analysis of the pattern of exchanges is shown in Figure 1. Four features can be noted. Firstly, the majority of tasks involved a few members (15 are engaged in 6 or more tasks) with a large number having been little involved. Secondly, most individuals were not in balance. There are those who supplied energy and those who consumed it. Since the number of offers always considerably exceeded the number of expressed wants, the consumers of work can be seen as having as important a function as the 'doers'; voluntary workers need clients. Following on from this, the third feature is that the 15 more active members tended to do more tasks than receive them (Ratio 94:63). The organization can be seen as satisfying a need for work in a relatively uncritical atmosphere. Fourthly, the medium of resource exchange was not a means of connecting most members with the core of the group to allow diffusion of ideology to take place. This is reflected in "commitment to organizational aims" (Table 4) which shows only moderate commitment to the aims of Network.

50% of those who enrolled did not take part in any exchange and these, together with those in Figure 1 whose exchange involvement was limited, will have had difficulty in relating to the 'core' group. This pattern has been followed throughout the life of Network with high activity levels being found among some 10% of members.

106

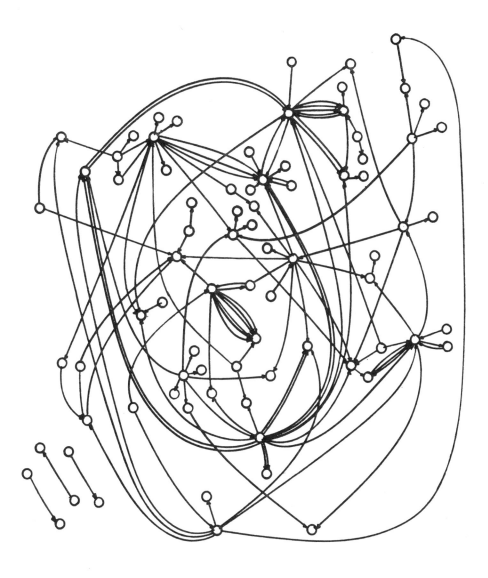

Figure 1. Sociogram of 125 Exchanges, Sept.1981 - May 1982.
Each arrow represents one exchange

More than half of the attendances at the weekly meetings have been by 14 members, a core group with a low turnover (2 per year). This stability has enabled learning to be incorporated into a set of organizational assumptions and unwritten procedures but it has made the meetings less open to newcomers, only 47 members attended over 5 meetings. It was decided, therefore, that one of the roles assigned to the salaried official from 1981 would be the induction of newcomers into organizational procedures. However, the commitment to democracy and the open style of meetings has enabled members to develop the confidence to speak and share the chairperson role.

50% of those interviewees who had attended meetings indicated positive attitudes towards the democratic structure and informality whilst the other 50% stressed disorganization, feelings of frustration and minority dominance as problems.

Content analysis of notes kept at meetings identified three main problems which are common in decision-making in voluntary bodies (Otto and Armstrong, 1978). Firstly, there has been the absence of clear operational goals by which day to day action may be guided. 80% of meetings have discussed at least one item in which conflict over goals was the dominant feature. For example the conflict between short-term and long-term aims has already been mentioned. Paton (1978) describes how a commitment to openness and democracy may result in high levels of manifest and latent conflict. This is because dissent is encouraged by the multiplicity of objectives on offer, members have heightened expectations of being able to influence decisions, they may be confused by the unfamiliar setting and yet the degree of voluntary and personal commitment which has been encouraged will tend to intensify even minor differences.

The second problem, again observed in 80% of meetings, has concerned the structure of, and procedures for, meetings. In nearly three years the group has, in the words of Tuckman (1965), formed, stormed (become aware of conflict and confusion as ambiguities appear), normed (established formal and informal rules towards becoming an efficient unit) and performed (carried out some tasks through these norms). But these stages are not clear cut and there are frequent returns to storming and norming as new procedures emerge and become custom and practice.

As the group has become more committed to performing, the third main difficulty has emerged. Indeed, some 65% of meetings have discussed the inadequacy or non-existence of procedures for the implementation of decisions and control. This concern for, but frustration with, 'aspects of management' is confirmed by interview responses as shown in Table 3. Since the appointment of an official with responsibility in this area, the record has improved. Indeed the full-time coordinator is significant for the survival and expansion of Network. Sarason et al. (1977) show how a leader's role was crucial to the success of a network in the United States. By means of appropriate cognitive ability and the power to remove blockages, a leader can ensure that success becomes habitual and continues through positive feedback. The task-orientated leader (Bales, 1955) becomes more important than the socio-emotional leadership hitherto provided by the core group.

Office work is a function which all members are invited to take part in. Of the total membership, throughout the three years, 127 members have worked in the office for varying periods and 32 members have worked in the office on more than 15 occasions. Even so, 50% of all visits involve only 14 members. Only four of these 14 figured as active members in the analyses of exchanges in Figure 1. This indicates that office work may be an alternative to other activity, perhaps appealing more to members needing temporal structure and defined tasks.

The low involvement of many members in the various Network activities indicates the organization's failure to provide for them the latent function of maintaining contacts outside the family. In addition, responses to the subscale 'organizational growth and development' in Table 3 show a similar failure to link individuals to wider goals and purposes.

Table 2 shows the responses for each factor developed from the 'Personal Needs Satisfaction' attitude scale. It indicates the high degree of importance attached to the satisfaction of social and psychological needs both by membership of Network and by conventional employment. Apart from the factor 'self-esteem needs', there is a correspondence between reported expectations from Network and from employment. Although people may not be joining Network for ideological reasons, participation seems to lead to an expectation that Network may be an alternative to employment, but a mean score of 5 to the subscale 'organizational loyalty and identification' in Table 4, indicates that there is some uncertainty.

Table 2 shows moderate satisfaction of the important need for activity. Data from participation rates in meetings, administration and resource exchange, shows that for a few people (no more than six at any one period) 'working' in Network approximates to half-time employment. However, for others, this important need has yet to be satisfied.

The need for autonomy (see Table 2) is fairly well satisfied. Members appear to appreciate the autonomy they personally enjoy. However, reference to 'supervision and control of activities' in Table 3 indicates that this aspect of organization is not entirely satisfactory. There is some difficulty in interpreting the responses to both these subscales when taken together. Impressions gained during interviews and observations suggest that members want autonomy for themselves but in an organizational sense want to see some more definite system of supervision and control.

The gap between importance of, and satisfaction with the 'knowledge' factor may relate to the lack of qualifications of most interviewees who saw this as a handicap in the employment stakes.

Membership can offer the important shared experiences outside the home. These are frequently early casualties of unemployment (Department of Health and Social Security, 1980; Morley-Bunker, 1982) so it is not surprising that, as Table 2 shows, the importance attached to satisfaction of social needs is quite high. Friendship analysis has shown that where few social bonds have been formed, the likelihood of dropping out has increased. 70% of those interviewed were unmarried and 74% had no children living at home. If it is to achieve its potential, Network will need to pay more attention to the processes of building social ties through activity.

CONCLUSION

A resource exchange may be an alternative to employment in that it can provide for most of its latent functions. The Network has recruited more members and survived for longer than many comparable organizations. It has achieved some success in that many members have had needs satisfied at the practical and socio-psychological levels. These satisfactions come not only from the exchange activity itself but also from participation in the decision-making and administrative process of the organization.

There is no evidence of great economic benefit. Exchange may be more of an idea which initially attracts and recruits people, and legitimates their involvement, but it is clear that this does not, for many, constitute a strong enough bond to ensure continuing commitment. A successful resource exchange could develop as one of a number of related activities which essentially provide the latent functions of employment, especially sharing and widening experience, time-structuring and the satisfaction of activity itself.

REFERENCES

Bales, R.F., How people interact in conferences. Scientific American, March, 1955.

Banks, M.H., C.W. Glegg, P.R. Jackson, N.J. Kemp, E.M. Stafford & T.D. Wall, The use of the general health questionnaire as an indicator of mental health in occupational studies. British Journal of Occupational Psychology, 1980, 53, 187-194.

Etzioni, A., A comparative analysis of complex organizations. New York: Free Press, 1975.

Hartley, J., Psychological approaches to unemployment. Bulletin of the British Psychological Society, 1980, 33, 412-414.

Hepworth, S.J., The psychological impact of unemployment. Journal of Occupational Psychology, 1980, 53, 139-145.

Hill, J., The psychological impact of unemployment. New Society, 19
    January, 1978.

Jahoda, M., The impact of unemployment in the 1930's and the 1970's.
    Bulletin of the British Psychological Society, 1979, 32, 309-314.

Kanter, R.S., Commitment and social organization: a study of commit-
    ment mechanisms in utopian communities. American Sociological
    Review, 1969, 33, 499-517.

Knoke, D., Commitment and detachment in voluntary associations.
    American Sociological Review, 1981, 46, 141-158.

MCVS., The Network: A mutual exchange of time and skills. Pamphlet,
    Merseyside Council for Voluntary Service, 1980.

Morley-Bunker, N., Perceptions of unemployment. Paper given to
    Occupational Psychology Section Annual Conference, January, 1982.

Otto, S. & F. Armstrong, The action research experiment. London:
    War on Want Press, 1978.

Paton, R., Some problems of co-operative organization. Co-operatives
    Research Unit, Open University, 1978.

Sarason, D.E., C. Carroll, K. Maton, S. Cohen & E. Lorentz, Human ser-
    vices and resource networks. London: Jossey-Bass, 1977.

Shepherd, G., Psychological disorder and unemployment. Bulletin of the
    British Psychological Society, 1981, 34, 345-348.

Snow, D.A., L.A. Zurcher & S. Ekland-Olsen, Social networks and social
    movements: a microstructural approach to differential recruitment.
    American Sociological Review, 1980, 45, 787-801.

Stark, R. & W.S. Bainbridge, Networks of faith: interpersonal bonds
    and recruitment to cults and sects. American Journal of Sociology,
    1980, 85 (6), 1376-1395.

Tuckman, B.W., Developmental sequence in small groups. Psychological
    Bulletin, 1965, 58 (6), 384-399.

APPENDIX 1. RESOURCE EXCHANGE

Examples of jobs done by members for other members:

Typing - repairing lawn mower - hair cutting - plastering - household
repairs - assistance with money management - transposing music for
blind member - transporting goods - sewing - electrical repairs -
gardening - motor-bike repairs - carpet laying - photography.

Examples of members teaching skills to each other:

French lessons - driving lessons - dog handling - candle making -
sewing lessons/workshop - electrical maintenance/workshop.

Examples of members doing jobs for other organizations:

Artwork for Friends of the Earth organization - distribution of leaflets
- office work (once a week) for a local theatre - erecting signs -
doing a sponsored swim to raise money for a sport centre - labouring,
construction work and canoe building for the Liverpool Water Sport
Centre.

June 1979 - June 1982, 191 members have been involved in 469 exchanges.

APPENDIX 2. OPEN-ENDED QUESTIONS

1. How did you find out about the Network?
2. Why did you join the Network?
3. What happened when you joined?
   - explore experience and events surrounding joining
   - what happened at initial contact
4. How did contacts, after joining, take place?
   - explore subsequent progress through Network
5. What wants have you had satisfied? When? How?
6. What offers have you had taken up? When? How?
7. How involved are you in members' meetings?
   - frequency of attendance
8. What opinion have you of the members' meetings?
   - explore decision taking procedures
9. How involved are you in the office administration?
   - frequency of rota duty
   - other office work
10. What opinion have you of the office administration and
    procedures for getting exchanges carried out?
11. What do you think about group projects?
    - management of them
    - involvement of self
12. Why did you leave the Network?
13. Is membership of the Network better or worse than doing
    a job ignoring the fact that Network involvement is not paid?

III
WORK DESIGN AND INDIVIDUAL BEHAVIOR

8. ERGONOMIC AND PARTICIPANTS IN DISPLAY WORK: AN EVOLUTION OF APPROACHES ACROSS THREE PROJECTS AT THE SOCIÉTÉ GÉNÉRALE DE BANQUE

A. Maasen

INTRODUCTION

The Société Générale de Banque, one of the main banks in Belgium, is organized into a Central Administrative Office and 16 Regional Offices. These offices are divided into an administrative and a commercial sector: the commercial sector is composed of branches. The bank has about 1.140 branches and employs 15.430 people: about 8.500 in the administrative and 7.000 in the commercial sector.

In the course of time, a number of automation projects have taken place, which have in many respects changed the administrative processes and hence the nature of the jobs of individual employees. Initially, branch personnel carried out mainly commercial activities with a minimum of registration (performed with the help of mechanical accounting machines) of incoming and outgoing amounts. The administrative processing itself was largely concentrated in large operational departments of the administrative units. In 1973 a start was made with the introduction into these departments of display terminals: the *Singer-Cogar project*. From then on the employees were to use these terminals for mass input of alphanumerical data.

To eliminate the monotonous jobs that were created in this way, it was decided, some years later, that data input had to be distributed among a large number of employees, constituting a component of each person's job. It was assumed, moreover, that the motivation of the employees would be enhanced and that the risk of error would decrease. In 1982 a start was made with equiping the branches with computers and terminals connected to a national network: the *branch terminal project*. This project brought along a number of changes. The fact that the execution of the administrative transactions was now partially transferred to the branches meant that the number of personnel in the commercial sector had to increase, while the large departments were partly dismantled. The administrative processing in the branch also made it possible for branch personnel to dispose of updated customer information at all times. Thus they were able to display a greater degree of commercial initiative.

Recently, another automation project has been launched. It concerns the introduction of *word processors* for secretarial work.

In this chapter we will describe these three projects in some detail, highlighting the approaches that have been followed with respect to ergonomical aspects and user participation. At the end we will discuss the trends that emerge from these projects.

THE SINGER-COGAR PROJECT

In 1975, in the operational departments of the regional offices of the bank, the punch card machines were replaced by displays and keyboards: the so-called 'Singer-Cogars'. Work on these Singer-Cogar terminals consisted in the input of alphanumerical data from cheques and transfers. The work cycles were short from 10 to 15 seconds. At this moment, the Singer-Cogar terminal is still operational, although it is gradually being replaced by polyvalent terminals in the departments and by terminals in the branches (see below: the branch terminal project).

Prior to the actual introduction, a start was made in '73/'74 with work groups in order to prepare the project. Personnel representatives participated in these groups. However, the problem areas tackled were of a very limited scope and oriented to the job. They concerned job and systems-analytical problems, the creation of new forms and a suitable search system, personnel replacements and the concrete planning of the installation. No attention was paid to the recognition of social and ergonomic problems at this early stage.

One year after the installation of the terminals a brief inquiry was held. The new technology had been experienced as a clear improvement, compared to the punch card machines. Reduction of the noise level appeared to be the determining factor in this overall positive judgement.

Some years later, several complaints emerged, however. They tended to be vague: fatigue, monotony. The attitude of the unions was very militant at that time, both in pamphlets and in questions in the consultative organs. There were several causes for their excitement. In the press, display work was presented as unhealthy and technology as a job-killer. At the same time, the study phase for the branch terminal was announced in the bank.

As a result, management decided to carry out a thorough investigation as to the nature and causes of the complaints in the Singer pools. In this study, three groups were compared: exclusively display work, display work alternating with traditional administrative work, exclusively administration. The areas investigated were: temporary and permanent fatigue, health, the ergonomic aspects of the work place and its environment, the general psychological climate. The main results may be summed up as follows.

Ergonomics of the work station and its environment

The general illumination was too strong (500 lux) and the reflection on the screen too bright. The dust produced by fitted carpets, the currents from the air-conditioning and the landscaped offices were disturbing factors. The screens showed the ergonomic shortcomings characteristic for the period in which they were designed. Measures were taken to reduce the overall level of illumination, to reorient the screens, to fit filters, to diminish air currents and dust. Although some of the complaints were well-founded, most of them were attributable to an over-sensitive reaction to environmental variables. In fact, these variables were very important for the overall work satisfaction, since the job itself was experienced as devoid of content and repetitive.

Fatigue and health

The complaints expressed were eyestrain, headache, tension and nervousness. Fatigue increased considerably after two hours uninterrupted display work. The eye complaints appeared to be reversible in nature. Complaints of nervousness were not caused by an exaggerated work-rhythm, but by the monotony of the repetitive job and the consequent lack of job satisfaction. To improve this situation, measures were proposed to introduce suitable arrangements of breaks and to integrate traditional administrative tasks in display work. The aim was to limit the duration of display work proper to $4\frac{1}{2}$ hours daily. Since that time, a longitudinal investigation for eye examinations has been set up among screen workers. The results over about ten years on a large group of persons of various ages have proved to be very satisfactory. Subjective complaints of functional eyestrain arise, but are reversible. Display work does not cause any organic eye damage nor any decrease of visual capacity. Preventive steps are also taken to exclude persons with congenital eye injuries for screen work.

Conclusion

For the Singer-Cogar project we can conclude that job satisfaction could be improved thanks to a close cooperation with a sample of users. Nevertheless, it must be noted that in this case the decision to involve users in the project was reached only after some years when complaints were generally expressed.

THE BRANCH TERMINAL PROJECT

The installation of displays in the branches started at the beginning of 1982. By mid-1985, all branches should be equipped with a minicomputer. Each counter should have a display terminal, with one printer for every two counters. The branch terminal project is the first step in the 'network project'. This latter project is aimed at the establishment of a network of telephone lines throughout Belgium connected in junctions. This network will permit the electronic exchange of data between the bank units (administration and accounts processing) and between the bank and the outside world (SWIFT, clearing house, customers).

The Singer-Cogar project had stimulated awareness that in subsequent automation projects attention should be given at an early stage to the quality of the work station and of the job content. In order to meet the needs of branch personnel as far as possible, a number of them were extensively consulted in the course of the project.

User participation

Various *work groups* were set up right from the preparatory phase. They were composed of union representatives, specialists and employees with the required banking knowledge. A large number of aspects were examined: the content of the programmes, the social consequences, the ergonomic hardware requirements, planning and logistics, security, etc.

The openness of the computer specialists to the contributions of non-computer trained employees was not present from the start onwards, but developed most favourably after the first test period.

By the way of *test case* 20 branches were equipped. The number of employees concerned consisted of 20 executive managers, their assistants, and 120 counter clerks. During the various inquiries and investigations in their branches, they could discuss their complaints, propose modifications and evaluate programmes for content and form. They contributed intensively to the definite shape of the project. Overall judgement on the project was very positive right from the start, both for the administrative and the commercial aspects.

Setting up a test case appeared to be an outstanding means of directly involving the users themselves in an automation project and of replacing the traditional curative treatment of complaints into a preventive one.

The bank has adopted an *information policy*, laid down in a formalized procedure for 'information and consultation on important technological and structural changes'. This procedure requires that the unions and the personnel involved are informed according to the lines of hierarchy, right from the start of the study phase at the work floor. An action plan is set up for implementing the changes after consultation of the different parties, while the decision-making remains with the management.

Thus, before the branch terminal project started, information was communicated in the national Works' Council concerning commercial, financial, social and organizational consequences. In the regional offices, this information was discussed in each local safety and health committee.

From 1975 onwards, employees regularly received brochures with information on the project and its development. In '81/'82, the year before the final installation of the terminals, a systematic information campaign was launched. A video film showing the aims of the project and giving experiences of employees in the test branches was shown to all staff. Heads of offices were given an extensive list of arguments to be used in guiding discussions after the film. The distribution of brochures continued, and in the meantime news was released in internal periodicals for the staff.

As proper *training* is crucial for the acceptance of new working equipment, much attention was paid to it.

To do justice to the specific needs and working methods of each regional office, employees from each office were trained to organize the regional training sessions. Those responsible for training were thus experienced a same kind of reality as the personnel in training. The conditions for involvement appeared optimal, in this way.

Moreover, based on the use that is being made of the terminal (daily input, occasional input, output only), a number of target groups were distinguished, and a specific training programme was provided for each. The duration of this training varied from one day (for commercial personnel executives) to four days (for counter clerks). The content varied from administrative processing-oriented (the counter clerks) to commercial management-oriented (the branch managers and their assistants).

Besides the organizers of the regional training sessions, one employee per regional office was put to work in the Organization and Computer Department of the bank from 1980 onwards. They collaborated in testing

out the software programmes and organized the national training and
information planning. They were also involved in the training of their
office colleagues as organizers of the local sessions. They returned to
their regional office a few months before the installation, in order to
coordinate the contacts with the engineers of the Organization and
Computer Department.

The organizers of the training sessions assisted the branch personnel
during the first operational week. It appeared in practice that this
prevented them to feel at a loss - something particularly important in
case of technical breakdowns.

Ergonomical aspects

The *ergonomics of the hardware* was given much weight. In purchasing the
equipment (display + keyboard + printer), the ergonomical criterion was
awarded the same value as the technical and financial criteria. In the
United States, the confrontation with the package of requirements pro-
voked the reaction from several constructors that - because of the ergonomic requirements - the cost price would become too high. But subsequently a number of them were willing to take account of the ergonomic
aspects, and they used this as a selling argument in their advertising.
Some ten brands were retained, since they simultaneously met the technical, ergonomical and financial criteria.

The equipment that was finally selected was ergonomically the most
suitable to the existing branch infrastructure. The ergonomic qualities
include: display and keyboard separated from each other; the keyboard
is 3 cm high (ideal, in view of the height of the existing counters),
weights only 2 kg and gives no disturbing reflections; the display is
adjustable in height and can be adjusted around 2 axes; the quality of
the picture and the legibility are very good (large screen, dark green
background, characters are 4.45 mm by 2.1 mm, distance between 2 lines
is 3.34 mm, matrix 7 x 9 gives the impression of a continuous line).
Concerning the printer, a system was adopted which extrudes ink; it
makes no disturbing noise and delivers only original printed matter,
thus increasing legibility.

The first evaluations of the hardware from users are very positive.

The necessary attention was also given to the *ergonomics of the installation* of the hardware in the branches. Those responsible for the branch buildings were handed documentation with advice concerning the placement of the equipment, the comfort of the areas, and the avoidance of reflections and noise. Apart from guidelines for transformations, some designs were presented - and are even tried out in practice - to build new branches with ergonomically optimal work stations.

Naturally, in practice, no budgets are provided for rebuilding work in all branches in the short term. Thus, compromises had to be reached in order to give priority, within the existing infrastructure, to certain well-determined environmental requirements above others.

Finally, attention was paid to the *ergonomics of the software*. It appeared that the programmes were quickly learned, and no complaints were expressed. Nor were there problems for older employees, except that the learning process tended to be slower.

The software configuration was approached in a totally different way, however, from that of the Singer-Cogar project. First of all, representatives from the user group were involved in determining the content of the programmes. Secondly, due to the experiences of the user group in the test branches, a large number of modifications were made. Their main complaints concerned a lack of autonomy, flexibility, uniformity and cancellation possibilities. Audible signals of fault indications or alarm-accounts were also experienced as disturbing.

The writing of the definitive programmes was then guided by the following principles.
- *Uniformity* was aimed at in the layout of the screen, in codes and in the logical value of the function keys through all bank transactions.
- The *autonomy* of users was increased by such things as the provision of possibilities of jumping screens and zones per screen, of interrupting and cancelling. Guidance programmes were built in accounting for different levels of knowledge and experience of the individual users.
- *Adaptation to the user* was, moreover, *optimized* by communication in his own language (Dutch, French), by simplicity in the messages, by limiting abbreviations to those generally accepted in the jargon,

124

and through visual indication of mistakes where correction was still possible.

Conclusion

The experiences with the system at work cover the short period of some eight months. Acceptance and evaluation of the system are good. Naturally, in each branch organizational adjustments are necessary during the running-in phase, but they need not become problematic. Technical breakdowns have remained under control and have been substantially anticipated.

The success of the project is largely due to the efforts described above, as a result of which the offices and the branches have been able to prepare themselves effectively and well beforehand to the new work organization.

THE WORD PROCESSING PROJECT

Word processing is part of the office automation project to be carried out in the future within the secretarial services. At the beginning, word processing will be approached in the same manner as the branch terminal. As a test, the credit secretaries in the offices have been equipped with hardware of the stand-alone type. Users were interviewed about the modalities of functioning, the technical possibilities, the quality of the printed layout, the ergonomic shortcomings of the work station, the printer, etc.

For different reasons, the stand-alone system will not be retained for general distribution:
- for financial reasons a shared-logic system has been opted for; however, the existing secretarial jobs will not be combined into pools; each work station will be equipped with the cheaper shared-logic terminals;
- ergonomically there were objections to the poorer quality of the screen, the currents from the ventilation system and the lack of room for the legs;

- for technical reasons a system compatible with the branch network
  has been chosen for.

The hardware adopted is the same as the branch terminal. The ergonomic
qualities of this hardware are well known.

To what extent the *user* is to be involved in this project will mainly depend on his involvement in the programmes. In the last half year,
only a few systems have been installed. The programmes for word processing have been tested out in a very limited group. An inquiry into the
experiences of a larger number of users is planned. Other partial projects in office automation, such as electronic mail, voice recognition,
storage of key words, etc. are still at the kindergarten stage. Complex
possibilities in this area will be tested out by computer experts, and
the unexperienced user will have little to contribute in this stage.

It is from the *ergonomic* science that an important evolution has
been launched: the user-friendliness of computer systems. The attempt
is to make the software specialists aware of the principles which optimize
the human-computer dialogue. That the computer specialists are not
insensitive to this, appears from the development of query languages
and basic frames within which each user can develop working programmes
in his natural language.

DISCUSSION

A comparison of the three project descriptions presented above, reveals
a clear evolution of the approaches that have been followed with respect
to ergonomical aspects and employee participation. Table 1 summarizes
the main trends.

As far as ergonomics is concerned, one may speak of an evolution in
two respects. First, there has been a shift from an a posteriori towards
an a priori approach. Secondly, the attention was at first focused on
the hardware and the physical surroundings, while only later, after the
first tests with the branch terminal, awareness began to grow of the
ergonomic qualities of the software.

	EVOLUTION FROM:	TOWARDS:
ERGONOMIC INVESTIGATION	A POSTERIORI of: - HARDWARE - ENVIRONMENTAL VARIABLES	A PRIORI + CONTINUOUS ADAPTED CORRECTIONS AND EVALUATIONS of: - HARDWARE - ENVIRONMENTAL VARIABLES - SOFTWARE

PARTICIPATION	WORK GROUPS
	- limited number
	- limited problem approach
	  . system-analytical
	  . planning
	
	USERS
	- once a posteriori investigation of complaints
	- 90 persons
	INFORMATION
	- once on installation
		WORK GROUPS
		- large number
		- broad range of problem areas
		  . system-analytical
		  . planning
		  . job content
		  . ergonomics
		  . software
		  . function-classification
		  . training
		USERS
		- continuous questioning a priori of users in the test phases
		- 160 persons
		INFORMATION
		- several periods
		- various media
		- all employees concerned

Table 1. Evolution of the approaches to ergonomics and participation

The involvement of users, a factor of great importance in building up a good man-machine dialogue, has also evolued. In the Singer-Cogar project, a limited number of users were consulted after the installation phase, so as to be able to make necessary improvements. On the other hand, in the branch terminal project, representative groups of users were brought together, from the study phase onwards, in order to give shape and content to the project together with specialists and technicians. Information on the project was given at an early stage to employee representatives and to future users. A large number of potential users was involved in planning and organizing of training sessions in the use of the hardware. In the word processing project a comparable approach has been chosen. The experiences from the latter project are still limited. It is clear, however, that the trend is towards an increased degree of user participation in the design and modification of his work station.

9. JOB CHARACTERISTICS AND JOB ATTITUDES: THE MODERATOR EFFECTS OF INDIVIDUAL NEEDS

L.A. Ten Horn

INTRODUCTION

In organizational psychological literature over the past ten years, much attention has been paid to the study of moderator effects. The job characteristics model proposed by Hackman and Oldham (1975, 1976) has been at the centre of this research effort. In this model five core job dimensions (skill variety, autonomy, task identity, task significance and feedback) are supposed to be of influence on three psychological states (experienced meaningfulness of the work, experienced responsibility for the outcome of the work, and knowledge of results). These psychological states are hypothesized to lead to certain work outcomes (high internal work motivation, high quality work performance, high satisfaction, low absenteeism and turnover). The two causal links in the model are hypothesized to be moderated by the need for personal growth on the job: for individuals with high growth need strength the links are supposed to be stronger than for low growth need strength individuals.

The *questionnaire* used for measuring most of the constructs (the Job Diagnostic Survey) appears to have acceptable psychometric properties. Hackman and Oldham (1974), Oldham (1976), Oldham, Hackman and Pearce (1976), Oldham and Brass (1979), Evans, Kiggundu and House (1979), Aldag and Brief (1979), Kiggundu (1980), Bhagat and Chassie (1980), Walsh, Taber and Beehr (1980), Vecchio and Keon (1981), Abdel-Halim (1981), Oldham and Hackman (1981) report good coefficients α for most

129

of the variables. There is also some evidence that the measurement of
the job characteristics has some validity. Judgements made by employees,
supervisors and observers converge moderately well, and analysis of
variance shows differences between jobs to contribute significantly to
overall variance (Hackman & Lawler, 1971; Hackman & Oldham, 1975; Brass,
1981). There is uncertainty, however, about the factorial structure of
the job characteristics (Dunham, 1976; Dunham, Aldag & Brief, 1977;
Pokorney, Gilmore & Beehr, 1980), possibly due to the use of different
item-formats (Green, Armenakis, Marbert & Bedeian, 1979) or sample-
fluctuations (Dunham, Aldag & Brief, 1977). The concepts underlying the
dimensions, however, are sufficiently different to warrant the distinction.
Hackman and Oldham combine the job dimensions into an overall Motivating
Potential Score (MPS). The formula used is open to criticism (Evans,
Kiggundu & House, 1979; Roberts & Glick, 1981), but this does not
entirely invalidate the MPS as a composite measure.

In its original form the *model* received only moderate support
(Hackman & Oldham, 1976). The hypothesized function of the psychological
states, between the job characteristics and the outcomes, has not been
supported. The moderator effect of growth need strength on *both* links
in the model has been questioned (Arnold & House, 1980; Wall, Clegg &
Jackson, 1978; Algera, 1980). It appears justified to leave the psychological states out of the model, as is done in most studies, and to
focus attention on the moderator effect that growth need strength has
on the relationships between the job characteristics and the outcomes,
directly.

The model received somewhat more support in this condensed form
(Oldham, Hackman & Pearce, 1976; Orpen, 1979), although the moderator
effect does not tends to be very strong in most cases and some results
can hardly be called positive (Evans, Kiggundu & House, 1979). Comparable
results were found with somewhat different instruments (Hackman & Lawler,
1971; Wanous, 1974; Brief & Aldag, 1975; Sims, Szilagyi & Keller, 1975;
Sims & Szilagyi, 1976; O'Reilly, 1977; Cherrington & England, 1980).
Summing up, the results so far are more or less in favour of the model.
Negative conclusions, like those drawn by White (1978), seem premature.

An important limitation of the model lies in the fact that only one moderator is studied: growth need strength. This concept undoubtedly stems from Maslow's ideas concerning the need for 'self-actualization' (Maslow, 1954). In this theory, however, Maslow mentioned a further number of four needs: the psychological, security, social and esteem needs.

The purpose of the study reported here is to investigate the moderating effects of the entire scale of needs taken from Maslow. The introduction of all Maslow-needs into the model may shed light on certain difficulties in interpreting results of recent studies. Brief and Aldag (1975) for instance report stronger relationships between job characteristics and extrinsic job satisfaction in *low* growth need strength individuals, than in respondents high in growth need strength. Oldham, Hackman and Pearce (1976) and Orpen (1979) report these effects as well. Hackman and Lawler (1971) and Sims and Szilagyi (1976) suggest, that respondents low in growth need strength might possibly be high in need for social contact. Generally, problems seem to arise in interpreting results from respondents low in growth need, who are actually defined in a negative way, i.e. by what they do *not* have. It is quite possible that this group of individuals is made up of persons with very diverse needs.

The relevance that lower Maslow-needs may have for organizational behaviour is demonstrated by two field studies done by Aronoff (1967, 1970) of work organization in different cultural groups in the Carribean and by a consecutive series of laboratory experiments (Aronoff & Messé, 1971; Messé, Aronoff & Wilson, 1972; Wilson, Aronoff & Messé, 1975; Michelini, Wilson & Messé, 1975; Wilson, 1976; Ward & Wilson, 1980). These studies showed that both the esteem and the security needs play an important part in people's reactions to their work situation. The difference in emphasis they place on the fulfilment of these two needs coincide with preferences for certain organization forms and leadership patterns. Moreover people tend to adjust their actual work situation according to these preferences, if they have freedom to do so. The fit or misfit between individual needs and the organizational set-up is also shown to have important effects on several outcome variables. The results of this series of studies and experiments as a whole are quite compelling and form a strong argument for considering more needs than growth need alone in studying organizational behaviour.

The present study investigates the moderator effects that the five needs coined by Maslow (1954) have on the relationships between job characteristics and job outcomes. The moderator variables used are the strengths of the physiological needs, the needs for security, social needs, esteem needs and self-actualization needs[*].

INSTRUMENTS

The *needs* were measured using an instrument developed and tested by Ten Horn (1983). It is based on the assumption of an U-shaped relationship between need-strength and need satisfaction/frustration, which had been demonstrated in a sample of 267 civil servants (Ten Horn, 1983; 70-92). Respondents were asked to rate a number of statements regarding their jobs. They indicated first whether they judged the statement to be true or not true with respect to their job. Next, they expressed how much they (dis)liked the presence (or the absence) in their job, of each aspect mentioned. A sample item: "In my work I can make full use of my abilities; yes, that is right/no, that is not right". "How do you feel about this state of affairs?"; followed by a 9-point scale ranging from 'I like it very much' to 'I dislike it very much', the middle of the scale being marked 'neither like nor dislike'.

Operationally the need-scores were calculated from these data using a simple algorithm, the essence being that the deviation from the neutral point on the like/dislike-scale is taken as an indicator of the strength of the need. Nine to fifteen items per need are used. The instrument compares favourably to questionnaires using 'importance-questions'. Coefficients α range from .70 to .89. Predictive validity is sufficient and the method is probably less prone to social desirability than other instruments.

---

[*] The social and esteem needs were subdivided in two subcategories each. These distinctions proved to be of little use, however, and will not be reported here. They can be found in Ten Horn (1983).

Two types of *job characteristics* were used.

Five characteristics were defined which corresponded to each of the need concepts: opportunity for personal growth, for esteem, for belongingness, for security and for physiological satisfaction. These 'Maslow-type' characteristics were measured using the 'true or untrue' answers to the statements mentioned above, i.e. the part of the answers respondents give, judging the statement to be a true description of their work situation or not. Coefficients α ranged between .70 and .86. It could also be demonstrated, that differences between jobs contribute significantly to observed variances.

A second set of characteristics was selected from organizational psychological literature in general and did not reflect Maslowian concepts. The characteristics chosen were: autonomy, variety, task identity, organizational climate (theory-X-style versus theory-Y-style), degree of specialization, opportunity for informal contacts, necessity of work related contacts, standardization (being tied down to regulations and procedures in the work) and the number of deviations from the normal course of events*.

These job characteristics were measured using self-report measures with 1 to 12 items in Likert-format. Coefficients α were in the range between .50 and .70 in different samples. It could be demonstrated that the variance of the job characteristics partly resulted from differences between jobs. The scores also correspond with ratings by outsiders. The number of jobs in these analyses, however, was limited to a total of ten.

The *outcome variables* were: general job satisfaction (4 items, α = .71), tendency to leave (3 items, α = .80), job involvement (7 items α = .65) and feelings of stress resulting from the job (3 items α = .83).

Items for the instruments were partly taken or adapted from Huizinga (1970), Hackman and Oldham (1975), Langdale (1974, 1976) and Schouten (1974). Further details are given by Ten Horn (1983).

---

* Feedback from the work itself was originally chosen for investigation as well. It was dropped from the study later on, because of unreliability of the instrument used.

A set of expectations was formulated answering the question which need could be expected to moderate which of the possible relationships between the job characteristics and the outcome variables. Part of these expectations had the status of hypotheses, based on research findings in the literature mentioned earlier. Another part had only exploratory value. For some relationships no explicit expectations could be formulated. The hypotheses and expectations are not given in full here, for the sake of brevity. However, they are marked by special characters in the tables reporting the results.

The moderator effects of each need-category were analysed separately, using a subgroup methodology. Three groups of respondents were formed, on the basis of the distribution of the need-strength scores of the particular need under investigation: one group comprising respondents with the highest need-strength scores, one group with low scoring respondents and one group in the middle of the distribution. Each group consisted of about ten to fifteen percent of the respondents. For each group the correlations were computed between each job characteristic and each outcome variable. The corresponding correlations in the three groups were compared. A moderator effect was claimed to exist if correlations between a characteristic and an outcome variable in the high-group differed significantly (5 percent one-sided) from the corresponding correlation in the low-group, the correlation in the middle-group laying in between.

Roberts and Glick (1981) have criticized this approach because of the elimination of data it implies. Several authors employ regression analysis instead (O'Reilly, 1977; Arnold & House, 1980; Champoux & Peters, 1980; Cherrington & England, 1980; Vecchio, 1980; Abdel-Halim, 1981). This type of analysis has the disadvantage, however, of presupposing a linear moderator effect. Subgroup analysis was judged to be more appropriate because no assumptions need to be made about the type of the relationships studied.

Samples

The questionnaire was completed by 921 respondents from three organizations in the Netherlands. One was a municipality employing some 130 persons partly working on clerical jobs and partly in the public works sector. The educational level varied from primary education only to university level. Most employees were men (82%). The second organization was an intermunicipal cooperation body performing a large number of rather diverse tasks like the collection of garbage, planning and management of recreational facilities, provision of health services and coordination of municipal policies. 29% of the 145 respondents were women and the educational level varied widely. The third organization was a large engineering office, active in the fields of civil engineering, urban planning, transportation, building construction, environmental protection etc. The higher educational levels were overrepresented (21% were academics). Only 12% of the employees were women. Response rates for the three organizations were 89, 64 and 63% respectively.

Results

The results are shown in Tables 1 to 5, one table for each need-category. Relationships *hypothesized* to be moderated are indicated by the letter 'h', exploratory expectations are marked by 'e'. For all other relationships no predictions were made.

One technical complication should be mentioned. The strength of a particular need (e.g. esteem) and the corresponding 'Maslow-type' job characteristic (opportunity for satisfying esteem needs) were measured using the same item-wordings. So, the two instruments may not be as independent as might be desirable. To circumvent this problem the items were divided into two sets, and two separate moderator analyses were done. In the first analysis item-set 1 was used for measuring need strength only and item-set 2 for the measurement of the Maslow-type job characteristics only. This means that need strength and the Maslow-type characteristics are assessed by completely different items. Contamination between scores on these grounds is therefore ruled out. In the second analysis the procedure is reversed: the items in set 1 are used for the Maslow-type characteristics and those of set 2 for measuring need strength. Wherever the contamination problem arose this double analysis was done. In the Tables the results of both are reported separately.

Table 1 gives the results for the *need for personal growth*. Most hypothesized and expected moderator effects are there, though not all are significant. Autonomy and variety are moderated in their relationships with general job satisfaction, tendency to leave and, to a certain extent, with involvement and stress as well. The task identity - job satisfaction relationship and the task identity - tendency to leave relationship show some moderator effect, but this does not reach significance. The effects on the climate - job satisfaction relationship and on the climate - tendency to leave relationship are also in the expected direction, but again not significantly so. The relationship of standardization to tendency to leave is moderated as expected (however, not significantly). The effect is absent in the standardization - job satisfaction relationship. The relationships of opportunity for personal growth are moderated as expected.

The findings for autonomy, variety and task identity are in accordance with those by Hackman and Lawler (1971), Wanous (1974), Brief and Aldag (1975), Sims and Szilagyi (1976), Evans, Kiggundu and House (1979), Orpen (1979) and Pokorney, Gilmore and Beehr (1980).

Table 2 gives the results of the *need for esteem from others*. The hypothesized effects on the relationships of opportunity to get esteem from others show up in one of the two analyses only. Of the exploratory expectations only the autonomy - tendency to leave relationship is moderated, and even there the effect is not quite clear, because the correlation of the middle-group is not in between the other two. An unexpected effect was found on the relationship of opportunity for satisfying security needs. The failure to find effects with the non Maslow-type job characteristics may be due to difficulty in finding characteristics related particularly to the esteem needs. Maybe, the quality of the interpersonal relations on the job is more pertinent to these needs, than are characteristics of the job itself.

Table 1. Correlations between job characteristics and four outcome variables for respondents with high, middle and low scores for growth need strength.

OUTCOME VARIABLES	Job satisfaction			Tendency to leave			Job involvement			Stress		
MODERATOR	growth need strength			growth need strength			growth need strength			growth need strength		
	high	middle	low	high	middle	low	high	middle	low	high	middle	low
Job characteristics												
Autonomy	$.28^h$	.33	-.10 *	$-.30^h$	-.04	.08 **	.17	.15	.07	.25	.19	.06
Variety	$.29^h$	.09	.04 *	$-.18^h$	-.02	.14 *	.43	.24	.10 **	.37	.25	.16
Task identity	$.14^h$	-.05	-.06	$-.09^h$	.08	.08	.04	-.09	-.00	.01	.19	.05
Org. climate	$.24^e$	.11	.06	$-.20^e$	.17	-.08	.18	-.04	.10	-.00	.23	-.26 *
Specialization	-.04	-.06	-.25	.05	.02	.14	.19	-.04	-.05 *	.28	.17	.20
Informal contacts	-.12	.08	-.03	.05	-.12	.01	-.09	-.08	-.02	.04	-.17	-.13
Work contacts	.05	.18	.07	-.07	-.09	-.00	.34	.10	.02 **	.24	.05	.14
Standardization	$-.04^e$	-.14	.17	$-.11^e$	-.10	.07	-.01	.10	-.10	-.39	-.19	-.13 *
Deviations	.06	-.10	-.13	.00	.08	.10	.20	-.10	-.02	.45	.21	.27
Opportunity for:												
growth 1	$.67^h$	.44	.08 **	$-.59^h$	-.35	-.11 **	.31	.32	.33	.02	-.04	.20
growth 2	$.67^h$	.62	.16 **	$-.56^h$	-.46	-.02 **	.46	.42	.45	.08	.06	.17
esteem	.40	.34	.12 *	-.50	-.08	-.14 **	.26	.31	.24	.17	.18	-.01
belongingness	.34	.50	.27	-.45	-.31	-.26	.15	.20	.20	-.30	-.12	-.31
security	.11	.22	.29	-.32	-.39	-.11	.04	.08	-.00	-.44	-.26	-.27
physiol. satisfactions	.05	.10	-.12	-.00	-.18	.10	-.10	-.03	.00	-.39	-.35	-.24

Note: h : hypothesized moderator effect, e: exploratory expectation
  * : difference between high/low groups is significant (5%)
 ** : difference between high/low groups is significant (1%)

137

Table 2. Correlations between job characteristics and four outcome variables for respondents with high, middle and low scores for need for esteem from others.

OUTCOME VARIABLES	Job satisfaction			Tendency to leave			Job involvement			Stress		
MODERATOR	need for esteem			need for esteem			need for esteem			need for esteem		
	high	middle	low	high	middle	low	high	middle	low	high	middle	low
Job characteristics												
Autonomy	.05^e	.12	.16	-.26^e	.08	.03 *	.00	.17	.12	.23	.27	.25
Variety	.10	.23	.17	.00	-.18	.06	.13	.37	.29	.32	.33	.31
Task identity	.07	.13	.05	.11	.11	-.04	.02	.08	.11	.06	.16	.09
Org. Climate	.31	.12	.28	-.07	.07	-.17	.15	-.05	.11	-.13	.19	-.05
Specialization	-.08^e	-.03	.05	.04^e	.16	.05	.08	-.01	.09	.24	.30	.06
Informal contacts	.03	-.12	.03	.07	-.05	-.01	.00	-.08	.07	.12	-.27	-.07
Work contacts	.05	.14	.26	.01	-.15	-.01	.15	.33	.03	.14	.34	.12
Standardization	-.01	-.05	.03	-.13	-.10	-.09	-.15	-.08	.03	-.35	-.26	-.32
Deviations	-.01	-.07	.21	.03	.09	.10	.14	.14	.20	.40	.39	.30
Opportunity for:												
growth	.50	.64	.37	-.49	-.42	-.22 *	.20	.37	.38	.12	.18	.17
esteem 1	.30^h	.25	.30	-.30^h	-.27	-.23	.12	.06	.22	-.03	-.09	-.20
esteem 2	.41^h	.41	.17 *	-.31	-.13	-.04 *	.35	.06	.27	.08	-.12	.30
belongingness	.45	.23	.23 *	-.40	-.31	-.22	.05	.15	.16	-.37	-.18	-.15 *
security	.27	.16	-.06 **	-.39	-.28	-.08 **	-.06	-.03	-.09	-.40	-.37	-.23
physiol.satisfactions	.05	-.09	-.14	-.12	-.04	.04	-.13	-.18	-.09	-.36	-.37	-.22

Note: h: hypothesized moderator effect, e: exploratory expectation
      *: difference between high/low groups is significant (5%)
    **: difference between high/low groups is siginficant (1%)

138

The moderator effect found with opportunity for belongingness may possibly be interpreted in this way.

The results of the *belongingness needs* are shown in Table 3. The hypothesis is only partly supported. The data do not fit the exploratory expectations either. There are, however, effects on the informal contact - involvement, the informal contact - stress and the work contacts - involvement relationships.

The moderator effects of the *security needs* are shown in Table 4. The hypotheses are supported. Most exploratory expectations find support as well. Deviations from the normal course of events, standardization and variety are moderated in their relationships to general satisfaction. The effects with tendency to leave are less clear, however. Neither is organizational climate moderated in the way expected. There are some interesting effects on the relationships of stress to standardization, opportunity for satisfying security, belongingness and growth needs.

Table 5 gives the effects of *physiological need strength* as a moderator. The hypotheses are not supported.

In evaluating the results, a few considerations should be borne in mind. First, the number of moderator effects per need may differ, due to difficulty in finding appropriate job characteristics related theoretically to each need. Growth need strength e.g. is much favoured by the fact that much research was done in this area. For the esteem, social and psychological needs the number of expectations that we were able to formulate was much smaller.

Secondly, moderator effects may be lacking due to limited sample variance. Data recently gathered in industrial settings show strength scores of the security and physiological needs that are much higher than in the present sample[*]. Thirdly, it should be noted that general satisfaction and tendency to leave are correlated phenomena ($r = -.54$ in this sample).

---

[*] Recent investigations by the author in a firm producing and installing electrical equipment and in a detergents factory in the Netherlands.

Table 3. Correlations between job characteristics and four outcome variables for respondents with high, middle and low scores for need for belongness.

| OUTCOME VARIABLES | Job satisfaction | | | Tendency to leave | | | Job involvement | | | Stress | | |
| MODERATOR | need for belongingness | | | need for belongingness | | | need for belongingness | | | need for belongingness | | |
	high	middle	low	high	middle	low	high	middle	low	high	middle	low
Job characteristics												
Autonomy	.21	.15	.20	-.27	-.00	.03 *	.21	.22	.15	.18	.13	.28
Variety	.13	.36	.24	.01	-.26	-.15	.40	.45	.32	.39	.20	.29
Task identity	-.00	.04	.18	.01	.01	-.03	-.00	-.05	.17	-.09	.14	.13
Org. climate	.34	.06	.33	-.35	-.01	-.09 *	.17	.07	.15	-.30	.02	-.04 *
Specialization	.19	.01	.05	-.04	.09	-.00	.15	.13	.11	.14	.19	.11
Informal contacts	.06e	-.08	.14	.04e	.05	-.02	.02	-.08	-.28 *	.06	-.14	-.35 **
Work contacts	.07e	.25	.11	-.06e	-.11	-.10	.35	.25	-.04 **	.13	.10	.11
Standardization	.00	.12	-.14	-.15	-.27	.06	-.14	.15	-.08	-.40	-.19	-.16 *
Deviations	.00	.16	.06	.04	-.13	.11	.16	.16	.04	.40	.25	.32
Opportunity for:												
growth	.49	.60	.49	-.44	-.40	-.36	.34	.47	.39	.07	-.03	.10
esteem	.47	.39	.23 **	-.44	-.32	-.14 *	.28	.33	.13	-.07	.08	.01
belongingness 1	.52h	.32	.42	-.41h	-.17	-.04 **	-.04	.13	-.04	-.43	-.13	-.22 *
belongingness 2	.22h	.31	.20	-.36h	-.31	-.18	.14	.09	.15	-.23	-.09	-.29
security	.28	.24	.04	-.25	-.36	-.19	.15	-.01	-.11	-.49	-.40	-.28
physiol. satisfactions	.06	-.02	-.05	-.30	-.07	.06 **	-.01	-.08	-.22	-.43	-.31	-.36

Note: h : hypothesized moderator effect, e: exploratory expectation
* : difference between high/low groups is significant (5%)
** : difference between high/low groups is significant (1%)

Table 4. Correlations between job characteristics and four outcome variables for respondents with high, middle and low scores for security need strength.

OUTCOMES VARIABLES	Job satisfaction			Tendency to leave			Job involvement			Stress		
MODERATOR	security need strength			security need strength			security need strength			security need strength		
	high	middle	low	high	middle	low	high	middle	low	high	middle	low
Job characteristics												
Autonomy	.24	.18	.38	-.20	-.19	-.06	.15	.23	.38	.06	.14	.20
Variety	.04^e	.33	.48 **	-.05^e	-.27	-.35 *	.17	.31	.52 **	.37	.07	.30
Task identity	.21	.09	.17	-.13	-.13	-.08	.16	.07	.14	-.11	.05	.02
Org. climate	.24^e	.18	.38	-.09^e	-.12	-.08	.18	.13	.18	-.21	.03	.06 *
Specialization	-.16	-.07	.28 **	-.06	.03	.14	.13	.17	.19	.22	.36	.11
Informal contacts	.09	-.06	-.04	.04	-.01	-.04	-.08	.11	.02	-.08	-.11	-.02
Work contacts	.08	.24	.32 *	-.03	-.14	-.27 *	.13	.17	.22	.01	.26	.20
Standardization	.07^e	-.16	-.24 *	-.02^e	.13	-.04	-.19	-.24	-.19	-.35	-.17	.07 **
Deviations	-.08^e	.06	.35 **	-.05^e	-.03	-.35 *	.09	-.00	.47 **	.34	.27	.28
Opportunity for:												
growth	.48	.56	.55	-.46	-.36	-.40	.40	.31	.56	.00	-.06	.27 *
esteem	.44	.44	.30	-.33	-.38	-.19	.43	.39	.43	-.18	-.05	.02
belongingness	.54^h	.35	.24 **	-.24	-.43	-.30	.21	.22	.22	-.45	-.13	-.04 **
security 1	.32^h	.02	-.09 **	-.33^h	.06	-.08 *	.07	-.05	-.12	-.50	-.02	-.12 **
security 2	.38^h	.12	-.13 **	-.25^h	-.08	.05 **	.20	-.11	-.31 **	-.41	-.33	-.24
physiol.satisfactions	.18	.01	-.26 **	-.24	.02	.22 **	.02	-.01	-.24 *	-.32	-.30	-.27

Note: h: hypothesized moderator effect, e: exploratory expectation
    *: difference between high/low groups is significant (5%)
    **: difference between high/low groups is significant (1%)

Table 5. Correlations between job characteristics and four outcome variables for respondents with high, middle and low scores for physiological need strength.

OUTCOME VARIABLES	Job satisfaction			Tendency to leave			Job involvement			Stress		
MODERATOR	Physiological need strength			Physiological need strength			Physiological need strength			Physiological need strength		
	high	middle	low	high	middle	low	high	middle	low	high	middle	low
Job characteristics												
Autonomy	.12	.28	.17	-.04	-.31	-.08	.07	.19	.12	.16	.08	.21
Variety	.07	.18	.30	-.15	-.13	-.13	.15	.22	.33	.18	.15	.19
Task identity	-.00	.14	.12	-.04	.02	-.11	-.06	.04	.04	-.04	-.04	.06
Org. climate	.28	.06	.11	-.21	-.17	-.10	.18	.09	-.01	-.20	-.02	.03
Spezialization	-.19	.16	-.16	.15	-.20	.28	-.02	.02	.00	.22	.11	.24
Informal contacts	.04	-.10	-.07	.03	.05	-.02	-.06	-.19	-.07	-.00	-.03	.01
Work contacts	.11	.12	.23	-.06	-.09	.02	.30	.14	.22	.06	.15	.14
Standardization	.24	.08	-.17 **	-.21	-.05	-.06	-.07	.05	-.06	-.34	-.13	-.22
Deviations	-.07	-.11	-.00	-.07	.14	.26	-.01	.01	.22	.39	.26	.24
Opportunity for:												
growth	.50	.56	.37	-.34	-.44	-.34	.35	.41	.38	.02	-.07	.08
esteem	.47	.42	.28	-.23	-.24	-.12	.24	.08	.25	-.05	-.08	.01
belongingness	.44	.25	.36	-.29	-.47	-.38	.26	.21	.28	-.39	-.18	-.16 *
security	.32	.27	.03 *	-.27	-.30	-.31	.12	.08	-.18 *	-.37	-.12	-.42
physiol. 1	.21[h]	.06	.01	-.09[h]	-.13	.10	.16	-.07	-.27 *	-.34	-.39	-.14
satisfactions 2	-.00[h]	.04	-.01	-.04[h]	-.13	-.04	-.04	.01	-.12	-.22	-.12	-.06

Note: h: hypothesized moderator effect, e: exploratory expectation
    *: difference between high/low groups is significant (5%)
    **: difference between high/low groups is significant (1%)

142

Hence, moderator tests using these as outcome variables will show some similarity in the results.

A final point to be mentioned is that several studies report rather high positive correlations between the strength of needs adjacent to each other in Maslow's model. The correlations drop off as the distance between needs in terms of Maslow's model grows larger (e.g. correlations between growth need and esteem need strength are larger than between growth need strength and strength of the security needs). This tendency was found by Ten Horn (1975) and Ten Horn and Vastenhouw (1975) in a secondary analysis of data gathered by Huizinga (1970), in the present sample and in secondary analyses of several other studies (Ten Horn, 1983: 270-273, 111). In this light, it is not surprising to find that moderator effects of adjacent needs are somewhat alike.

DISCUSSION

It was the purpose of this study to investigate all five Maslow-needs as possible moderators of the job characteristics - outcome relationships. In recent literature attention has been focused almost exclusively on growth need strength. The significance of this need was supported in the present study. The results, however, suggest at least one other need to be important in shaping people's reactions to their jobs: the need for a secure and predictable work situation. This finding fits in very well with the results from research by Aronoff and his colleagues. If corroborated by further research, the consequences for organizational practice may be profound. E.g. the failure of certain job redesign projects may be partly caused by the fact, that the subjects concerned are perhaps more concerned with security than with growth. Departments employing people with relatively strong security needs require a different type of management than departments populated by persons emphasizing growth needs. These practical consequences, which are far reaching indeed, make a call for further research particularly urgent.

The necessity to incorporate the other needs from Maslow's theory in our models of job satisfaction, is less clear. The moderator effects of the esteem, social and physiological needs are not very pronounced.

This may be due to failure to identify proper job characteristics for these needs. There are, however, several moderator effects, although not predicted from theory. Furthermore the effects appear to run parallel to those of the adjacent needs.

This phenomenon and the pattern of correlations between needs suggest a certain graduality in the scala of needs. Mitchell and Moudgill (1976) therefore rightly conclude, that the choice of the number of needs is an arbitrary one and depends on the level of specifity desired. It seems prudent not to limit that number too drastically, considering the present state of research. For practical purposes a limitation to three categories (security, social, growth) could have advantages. In fundamental research the use of all five categories seems available for the time being.

There are some more suggestions to make with respect to further research. The present study shows several weaknesses. The job characteristics were measured by self-report questionnaires. Most research in this area has been done in this way. These measures should be supplemented by really objective ones. Although the objective characteristics of the jobs partly seem to determine the scores obtained by the present methods, subjective influence is not ruled out. Instruments like the one developed by Algera (1980) may bring us some way in this direction. A second limitation of our study was its correlational nature. The causal problem cannot be properly tackled in that way. Experiments, changing the work structure in accordance to the needs of those employed are required. Experiments in which things are changed in an adverse way (worsening the job-person-fit) would be required as well. Ethical principles run contrary to the latter experiments, but perhaps some naturally occuring changes in organizations may be found that fit these methodological exigencies.

REFERENCES

Abdel-Halim, A.A., Personality and task moderators of subordinate responses to perceived leader behavior. Human Relations, 1981, 34 (1), 73-88.

Aldag, R.J. & A.P. Brief, Examination of a measure of higher-order need strength. Human Relations, 1979, 32 (8), 705-718.

Algera, J.A., Kenmerken van werk; de constructie van een instrument voor het meten van taakkenmerken die van invloed zijn op de motivatie, satisfactie en prestaties van taakuitvoerenden. Meppel, 1980.

Arnold, H.J. & R.J. House, Methodological and substantive extensions to the job characteristics model of motivation. Organizational Behavior and Human Performance, 1980, 25, 161-183.

Aronoff, J., Psychological needs and cultural systems. Princeton N.J., 1967.

Aronoff, J., Psychological needs as determinants in the formation of economic structures: a confirmation. Human Relations, 1970, 23 (2), 123-138.

Aronoff. J. & L. Messé, Motivational determinants of small-group structure. Journal of Personality and Social Psychology, 1971, 17 (3), 319-324.

Bhagat, R.S. & M.B. Chassie, Effects of changes in job characteristics on some theory-specific attitudinal outcomes: Results from a naturally occuring quasi-experiment. Human Relations, 1980, 33 (5), 297-313.

Brass, D.J., Structural relationships, job characteristics, and worker satisfaction and performance. Administrative Science Quarterly, 1981, 26, 331-348.

Brief, A.P. & R.L. Aldag, Employee reactions to job characteristics: a constructive replication. Journal of Applied Psychology, 1975, 60 (2), 182-186.

Champoux, J.E. & W.S. Peters, Applications of moderated regression in job design research. Personnel Psychology, 1980, 33, 739-783.

Cherrington, D.J. & J.L. England, The desire for an enriched job as a moderator of the enrichment-satisfaction relationship. Organizational Behavior and Human Performance, 1980, 25, 139-159.

Dunham, R.B., The measurement and dimensionality of job characteristics. Journal of Applied Psychology, 1976, 61, 404-409.

Dunham, R.B., R.J. Aldag & A.P. Brief, Dimensionality of task design as measured by the job diagnostic survey. Academy of Management Journal, 1977, 20, 209-223.

Evans, M.G., M.N. Kiggundu & R.J. House, A partial test and extension
    of the job characteristics model of motivation. Organizational
    Behavior and Human Performance, 1979, 24 (3), 354-381.

Green, S.B., A.A. Armenakis, L.D. Marbert & A.G. Bedeian, An evaluation
    of the response format and scale structure of the job diagnostic
    survey. Human Relations, 1979, 32 (2), 181-188.

Hackman, J.R. & E.E. Lawler, Employee reactions to job characteristics.
    Journal of Applied Psychology, 1971, 55 (3), 259-286.

Hackman, J.R. & G.R. Oldham, The job diagnostic survey; an instrument
    for the diagnosis of jobs and the evaluation of job redesign
    projects. Yale University, Department of Administrative Science,
    technical report, no. 4, 1974.

Hackman, J.R. & G.R. Oldham, Development of the job diagnostic survey.
    Journal of Applied Psychology, 1975, 60 (2), 159-170.

Hackman, J.R. & G.R. Oldham, Motivation through the design of work;
    test of a theory. Organizational Behavior and Human Performance,
    1976, 16 (2), 250-279.

Horn, L.A. ten, Maslow's theorie van fundamentele behoeften nader
    onderzocht. Sociale Wetenschappen, 1975, 18 (1), 59-76.

Horn, L.A. ten, Behoeften, werksituatie en arbeidsbeleving. Pijnacker,
    1983.

Horn, L.A. ten & J. Vastenhouw, Maslow's theorie van fundamentele
    behoeften, ééndimensionale "unfolding" en principale komponenten
    en analyse. Sociale Wetenschappen, 1975, 18 (3), 214-223.

Huizinga, G., Maslow's need hierarchy in the work situation. Groningen,
    1970.

Kiggundu, M.N., An empirical test of the theory of job design using
    multiple job ratings. Human Relations, 1980, 33 (5), 339-351.

Langdale, J.A., Assessment of work climates; the appropriateness of
    classical-management theory and human relations theory under
    various contingencies. New York University, unpublished doctoral
    dissertation, 1974.

Langdale, J.A., Toward a contingency theory for designing work orga-
    nizations. Journal of Applied Behavioral Science, 1976, 12 (2),
    199-214.

Maslow, A.H., Motivation and Personality. New York, 1954.

Messé, L.A., J. Aronoff & J.P. Wilson, Motivation as a mediator of the mechanisms underlying role-assignment in small groups. Journal of Personality and Social Psychology, 1972, 24, 84-90.

Michelini, R.L., J.P. Wilson & L.A. Messé, The influence of psychological needs on helping behavior. Journal of Psychology, 1975, 91, 253-258.

Mitchell, V. & P. Moudgill, Measurement of Maslow's need hierarchy. Organizational Behavior and Human Performance, 1976, 16 (2), 334-349.

Oldham, G.R., Job characteristics and internal motivation: the moderating effects of interpersonal and individual variables. Human Relations, 1976, 29 (6), 559-569.

Oldham, G.R. & D.J. Brass, Employee reactions to an open-plan office; a naturally occuring quasi-experiment. Administrative Science Quarterly, 1979, 24 (2), 267-284.

Oldham, G.R. & J.R. Hackman, Relationships between organizational structure and employee reactions; comparing alternative frameworks. Administrative Science Quarterly, 1981, 26, 66-83.

Oldham, G.R., J.R. Hackman & J.L. Pearce, Conditions under which employees respond positively to enriched work. Journal of Applied Psychology, 1976, 61 (4), 395-403.

O'Reilly, C.A., Personality-job fit: implications for individual attitudes and performance. Organizational Behavior and Human Performance, 1977, 19, 36-46.

Orpen, Ch., The effects of job enrichment on employees satisfaction, motivation, involvement and performance: a field experiment. Human Relations, 1979, 32 (3), 189-217.

Pokorney, J.J., D.C. Gilmore & T.A. Beehr, Job Diagnostic Survey dimensions: Moderating effect of growth need and correspondence with dimensions of Job Rating Form. Organizational Behavior and Human Performance, 1980, 26 (2), 222-237.

Roberts, K.H. & W. Glick, The job characteristics approach to task design: a critical review. Journal of Applied Psychology, 1981, 66 (2), 193-217.

Schouten, J., Vrijheid in het werk; over organisatiestruktuur en het welzijn van produktiewerkers. Meppel, 1974.

Sims, H.P. & A.D. Szilagyi, Job characteristic relationships; Individual and structural moderators. Organizational Behavior and Human Performance, 1976, 17 (2), 211-230.

Sims, H.P., A.D. Szilagyi & R. Keller, The measurement of job characteristics. Academy of Management Journal, 1975, 19, 195-212.

Vecchio, R.P., Individual differences as a moderator of the job quality-job satisfaction relationship; evidence from a national sample. Organizational Behavior and Human Performance, 1980, 26, 305-325.

Vecchio, R.P. & T.L. Keon, Predicting employee satisfaction from congruency among individual need, job design and system structure. Journal of Occupational Behaviour, 1981, 12, 283-292.

Wall, T.D., C.W. Clegg & P.R. Jackson, An evaluation of the Job Characteristics Model. Journal of Occupational Psychology, 1978, 51 (2), 183-196.

Walsh, J.T., T.D. Taber & T.A. Beehr, An integrated model of perceived job characteristics. Organizational Behavior and Human Performance, 1980, 25, 252-267.

Wanous, J.P., Individual differences and reactions to job characteristics. Journal of Applied Psychology, 1974, 59 (5), 616-622.

Ward, L. & J.P. Wilson, Motivation and moral development as determinants of behavioral acquiescence and moral action. Journal of Social Psychology, 1980, 112 (2), 271-286.

White, J.K., Individual differences and job quality-worker response relationship; review, integration, and comments. Academy of Management Review, 1978, 3, 267-280.

Wilson, J.P., Motivation, modelling, and altruism; a person X situation analysis. Journal of Personality and Social Psychology, 1976, 34 (6), 1078-1086.

Wilson, J.P., J. Aronoff & L.A. Messé, Social structure, member motivation and group productivity. Journal of Personality and Social Psychology, 1975, 32 (6), 1094-1098.

10. PERSONALITY AND JOB CONDITIONS: AN ANALYSIS OF THE INTERACTION BETWEEN PERCEIVED PERSONAL CONTROL VARIABLES AND OBJECTIVE CONTROL PATTERNS

H.-U. Hohner

INTRODUCTION

If one tries to analyse the relationship between job conditions and personality with regard to the dimensions of control, it is helpful to differentiate between objective control, perceived control, and personality-specific locus of control.

Objective control characterizes the measure of restriction (i.e. room for action) imposed on the employee by the type of occupation and the situation at his place of work. Objective control can be ascertained 'strictly' independent of the particular workers (e.g. by the analysis of work and occupation). But it can also be assessed 'loosely', by interviewing the individual workers or having them complete questionnaires. However, the danger exists that, when the objective facts are 'loosely' recorded, they are influenced by the subjective perception of the worker himself (cf. Gablenz-Kolakovic et al., 1981).

In the case of *subjective control* it is necessary, to distinguish two different classes of variables. On the one hand, there is the subjective perception of working conditions relevant for control. On the other hand, the individual's locus of control as a characteristic of the personality must be considered.

This chapter starts with a general review of the empirical findings on the relationship between work and locus of control. Some relevant studies are briefly introduced. Next the different practical implications to be drawn from the empirical results are discussed. Finally a model is presented which integrates objective and subjective dimensions of control into a joint theoretical framework.

LITERATURE REVIEW: STUDIES ON THE RELATIONSHIP BETWEEN OCCUPATIONAL CHARACTERISTICS AND LOCUS OF CONTROL

In December 1982, almost 3800 articles dealing with 'locus of control' had been listed in the *Psychological Abstracts*. Between one and two percent of these studies relate to the relationship of interest here, i.e. between locus of control and occupational variables.

Locus of control has as a rule been measured by Rotter's (1966) I-E scale or by related instruments. The locus of control scale assesses personal beliefs (generalized expectations) about whether certain occurrences are seen as being more due to one's own actions (internal locus of control) or to the actions of other persons, external forces, or chance (external locus of control). The empirical studies which examine the relationship between objective and subjective control are inflicted with a specific dilemma: in studies where objective control has been ascertained independently from the workers, subjective control variables have often been neglected (e.g. Gardell, 1971, 1977a; Oesterreich, 1981). On the other hand, the objective aspects of jobs in studies of locus of control - if they are treated at all - are assessed 'loosely' instead of 'strictly' with respect to the workers concerned. This is also the case for all the studies mentioned here.

Job aspects and locus of control

Global indicators

There are indicators such as 'occupational level' which above all relate to the occupational position within the organization or which mark the affiliation to a certain occupational and status group (e.g. blue-collar or white-collar workers). That such indicators of occupation are suitable for characterizing control potential (i.e. restriction at the work place) is supported by a whole series of studies (Denison, 1981; Karasek, 1981; Oegerli and Udris, 1981; Wilpert and Rayley, 1983; Zündorf and

150

Grunt, 1980). According to these studies a high occupational level corresponds with more opportunities to influence the tasks, whereas a low occupational level characterizes more restrictive working conditions. Therefore, the occupational level can function as a 'quasi-objective' indicator of objective control at the place of work.

It appears that a relationship exists between high occupational level (which implies autonomous working conditions) and an internal locus of control, whereas a low level (which indicates restrictive working conditions) corresponds to an external locus of control (Hohner and Walter, 1981; Jurkuhn, 1978; Mitchell, Smyser and Weed, 1975; Ryckman and Malikiosi, 1974; Pestonjee, 1979; Szilagyi, Sims and Keller, 1976). The studies relate to several cultures, i.e. West Germany, India, and the USA. The samples include between 200 and more than 1000 subjects. Locus of control is recorded mainly by (partially modified or shortened) I-E scales but also to some extent by instruments developed by the authors. The relationship between occupational indicators and locus of control has been examined by rank correlations (Szilagyi et al., 1976), T-tests (Mitchell et al., 1975), ANOVA (Hohner and Walter, 1981; Jurkuhn, 1978; Pestonjee, 1979; Ryckman and Malikiosi, 1974) and discriminant analysis (Jurkuhn, 1978). Those persons with managerial functions (managers) and higher qualifications (professionals) attained higher internal scores than subordinates or less qualified employees (Mitchell et al., 1975; Pestonjee, 1979; Ryckman and Malikosi, 1974; Szilagyi et al., 1976; see Table 1).

In comparison to blue-collar workers, white-collar workers attained higher internal scores (Hohner and Walter, 1981; Jurkuhn, 1978). One must note, that among the white-collar workers, top positions are included for which the blue-collar jobs have no equivalent. When the samples are adjusted by deleting the former group, the differences with respect to locus of control remain however (Hohner and Walter, 1981, p. 398). When comparing locus of control with the earnings of the subjects a correspondence between higher income and more internal locus of control can be seen (Hohner and Walter, 1981; Jurkuhn, 1978; Vecchio, 1981).

Indicators	Locus of Control	Authors
A. Rough vocational indicators		
High occupational level	←——→ internal	
- administrative e.g. head of department professional e.g. medical technologists nurse's technical e.g. licensed practical nurses clerical service e.g. nurse's aides	" (1)	Szilagyi, Sims,& Keller 1976
- managers subordinate employees	" (1)	Mitchell, Smyser,& Weed 1975
- professional e.g. professor worker e.g. painter	" (2)	Ryckman & Malikiosi 1974
- registered master subordinate labourers	" (4)	Pestonjee 1979
- white-collar workers blue-collar workers	" (3)	Hohner & Walter 1981
High income	←——→ internal (3)	Hohner & Walter 1981
	(3)	Jurkuhn 1978
	(3)	Vecchio 1981
B. Job dimensions		
High complexity	←——→ internal	
- complex vs. routine	" (1)	Hammer & Vardi 1981
- qualified vs. routine	" (3)	Jurkuhn 1978
- relations with people vs. things	" (3)(a)	Hohner & Walter 1981
Extensive room for disposition	←——→ internal	
- influence on planning, execution, and length of task	" (3)	Hohner & Walter 1981
- leeway in working and occupational decisions	" (3)(b)	Jurkuhn 1978
	" (1)	Mitchell, Smyser,& Weed 1975
Extensive variety	←——→ internal (3)	Hohner & Walter 1981
High workload	←——→ external	
- noise, dirt	" (3)(b)	Jurkuhn 1978
- noise, dust, heat, cold, chemicals, risk of accidents, physical and psychic demands, concentration, pressure of time, control at the place of work	" (3)	Hohner & Walter 1981

(1) locus of control according to Rotter   (a) only for 3 of the 6 scales
(2) locus of control according to Levenson   (b) only for 1 of the 3 scales
(3) instruments developed by the authors
(4) alienation

Table 1. Vocational indicators and their empirical relation to locus
of control

An additional type of indicator, such as complexity or room for action, relates directly to the situation at the place of work. In their studies Kohn and Schooler (1982) identified job aspects relevant for control, "that have been shown to have substantial impact on men's psychological functioning, independent of other pertinent job conditions and of education" (p. 1259). These features refer to one's place within the organizational structure, to the opportunities for self-direction (complexity and routinization of work, degree of supervision), to the basic work load (time pressure, dirt, burdens, number of hours per week) and to the occupational risks and gratuities (income, risk of losing one's job, etc.). According to the most important findings, aspects of the job and personality influence each other reciprocally with time. Therefore, jobs which encourage self-direction also support a self- -directed orientation. On the other hand jobs with restrictive working conditions are more likely to promote conformist attitudes. Conversely, the self-directed attitude leads in due time to jobs which objectively also have more room for action (Kohn and Schooler, 1982, p. 1281-1282).

As Table 1 shows, the relevance of some of these 'structural impera- ratives of the job' could also be demonstrated for locus of control. In this way *high complexity*, extensive *room for action*, few *job pressures* and great *variety* correspond with internal locus of control and vice versa.

The studies described here point unanimously in the same direction. Employees who have a certain room for control at their place of work attain higher internal locus of control scores than employees with working conditions which are to a large extent restrictive. One must be aware that jobs with a large amount of room for control characterize especially those positions which are above average with respect to education as well as income. As is well known, the type of school and vocational education correspond with social background. Thus, the occupational level represents an indicator which exceeds the working conditions in the narrow sense.

Indicators of work experience and locus of control

Table 2 shows those studies in which variables of work experience are related to locus of control. The first variable to be considered is *job satisfaction*. A small sample of scientists and engineers (Organ and Greene, 1974), people who work on an hourly basis (Runyon, 1973), as well as more than a thousand male employees (Vecchio, 1981) were examined. With the exception of the Runyon's findings, a correlation can be seen between internal locus of control and greater job satisfaction.

In two longitudinal (Andrisani, 1977; Frantz, 1980) and two cross-sectional studies (Hammer and Vardi, 1981; Heisler, 1974) the relationship between *occupational success* and locus of control was analyzed. Locus of control was assessed by items from the Rotter I-E-scale. The panels incorporated 960 (Frantz, 1980) and 7683 (Andrisani, 1977) subjects from the National Longitudinal Surveys (NLS). In the cross-sections, 560 blue- and white-collar workers as well as 200 civil servants were questioned. The connection between internal orientation and occupational success was shown consistently. Both longitudinal studies showed an interaction between locus of control and objective occupational aspects (income), as seen with Kohn & Schooler (1982).

Job involvement was investigated cross-sectionally in limited samples of employees working on an hourly basis (Runyon, 1973), managers (Kimmons and Greenhaus, 1976), as well as 300 employees from six countries (Reitz and Jewell, 1979). In all three studies more internal scores corresponded with greater job involvement.

The relationship between locus of control and additional dimensions of work experience was analyzed in the following studies: Becker and Krzystofiak (1982) examined a subgroup out of the NLS on whether, and how strongly, especially black people perceive *occupational discrimination*. In their study perceived discrimination corresponded with external locus of control. Brousseau and Mallinger (1981) found no direct relationship between locus of control and *perceived occupational stress* in a study with about 100 dentists. Instead a moderate correspondence was shown between internal orientation and physiological health indicators. Blue- and white-collar workers who are *active in the firm's politics* (e.g.

154

Indicators	Locus of Control	Authors
High job satisfaction	⟵⟶ internal	
- ... with the actual content of the job; ... with the organization and its management	" (1)	Organ & Greene 1974
- overall job satisfaction	" (2)	Vecchio 1981
- satisfaction with supervision	(no direct (1) connection)	Runyon 1973
Occupational success	⟵⟶ internal	
- growth in earnings; occupational advancement	" (1)	Andrisani 1977
- wage's change; job and labor market experience et al.	" (1)	Frantz 1980
- career activities, efforts spent on job mobility, use of strategies et al.	" (1)	Hammer & Vardi 1981
- number of promotions, salary increases, awards received et al.	" (1)	Heisler 1974
Extensive job involvement	⟵⟶ internal	
- work involvement sensu Lodahl & Kejner	" (1) " (1)	Kimmons & Greenhaus 1976 Runyon 1973
- job involvement scale (Greene 1967)	" (1)	Reitz & Jewell 1979
High job performance	⟵⟶ internal (3)	Broedling 1975
		Hersch & Scheibe 1967
		Lied & Pritchard 1976
		Majumder, MacDonald, & Greever 1977
Perception of labor market discrimination	⟵⟶ external (1)	Becker & Krzystofiak 1982
Perceived occupational stress	⟵⟶ (no connection) (1)	Brousseau & Mallinger 1981
Involvement in firm policies	⟵⟶ internal (4)	Hohner 1982

(1) locus of control sensu Rotter
(2) instrument developed by the author
(3) quoted according to Spector (1982, p. 489)
(4) on the locus of control subscale "firm policy"

Table 2. **Indicators of work experience and their empirical relation to locus of control**

active unionists) showed a more internal orientation in the domain of 'firm politics' than their non-active colleagues (Hohner, 1982).

Spector (1982) points at four empirical studies which all report a positive relationship between internal locus of control and good *occupational performance* (Broedling, 1975; Hersch and Scheibe, 1967; Lied and Pritchard, 1976; Majumder, MacDonald and Greever, 1977). Performance here was not only recorded 'loosely' by the respective subjects, but also in part 'strictly' by their superiors.

Locus of control as a moderator variable

Whether locus of control moderates the relationship between job satisfaction and job aspects was examined by several authors (Evans, 1973; Kimmons and Greenhaus, 1976; Mitchell e.a., 1975; Runyon, 1973; Sims and Szilagyi, 1976; Vecchio, 1981). In this way, internals were for example more satisfied with a participative and democratic style of supervision than externals; conversely, externals were more satisfied with a directive style of supervision than internals. However, in these studies contradictory results were found concerning the moderating function of locus of control. In a representative study in Australia, Kabanoff and O'Brien (1980) found indications of a moderating effect of locus of control in the domains of work and leisure. In the discrimination analyses conducted, the variables of age and income proved, however, to be more significant than that of locus of control.

Indicators of the 'cognitive control' of the employees (labeled with items of locus of control according to Levenson and with items developed by the authors) moderating between working conditions which stimulate stress and psychic well-being were reported by Frese, Schmidt-Hieber and Leitner, 1981). All in all, one can find only little and somewhat inconsistent evidence on the role of locus of control as a moderator between various aspects of work and/or persons (cf. on this White, 1978).

Summary evaluation

The appraisal of the outlined studies has proved to be ambiguous. On the one hand, the studies show the relevance of the locus of control variable. On the other hand, the proportion of variance which has been accounted for by locus of control is generally very small. The individual findings of the studies result in a jig-saw puzzle in which a structure of relationships can be recognized but which remains on the whole relatively unclear. With the exception of the longitudinal studies, the other results inform us only of correlations between locus of control and specific job variables at single time points.

In the bivariate analyses one can continually see the pattern of autonomy-supportive working conditions and internal locus of control, and conversely, restrictive working conditions and external locus of control; the question to what degree work and occupation contribute to the individuals' development of locus of control cannot, however, be answered satisfactorily on the basis of such findings. One can only record that attractive positions are held by more internal people. Whether restrictive working conditions generate or support a more external orientation and jobs with a great amount of room for action more internal orientations, or whether internal people are more likely to attain better positions than external people, or whether both are, true cannot be decided from these studies. Only when the existing longitudinal studies on the connection between work and personality (i.e. the relationship between locus of control and occupational advance; Andrisani, 1977; Frantz, 1980) are systematically combined with the appropriate cross-sectional results, a framework can be constructed which shows the interactive influence of objective and subjective dimensions of control. There are two longitudinal studies which deal with the relationship between objective and subjective control dimensions, but these are not yet complete (Project 'Psychic stress at the place of work', 1981; project 'Socialization as a function of work', cf. the last section of this chapter). Of course several detailed analyses are needed to provide the hypothesized framework with a solid theoretical foundation and with 'meat' from controlled empirical studies.

157

APPLICATIONS AND CRITICISM

Implications for practice

Turning to the field of practical applications one finds in the pertinent literature two positions, which can be combined with each other only with difficulty.

- The first position is emphasized by Spector (1982). The locus of control variable is used as an instrument of selection and classification. By following the empirical results, 'internals', for example, would be assigned to complex jobs and to departments with a participatory style of supervision, whereas 'externals' should receive easier jobs and would be assigned to places of work more strictly controlled by superiors.

- The second position is represented by such authors as Gardell (1977b) or Ulich (1981; Ulich and Frei, 1980). They plead for an increase in objective occupational leeway in those places of work which are marked by their strictly restrictive working conditions.

Selection and placement

Some comments should be given on the first position, as described by Spector in a review in the *Psychological Bulletin*. The following quote illustrates his point of view clearly:

> "The nature of a job within the context of organizational factors and demands would determine whether an internal or external would be best suited. If a job requires complex information processing and frequent complex learning, internals would be expected to perform better; for simple tasks, however, the performance differential would disappear. When tasks or organizational demands require initiative and independence of action, the internal would be more suitable; when the requirement is for compliance, however, the external would be more appropriate. Finally, for jobs requiring high motivation, internals would be more likely to believe that their efforts will lead to rewards, especially when they actually do, and thus internals would tend to exhibit higher motivation. Therefore, it would seem that internals are best suited for highly technical or skilled jobs, professional jobs, and managerial or supervisory jobs. Externals would be more suited to factory line jobs, unskilled labor jobs, and jobs of a routine nature" (Spector, 1982, p. 486).

158

As will be shown, many of the studies referred to in Spector's assignment model should be criticized both methodologically and theoretically. In addition to this, problems could arise with this model due to the fact that many jobs are not formed in such a way that they may be fitted into these simple assignment patterns. For example, Spector himself specifies the problem in the field of modern military where both the 'external' ability of subordination and the 'internal' ability of initiative are necessary to the same extent. But even ignoring these problems, several arguments must be put forward against the use of the personality dimension of locus of control as a criterion for the hiring and assignment of workers.

- Thus it appears problematic on ethical grounds with respect to the protection of the individual's privacy, when personality variables (such as locus of control) are treated as qualifying characteristics by the employing firm.

- Further it seems questionable to place those employees identified as 'externals' into restrictive and dead-end jobs and for this reason not to provide the chance to develop an internal orientation. As noted before, there are reinforcing mechanisms which appear to be built into the jobs meant for 'internals' and with them the potential for vocational advances.

- Spector's model seems to be a static one, which ignores, at least as far as the restrictive working conditions are concerned, the long term effects of the occupation on the employee's personality. Aside from this, it overestimates the predictive quality of the locus of control instruments and treats the locus of control as being invariant to a certain extent and resistent to change. For example, several employees can be found, who at a certain point in time were diagnosed as 'externals', but who have developed an internal orientation under suitable stimulation (e.g. a certain degree of responsibility). A completely different question, to be treated below, is whether one should aim principally at an internal orientation.

- The last point stresses the relevance of the quality and reliability of diagnosis. If one were to follow Spector's suggestion it would have considerable consequences for the employee, whether he or she is assigned to the group of internals and thus receives more stimulating jobs which are conducive to the personality, or whether he or she is classified as being an external and thus receives more restrictive working conditions. The standard which appears throughout, namely that the internals are the 'good guys' and the externals the 'bad guys' has, incidentally, already been criticized by Rotter (1975) as not being appropriate for the locus of control construct nor the theory of social learning underlying it. Although the locus of control scale was developed within the field of clinical psychology, the pertinent findings were mainly gained from questionnaire studies or laboratory experiments. Thus the use of such findings for non-clinical single case diagnosis seems, to say the least, problematic.

Job redesign

Spector's proposal can be restricted to certain conditions (e.g. Hammer and Vardi, 1981) - i.e. when reorganization of the job is out of the question. These authors, however, stress the necessity of changes in the working and organizational structure as a primary task. "If organizations want employees with drive and initiative on all hierarchical levels, they could benefit from the initiative already present by not thwarting it through constraints which can be removed, such as company policies governing upward mobility" (p. 28). In this, they are moving toward a position which also takes the interests of the employees into consideration and stresses them.

The fundamental idea of this second position is to reduce restrictive working conditions and to extend the participatory opportunities of the employees. In doing this, particular modifications in the job or the departmental structure should be carried out with respect to the viewpoint of their 'conduciveness to the personality' (Persönlichkeitsförderlichkeit; Ulich and Frei, 1981) and in cooperation with the employees concerned. Such modifications, with the aid of the so called 'subjective analysis of work' method (Subjektive Tätigkeitsanalyse; Ulich, 1980), have already been successfully carried out with respect to the interests of both company and employees. In the years to come, there is a great

160

opportunity for such ideas to be realized as technological advances
force modifications of work structures. Those modifications which are
directed more towards autonomy might also stimulate, especially over a
longer period of time, more personal responsibility and a greater readi-
ness to qualify oneself further, as well as lead to greater job involvement and greater job satisfaction, thus promising profit for both company and employees.

Criticism of the studies

The studies can be criticized with respect to their practical implications. Here one should ask how much the formulation of the questions
and the designs of the studies must be supplemented and made more precise,
in order to provide an adequate basis for decisions on the modification
of work and organizational structure. Another question concerns the
scientific elucidation of the process of occupational socialization. Or
expressed more precisely: it is a question of the analysis of the interaction between work and personality within a developmental perspective.
With this perspective in view, several types of criticism can be differentiated which concern to a greater or lesser extent the studies reviewed
here.

A first line of criticism stems from the evaluation of the studies
according to conventional methodological criteria for the quality of
empirical social research. This concerns for example the question of
the measurement qualities of the instruments' information about the external and internal validity of the research designs, and a comprehensible
documentation of the findings.
In this chapter only two main points will be stressed.
- Several studies are based on relatively small samples (e.g. Runyon,
  1973). Depending on the method of evaluation, the subjects must be
  divided into further sub-groups so that the cell-assignment in the
  ANOVAs then amounts only to e.g. n=10. Admittedly, one still has the
  formal criterion of statistical significance. However, when the formal
  confirmation of the 'null-hypothesis', which is due to the small number
  in the sample, receives the same emphasis in the interpretation as

the confirmation of the alternative hypothesis, this seems to be questionable with regard to the research questions.

- A second point concerns the external validity of the studies. In several studies only a relatively small number of those asked actually took part in the study. One may, however, assume that in such studies internal persons are overrepresented (Hohner, 1983).

The second type of criticism relates to the research practice regarding the locus of control-variable.

- The I-E scale developed by Rotter was used most. In doing this, the long version of the scale with 23 items was not always put into use, presumably for reasons of research economy, and instead one was often confronted with a shortened and partially modified scale with, for example, 4, 11, or 14 items. Apart from this, the format of answers to the items was varied (e.g. forced-choice-items, four-stage Likert-scales). A problem exists because a locus of control scale of, for example, 4 items may possibly assess a different construct than that of the long version of the Rotter-scale. In order to be able to assess this problem, more information about the correlation between the particular shortened scales and the long version would be necessary. On the other hand, the findings gained by various modifications of the Rotter-scale and of the Levenson-Scales and by further locus of control scales confirm the validity of the locus of control construct.

- Locus of control scales are used in several evaluation designs as independent variables. In these cases extreme groups of internals versus externals are formed. This classification is not attached to normed absolute values, but is dependent on the particular sample. In many cases, however, these samples are homogeneous (e.g. managers, unskilled workers, prisoners, etc.). Even in the comparison of groups, a certain amount of arbitrariness exists concerning whether one falls into the group of internals or that of the externals, as this indeed depends on the other persons in the sample. The problem of assignment appears especially problematic within the framework of individual diagnosis. In order to pursue this question further, it would be necessary to know the absolute scores of the various subject groups in the individual studies. These have, however, for the most part not been published. In fact, it would be valuable to collect the essential findings and to set up norms.

- A further problematic point relates to the dimensions of the locus of control construct. There is especially the question as to the confounding of the factors of 'control ideology' versus 'personal control' (see below).

- Furthermore, there is the problem of the domain specifity of the locus of control. In the analysis of the relationship between locus of control as a generalized construct, as ascertained by Rotter's I-E scale (or by the Levenson-scales), and specific work aspects, no strong empirical correlations are expected a priori. One can even assume that the lower correlations reported between locus of control and specific working conditions can be partially due to the fact that internal subjects perceive more room for movement than external subjects. The findings reported here relating to job satisfaction also support this assumption. This question can, however, only be clarified empirically if one investigates objective control at the place of work in a 'strict' manner, i.e. independent of the employees concerned. If one were to develop locus of control scales for specific job conditions or specific domains of experience particularly, then the examined sub-relation could also be worked out empirically in a more precise manner (cf. Hohner and Walter, 1981, p. 404).

The third type of criticism relates to the growth in knowledge about the question of vocational socialization.

- In order to analyse the interaction between the variables at the place of work and personality variables (in this case locus of control) over a longer period of time, longitudinal studies are recommended (Frese, 1982; Hohner, in press). Although unsatisfactory, one could, by way of substitution interpret the data from cross-sectional studies by analogy with comparable samples and instruments in which, however, the characteristics (e.g. age) vary. Admittedly, one can find a series of studies on the same question (e.g. with respect to the connection between job satisfaction and locus of control); however, these studies do not satisfy the above criteria, as in many cases neither the instruments nor samples can be directly compared.

- Objective control variables have not been assessed 'strictly' in any of the reviewed studies. Yet the findings described before show that the quasi-objective indicators (occupational level) and the job indicators recorded in a 'loose' manner, correspond to a great extent in their findings concerning locus of control. One can presume, though, that by analyzing individual cases of several persons one could ascertain extensive differences between objective and per- ceived control. In group comparisons, such intra-individual differen- tiation could be overlooked.

The fourth type of the criticism relates to the nature of the locus of control construct. It refers to the determinative view which comes to light in, for example, the original Rotter scale. The items there must be answered in an either external or an internal manner. Items which aim at the simultaneous assessment of internal *and* external in- fluences are not included in any of the scales reported on.

Whether such forms of an 'interactive' locus of control (Hoff, 1982) can indirectly be identified on the basis of the Rotter scale and re- lated instruments is doubtful. In this way, people who attain scores in the middle range of the scale have answered some of the items ex- ternally and the rest internally. This, however, doesn't mean that they are convinced of having 'one as well as the other'. Besides, a person with an interactive locus of control could answer all Rotter items for example internally, crossing them off according to the strongest influ- ence. Even if one ascertains the locus of control with multi-dimensional instruments (e.g. Levenson, 1974), one cannot establish with certainty whether it has a determinative or an interactive orientation. One can at most attain indications from certain profiles (e.g. personal control is very high; chance and control by others is very low --> determinative internal orientation). What does one do with those who attain high scores in all three dimensions? These persons could have an interactive orientation, i.e. see various influences in the same situation; however, it could also be a question of causal attribution in a specific domain or situation.

With this in mind, further empirical work is necessary. One can assume that with suitable recording not only of determinative (internal or external) but also of interactive control orientations, clearer empirical relationships could be discovered between locus of control and job variables.

SKETCH OF A MODEL WHICH INTEGRATES BOTH OBJECTIVE AND SUBJECTIVE DIMENSIONS OF CONTROL

In order to improve the analysis of the interaction between work and personality, it seems to be advisable to integrate objective factors of control, the subjective perception of these factors, and the personality variable of locus of control into an interactive theoretical framework (Hoff, 1981). Such a model should then be tested in a longitudinal study. The three named groups of variables act as the main components of the model (Figure 1).

Objective factors of control. Here characteristics of work and organizational structure are meant insofar as they are seen to be relevant for control. On the one hand, there are factors which mark the amount of restriction and of room for control *directly*, like dimensions describing the opportunities for the employee to have influence on the planning, on the carrying out, and on the length of time of job tasks, but also on variables such as participation and responsibility for colleagues, machines, and products. On the other hand, there are factors relating to the degree of restriction and the room for control which is *indirectly* at the employee's disposal, like for example, the job's complexity, variety, degree of routinization, the amount of intellectual stimulation and stressors and strains.

Dimensions of objective control can be ascertained by both 'strict' and 'loose' methods, for example by objective work and occupational analyses (Lappe, 1981), by asking experts or by qualitative or standardized questioning of the employees concerned (Hoff, Lappe and Lempert,

1983). Because in questioning those concerned, information on objective control may be more or less confounded with subjective perceptions the following model requires 'strict' methods of recording. This is the case at least as long as the relationship between objective control and subjective perception of control is not elucidated empirically for more detailed aspects of work and for individual persons (Landeck, 1981).

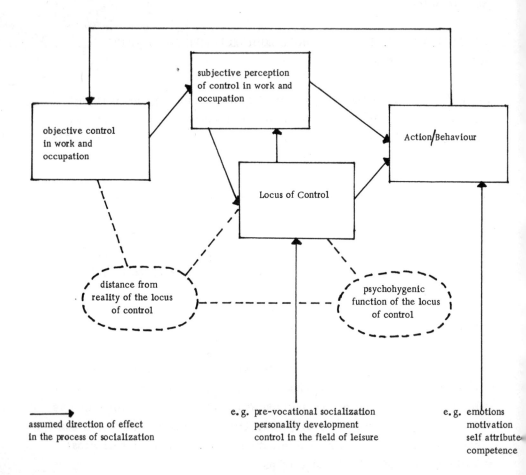

Figure 1. Model sketch on the analysis of objective and subjective control

Subjective perceptions of work and organizational aspects relevant for control act as the second main component of this model. The employee's perception of the objective control factors falls into this category. Here one can distinguish between the employee's views relating to the characteristics of his occupation and work place (e.g. "my work is very varied") and those relating to his own experience (e.g. "I find my job quite boring").

The third main component is represented by the *locus of control* construct. This construct should be differentiated according to several points of view. The most important differentiations (cf. Hohner, in press) concern:

- the dimensions of the construct, distinguishing 'personal control' and 'control ideology' on the one hand an external versus fatalistic elements of the locus of control on the other hand. This means that beliefs referring to a 'modal' person and his influence ("*one* can ...") must be separated from those which refer to the person himself ("*I* can ..."). And further, that personal control (internality), control by other persons (externality), and control by chance or fate (fatalism) should be recorded as separate dimensions;

- the domain specificity of the construct. Here the extent to which control beliefs are structured according to various domains of experience must be examined. In our model this refers especially to the fields of 'work' and 'leisure'. The Rotter concept proceeds on the assumption that the locus of control concerning various situations and domains of experience is generalized (i.e. that people have the same internal or external beliefs respectively for all domains of experience);

- determinative versus interactive locus of control (Hoff, 1982; Hoff and Hohner, 1982). This highly important difference refers to whether a person emphasizes mainly a certain class of influences (e.g. only his own influence or only external influence) or the simultaneous intrasituative interaction of internal and external influences. It is to be assumed that control beliefs in specific domains of experience are related to an interactive locus of control.

A further component of the model is the *distance from reality* of perceived control and of locus of control (cf. detailed by Hohner and Hoff, 1983), being an indicator of the agreement or the discrepancy between objective control on the one hand and perceived control or locus of control on the other hand. This construct promises to be fruitful on three accounts.

- It allows detailed analyses of interaction between work and personality. For example, one can compare the degree and direction of the distance from reality of 'perceived control' and 'locus of control' and by doing this gain information as to the role of perceived control: whether perceived control should be attributed to the work or to the personality; by which persons and why; etc..

- It opens the opportunity to approach the psychic and psychohygienic functions of locus of control with specially focused questions (cf. Hoyos e.a., 1982; Lefcourt, 1980). Thus, for example, the psychic benefit of an internal locus of control which is far from reality could appear to lie in the fact that the individual can stabilize his endangered self-esteem by a cognitive reduction of the dissonance, attributing himself personal effectiveness which is in fact not present.

- It makes it possible to restructure the normative evaluation of the locus of control. As has already been described, the desired characteristics and demeanour, which show the norm, seem to be those of internal locus of control. This fact can lead to pedagogical, pre-ventive, or therapeutic intervention taking an internal orientation as its desired criterion and then promoting it particularly. However, if one examines the ideas of control according to distance from reality or according to aspects of personal fitness, then one will arrive at a different evaluation in several cases. For example, an internal orientation would be far from reality in a working situation which is determined by external influences and could promote an illusionary attitude which could at length lead to painful conflicts for the person concerned.

In conclusion, several further components of this model should be pointed out. In previous studies the role of the locus of control as a component which directs behaviour is neglected. It is, however, just this research on the locus of control which promises to be a relevant contribution to the field of actions or behaviour (Hohner and Hoff, 1983; cf. Chapman, Skinner and Baltes, 1982; cf. on the concept of the style of action, Frese, 1983).

One must also incorporate the variables of *prevocational socialization* and *personal development* as background conditions for the model, as well as concurrent conditions and experiences in those domains of life *not* connected with the job. Finally, one must study change or stability in the objective and subjective dimensions of control.

This model has been put into use within the framework of a longitudinal study of young skilled workers that was started in 1980 (Hoff, Lappe and Lempert, 1982; 1983). The aim of this study, which focuses on individual case analyses, lies especially in the specification of an interactive theory of occupational socialization and personality development. Results already at hand indicate the empirical fruitfulness of at least a part of the model (Hohner, in press). Thus a number of workers evaluate the result of their occupational choice as being due to their own efficacy, where in fact external influences (parents, employment office) have played a major role.

Further effort will focus on empirical tests of the model to establish its validity.

* The author would like to thank the following individuals for their help: Hiltrud Albat, Ernst Hoff, Samantha J. Hume, Lothar Lappe, Wolfgang Lempert, Amy Jo Michele, Barbara Redlitz, Ellen Skinner, and Wilfried Spang.

REFERENCES

Andrisani, P.J., Internal-external attitudes, personal initiative, and
the labor market experience of black and white men. Journal of
Human Resources, 1977, 12, 309-328.

Becker, B.E. & F.J. Krzystofiak, The influence of labor market discrimination on locus of control. Journal of Vocational Behavior, 1982,
21, 60-70.

Broedling, L.A., Relationship of internal-external control to work
motivation and performance in an expectancy model. Journal of
Applied Psychology, 1975, 60, 65-70.

Brousseau, K.R. & M.A. Mallinger, Internal-external locus of control,
perceived occupational stress, and cardiovascular health. Journal
of Occupational Behavior, 1981, 2, 65-71.

Chapman, M., E.A. Skinner & P.B. Baltes, Action, intelligence, and
control in a developmental perspective (project prospectus).
Unpublished manuscript. Berlin: Max Planck Institute for Human
Development and Education, August, 1982.

Denison, D.R., Sociotechnical design and self-managing work groups:
The impact on control. Journal of Occupational Behavior, 1982, 3,
297-314.

Evans, M.G., The moderating effect of internal versus external control
on the relationship between various aspects of job satisfaction.
Studies in Personnel Psychology, 1973, 5, 37-46.

Frantz, R.S., The effect of early labor market experience upon internal
-external locus of control among young male workers. Journal of
Youth and Adolescence, 1980, 9, 203-210.

Frese, M., Occupational socialization and psychological development:
An underemphasized research perspective in industrial psychology.
Journal of Occupational Psychology, 1982, 55, 209-224.

Frese, M., Der Einfluss der Arbeit auf die Persönlichkeit. Zum Konzept
des Handlungsstils in der beruflichen Sozialisation. Zeitschrift
für Sozialisationsforschung und Erziehungssoziologie, 1983, 3,
11-28.

Frese, M., E. Schmidt-Hieber & K. Leitner, Arbeitsbedingungen, kognitive Kontrolle und psychisches und psycho-physiologisches Befinden:

Welcher Erkenntnisfortschritt lässt sich aus einer quantitativen
Querschnittsuntersuchung ziehen? In: Michaelis, W. (Ed.), Bericht
über den 32. Kongress der DGfPs in Zürich 1980. Göttingen: Hogrefe,
1981, S. 549-552.

Gablenz-Kolakovič, S., T. Krogoll, R. Oesterreich & W. Volpert,
Subjektive oder objektive Arbeitsanalyse? Zeitschrift für Arbeitswissenschaft, 1981, 35, 217-220.

Gardell, B., Alienation and mental health in the modern industrial
environment. In: L. Levi (Ed.), Society, stress and disease (Vol. I).
London: Oxford University Press, 1971, 148-180.

Gardell, B., Autonomy and participation at work. Human Relations, 1977a,
30, 515-533.

Gardell, B., Psychological and social problems of industrial work in
affluent societies. International Journal of Psychology, 1977b,
12, 125-134.

Hammer, T.H. & Y. Vardi, Locus of control and career self-management
among nonsupervisory employees in industrial settings. Journal of
Vocational Behavior, 1981, 18, 13-29.

Heisler, W.J., A performance correlate of personal control beliefs in
an organizational context. Journal of Applied Psychology, 1974,
59, 504-506.

Hersch, P.D. & K.E. Scheibe, Reliability and validity of internal-
external control as a personality dimension. Journal of Consulting
Psychology, 1967, 31, 609-613.

Hoff, E., Sozialisation als Entwicklung der Beziehung zwischen Person
und Umwelt. Zeitschrift für Sozialisationsforschung und Erziehungssoziologie, 1981, 1, 91-115.

Hoff, E., Kontrollbewusstsein: Grundvorstellungen zur eigenen Person
und Umwelt. Kölner Zeitschrift für Soziologie und Sozialpsychologie,
1982, 34, 316-339.

Hoff, E. & H.-U. Hohner, Zur Operationalisierung von Kontrollbewusstsein. In: S. Preiser (Ed.), Kognitive und emotionale Aspekte
politischen Engagements. Fortschritte der Politischen Psychologie,
Band 2. Weinheim: Beltz, 1982, 125-129.

Hoff, E., L. Lappe & W. Lempert, Sozialisationstheoretische Überlegungen
zur Analyse von Arbeit, Betrieb und Beruf. Soziale Welt, 1982, 33,
508-536.

Hoff, E., L. Lappe & W. Lempert, Methoden zur Untersuchung der Sozialisation junger Facharbeiter. Berlin: Max Planck Institut für Bildungsforschung (Materialien aus der Bildungsforschung, Band 24), 1983.

Hohner, H.-U., Ursachenzuschreibung (locus of control) und betriebspolitisches Engagement. In: S. Preiser (Ed.), Kognitive und emotionale Aspekte politischen Engagements. Fortschritte der politischen Psychologie, Band 2. Weinheim: Beltz, 1982, 130-147.

Hohner, H.-U., Das Dilemma der externen Validität bei psychologischen Fragebogenuntersuchungen. Ein empirischer Beitrag zur Artefaktforschung. Diagnostica, 1983, 29, 26-39.

Hohner, H.-U., Zwischen Kontrolle und Ohnmacht. Thesen zur psychologischen Bestimmung von Kontrollbewusstsein in einem zunehmend restriktiven Arbeitsmarkt. In: H. Moser & S. Preiser (Eds.), Umweltprobleme und Arbeitslosigkeit. Fortschritte der politischen Psychologie. Band 4. Weinheim: Beltz (in press).

Hohner, H.-U. & E.H. Hoff, Prävention und Therapie. Zur Modifikation von objektiver Kontrolle und Kontrollbewusstsein. Psychosozial, 1983 (in press).

Hohner, H.-U. & H. Walter, Ursachenzuschreibung (locus of control) bei Arbeitern und Angestellten. Einige empirische Befunde. Psychologische Beiträge, 1981, 23, 392-407.

Hoyos, Graf C., H. Metzen, H. Dvorak, E. Hausmann & R. Leitmeier, Belastung und Beanspruchung bei Steuerungs- und Überwachungstätigkeiten. Berichte aus dem Institut für Psychologie und Erziehungswissenschaft der Technischen Universität München, Nr. 9, München, Juni, 1982.

Jurkuhn, D., Arbeitssituation und Selbstverantwortlichkeit. Eine empirische Untersuchung über die Zusammenhänge zwischen Arbeitsbedingungen, Arbeitszufriedenheit und Selbst-, Fremd- und Zufallskontrolle. Dissertation, Trier, 1978.

Kabanoff, B. & G.E. O'Brien, Work and leisure: A task attributes analysis. Journal of Applied Psychology, 1980, 65, 596-609.

Karasek, R.A., Zum Vergleich arbeitsplatzbedingter Stressfaktoren bei Arbeitern und Angestellten: Beziehungen zwischen sozialer Schicht, Arbeitsplatzmerkmalen und psychischer Beanspruchung. In: M. Frese (Ed.), Stress im Büro. Bern: Huber, 1981. 22-44.

Kimmons, G. & J.H. Greenhaus, Relationship between locus of control and reactions of employees to work characteristics. Psychological Reports, 1976, 39, 815-820.

Kohn, M.L. & C. Schooler, Job conditions and personality. A longitudinal assessment of their reciprocal effects. American Journal of Sociology, 1982, 87, 1257-1286.

Landeck, K.J., Zur Gültigkeit subjektivistischer Arbeitsplatz-Analyseverfahren - Ergebnisse einer quasi-experimentellen Untersuchung. Psychologie und Praxis, 1981, 25, 155-165.

Lappe, L., Die Arbeitssituation erwerbstätiger Frauen. Frankfurt: Campus, 1981.

Lefcourt, H.M., Locus of control and coping with life's events. In: E. Staub (Ed.), Personality. Basic aspects and current research. Englewood Cliffs: Prentice-Hall, 1980, 200-235.

Levenson, H., Activism and powerful others: Distinctions within the concept of internal-external control. Journal of Personality Assessment, 1974, 38, 377-383.

Lied, T.R. & R.D. Pritchard, Relationships between personality variables and components of the expectancy-valence model. Journal of Applied Psychology, 1976, 61, 463-467.

Majumder, R.K., A.P. MacDonald & K.B. Greever, A study of rehabilitation counselors: Locus of control and attitudes toward the poor. Journal of Counseling Psychology, 1977, 24, 137-141.

Mitchell, T.R., C.M. Smyser & S.E. Weed, Locus of control: supervision and work satisfaction. Academy of Management Journal, 1975, 18, 623-631.

Oegerli, K. & I. Udris, Angestellte oder Büroarbeiter? Untersuchungen zur Tätigkeitsklassifikation, zu Beanspruchungs- und Zufriedenheitsstrukturen im Bürobereich. In: M. Frese (Ed.), Stress im Büro. Bern: Huber, 1981, 96-124.

Oesterreich, R., Handlungsregulation und Kontrolle. München: Urban & Schwarzenberg, 1981.

Organ, D.W. & Ch.N. Greene, Role ambiguity, locus of control, and work satisfaction. Journal of Applied Psychology, 1974, 59, 101-102.

Pestonjee, D.M., Alienation, insecurity, and job satisfaction. Vikalpa, 1979, 4, 9-14.

Projekt "Psychischer Stress am Arbeitsplatz" Darstellung der Konzeption und der Skalenentwicklung. Berliner Hefte zur Arbeits- und Sozialpsychologie. Oktober, 1981.

Reitz, H.J. & L.N. Jewell, Sex, locus of control, and job involvement: A six-county investigation. Academy of Management Journal, 1979, 22, 72-80.

Rotter, J.B., Generalized expectancies of internal versus external control of reinforcement. Psychological Monographs, 1966, 80, (whole No. 609).

Rotter, J.B., Some problems and misconceptions related to the construct of interna versus external control of reinforcement. Journal of Consulting and Clinical Psychology, 1975, 43, 56-67.

Runyon, K.E., Some interactions between personality variables and management styles. Journal of Applied Psychology, 1973, 57, 288-294.

Ryckman, R.M. & M. Malikiosi, Differences in locus of control orientation for members of selected occupations. Psychological Reports, 1974, 34, 1224-1226.

Sims, H.P. & A.D. Szilagyi, Job characteristic relationships: Individual and structural moderators. Organizational Behavior and Human Performance, 1976, 17, 211-230.

Spector, P.E., Behavior in organizations as a function of employee's locus of control. Psychological Bulletin, 1982, 91, 482-497.

Szilagyi, A.D. Jr., H.P. Sims & R.T. Keller, Role dynamics, locus of control, and employee attitudes and behavior. Academy of Management Journal, 1976, 19, 259-276.

Ulich, E., Subjektive Tätigkeitsanalyse als Voraussetzung autonomieorientierter Arbeitsgestaltung. In: F. Frei & E. Ulich (Eds.), Beiträge zur psychologischen Arbeitsanalyse, Bern: Huber, 1980, 327-347.

Ulich, E., Möglichkeiten autonomieorientierter Arbeitsgestaltung. In: M. Frese (Ed.), Stress im Büro. Bern: Huber, 1981, 159-178.

Ulich, E. & F. Frei, Persönlichkeitsförderliche Arbeitsgestaltung und Qualifizierungsprobleme. In: W. Volpert (Ed.), Beiträge zur Psychologischen Handlungstheorie. Bern: Huber, 1980, 71-86.

Vecchio, R.P., Workers belief in internal versus external determinants of success. Journal of Social Psychology, 1981, 114, 199-207.

White, J.K., Individual differences and the job quality - worker response relationship: review, integration, and comments. The Academy of Management Review, 1978, 3, 267-280.

Wilpert, B. & J. Rayley, Nationale Mitbestimmungssysteme und ihre Wirkungen auf Partizipationsverhalten. Psychologie und Praxis. Zeitschrift für Arbeits- und Organisationspsychologie, 1983, 27 (N.F.1), 3-12.

Zündorf, L. & M. Grunt, Hierarchie in Wirtschaftsunternehmen. Frankfurt: Campus, 1980.

11. TYPE A BEHAVIOUR PATTERN AS A MODERATOR IN THE STRESSOR-STRAIN RELATIONSHIP

J.A.M. Winnubst, F.H.G. Marselissen, A.M.L. van Bastelaer
Ch.J. de Wolff & A.E. Leuftinck

INTRODUCTION

Type A behaviour is nowadays considered in medicine and social science
as an important factor related to the impact of stress on cardiovascular
disease (Cooper et al., 1981). This style of behaviour possibly strengthens the adverse effects of psychosocial stress. Persons under stress
with excessive Type A behaviour will run an increased risk of developing
illness. Although there is a growing body of research evidence regarding
the relationships between Type A behaviour, stress and health, there
are still many conceptual and empirical issues that remain unclear. This
chapter examines the role of Type A behaviour in relation to the stres-
sor-strain-illness model of organizational stress. This model has been
developed, in the course of many years, by members of the Institute for
Social Research at the University of Michigan (Kahn et al., 1964;
French & Caplan, 1972). Recently, it has generated a great deal of research in the Netherlands (Van Dijkhuizen, 1980; Reiche, 1982; Van
Bastelaer & Van Beers, 1982). We shall analyse Dutch data with regard
to the hypothesis that Type A behaviour strengthens the impact of organizational stressors on perceived strain and illness. This study is
based on research by LaRocco, House and French (1980) and Winnubst,
Marcelissen and Kleber (1982) on social support.

Conceptual framework

The Michigan model starts with an objective work situation that may give rise to perceived job stressors. According to Van Dijkhuizen (1980, p. 25) stressors are "... those elements in the environment which, in the opinion of the person himself (by his perception) influence his daily routine, his psychological and physical health". Examples are role conflict, role ambiguity, workload etc. Stressors can cause psychological, behavioural and physiological strains. The term strain is used "... to denote the directly measurable effects of internal stress, being the consequence of the actions of one or several stressors" (Ibid, p. 30).

Several strains are considered as precursors of disease. For instance, high blood pressure, cigarette smoking, high cholesterol level etc. are often mentioned in cardiological literature as important factor of ischaemic heart disease (Mietinnen, 1973, Buell & Eliot, 1980).

In most of the medical research these risk factors are, however, treated as isolated variables. The advantage of the Michigan model lies in the integrative view of stress. A good definition of stress in this view is: Stress is a "perceived substantial imbalance between demands and response capability, under conditions where failure to meet demands has important perceived consequences" (McGrath, 1970). Stress is, therefore defined as a relationship between the person and the environment. This view on stress is in line with modern interactionist perspectives on personality (Ekehammer, 1974). Two other aspects of this Michigan model are the moderating variables: 1) personality (Type A behaviour, rigidity) and 2) social support. Type A behaviour - a style of coping with stress characterized by competitive, hurried and aggressive striving - has a central place in our study. As the level of type A behaviour increases, the relationship between job stressors and strain should become stronger. Social support is the other main intervening factor. Social support should be able to 'buffer' the negative consequences of psychosocial stress. This stress model has been further validated and elaborated in research in the Netherlands.

Type A behaviour

Friedman and Rosenman (1974) are the pioneers of the behavioural approach of cardiovascular disease. In the late 1950's they 'discovered' the typical behavioural style of many of their patients. These cardiologists

called Type A behaviour an action-emotion complex of enhanced hostility, ambitiousness, time urgency, competitiveness. Type A individuals are placing themselves in a chronic struggle to reach an ever-expanding number of goals in the shortest period of time often against opposing environmental forces. Persons are labelled Type A when they:
- are hard-driving;
- exhibit high levels of impatience;
- experience a chronic time pressure;
- are very competitive and ambitious;
- work harder at challenging tasks;
- often express hostility and irritation;
- suppress physical and psychological symptoms.
Persons showing the opposite behaviour pattern are called Type B persons.

Recent studies have shown the importance of this energetic behavioural style as a risk factor for coronary heart disease (CHD). In large-scale epidemiological research the hypothesized relationship between type A behaviour and CHD was investigated. In one of these studies - the Western Collaborative Group Study (WCGS) - more than 3000 men from 11 corporations were examined for the presence of CHD during a period of $8\frac{1}{2}$ years. In several follow-up reports Rosenman et al. (1970, 1975) proved that Type A behaviour is an important risk factor for CHD. In the 39-49 year-old group, the incidence of CHD was $6\frac{1}{2}$ times higher for men possessing the Type A behaviour than for those with the non-type A pattern. The behavioural style showed a predictive power apart from blood-pressure, cholesterol-level and other well known medical risk factors. After $4\frac{1}{2}$ years Rosenman et al. (1970) reported that the pre-dictive link between Type A behaviour and CHD was still present with statistically higher incidences of CHD in both age groups (39-49, 50-59) among men showing the behavioral style (see also: Matteson & Ivancevich, 1980).

In 1975 Rosenman et al. confirmed again the former conclusions after a follow-up study of $8\frac{1}{2}$ years. Those subjects judged to be Type A had twice the rate of CHD and were five times as likely to have a second infarction. According to the 'Review Panel on Coronary-prone Behaviour and Coronary Heart Disease' the WCGS and the Framingham Study (another epidemiological study) demonstrated, that Type A behaviour

"... is associated with an increased risk of clinically apparent CHD in employed, middle-aged U.S. citizens. The risk is greater than that imposed by age, evaluated values of systolic blood pressure and serum cholesterol, and smoking and appears to be of the same order of magnitude as the relative risk associated with the latter three of these other factors" (Cooper, 1981, p. 1200).

The oldest way of measuring Type A behaviour is the Structured Interview (SI). This interview was developed by Friedman and Rosenman and elicits Type A behaviour characteristics: fist clenching, speech hurrying, signs of impatience etc. To avoid the possible subjectivity and cost of the SI, Jenkins (1967) developed a paper and pencil questionnaire. His Jenkins Activity Survey is the most used device of this moment and has demonstrated its ability to predict CHD in several studies. After factor analysis three subscales were derived: hard driving, job involvement, and speed/impatience. However, only the total JAS score is predictive of CHD. Other scales are the Bortner Short Rating Scale and the Sales Type A scale. Several authors mentioned that these scales are not valid and unreliable (Chesney & Rosenman, 1980; Matteson & Ivancevich, 1980).

Chesney and Rosenman (1980) see Type A behaviour as the personification of the Western work ethic and reviewed the occupational stress literature about this subject. They point out a dozen studies but sometimes the results are inconsistent. Caplan et al. (1975) studied Type A behaviour in the occupational environment and examined its relationship to job stressors and psychological strains. His sample counted 2.010 persons from 23 occupational groups. He did not find any relationship of interest between Type A behaviour on the one hand and job stressors like work overload and job satisfaction and strains like anxiety, depression, and somatic complaints on the other hand. Caplan et al., however, used the Type A scale of Sales which has not been empirically validated.

Mettlin (1976) studied 943 white-collar, middle-class males from five work organizations in New York using the Jenkins Activity Survey. Type A behaviour now was related to occupational status, prestige and rapid career achievement. Howard, Cunningham and Rechnitzer (1977) found that Type A managers experienced heavy work load, difficulty in satisfying conflicting demands, much work competition and a heavy supervisory responsibility.

These findings suggest that Type A behaviour is related with some work stressors. Not clear however, is the relationship between Type A behaviour, work stressors and physiological parameters as blood-pressure and cholesterol. Laboratory studies have found that Type A's, when confronted with a challenging and difficult situation, show an increase in blood-pressure and catecholamines (Dembroski, 1978). Chesney and Rosenman (1980) have the opinion that Type A workers when confronted with challenging work in the laboratory, show increase in physiological arousal, that, over the years, may enhance the coronary atherosclerotic process. However, they state about stress research done in the occupational environment that "it ... would not be expected to show evidence of psychological distress and physiological arousal unless it was performed at times when, or in settings where, the workers felt particularly challenged" (p. 203).

In our study we have had the opportunity to test some hypotheses. We used the Jenkins Activity Survey, which is the best validated measure of Type A behaviour until now, in a large-scale longitudinal research project. In the design we combined stressor- and strain-measures with The JAS and with physiological measures. Therefore we are in a rather unique position to be able to study main and interaction effects of Type A behaviour in the stressor - strain relationship. We agree with Chesney and Rosenman (1980) when they say: "... if future research in the laboratory and the work environment confirms the dynamic relationships among the worker, environmental challenge, and physiological arousal that are found ..., then interventions to modify Type A behaviour could focus on only those aspects of the behaviour pattern that are associated with risk of CHD" (p. 207).

HYPOTHESES

In the introduction of this paper we have presented a conceptual framework for the study of job stress, based on the research of French and

180

Caplan (1972) and further elaborated in Dutch research (Kleber, Winnubst & De Wolff, 1980). This model is presented in Figure 1. Objective stressors, social support variables and illness are left out of this model as they are not involved in this study.

The model predicts that Type A behaviour plays a conditioning role: it aggravates the effects of perceived job stressors on job strain and health. The hypothesized aggravating effects of Type A behaviour are presented in Figure 1.

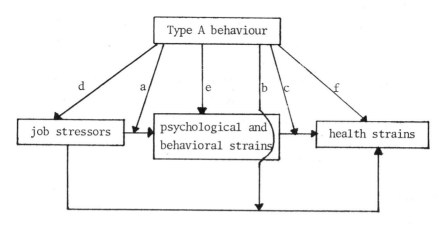

Figure 1. Model of the hypothesized effects between stressors, strains and health (arrow a, b and c represent the aggravating effects of Type A behaviour; arrow d, e and f represent the main effects of Type A behaviour)

As the level of Type A behaviour increases, the relationship between job stressors and job strains should also increase. However, Reiche (1982) mentions some controversy: some research supports the moderator position, and some supports both positions. The present study is concerned with this question, which may be stated as follows: what are the main or additive effects on the one side, and what are the moderating effects on the other side of Type A behaviour, in the 'causal' chain of stressors → strains → health?

As an analogue to the LaRocco et al. (1980) study about social support, we formulate six hypotheses about effects of Type A behaviour:

Main effects:

Hypothesis 1: Type A behaviour is positively correlated with stressors (arrow d in Figure 1)

Hypothesis 2: Type A behaviour is positively correlated with psychological and behavioural strains (arrow e in Figure 1)

Hypothesis 3: Type A behaviour is positively correlated with health strains (arrow f in Figure 1).

Interaction effects:

Hypothesis 4: Type A behaviour aggravates the relationship between stressors, and psychological and behavioural strains (arrow a in Figure 1)

Hypothesis 5: Type A behaviour aggravates the relationship between stressors and health strains (arrow b in Figure 1)

Hypothesis 6: Type A behaviour aggravates the relationship between psychological, behavioural, and health strains (arrow c in Figure 1).

METHODS

Sample

The sample consisted of 1.246 employees of 13 different industrial organizations and comprised 1.167 males and 79 females, all living in the south-eastern part of the Netherlands and all were native Dutch. Both blue and white collar occupations were represented. The original sample counted 1.600 employees, of which 80% were willing to participate. The employees were between 34-65 years of age and the mean age was 45 years. The sample was part of a large-scale longitudinal study on the social and psychological causes of ischaemic heart disease by the University of Nijmegen, Department of Work and Organizational Psychology, the Department of Social Medicine and the Occupational Health Bureau, Doetinchem. The medical check up was part of another large-scale research project, the COPIH project.

Measures

Inspired by the Michigan model, a Dutch team (The Stress Research Group Nijmegen) developed a comprehensive instrument 'The Organizational Stress Questionnaire', called the V.O.S. It measures several aspects of perceived job stressors, strains, personality and social support. Modified versions of this instrument have been used in a variety of studies and in several organizations in the Netherlands: hospitals, industry, the army and schools. It has been validated extensively (Kleber, Winnubst & De Wolff, 1980). Five indices of *perceived stress* in the work environment were used. Role conflict, a 2-item scale, measured the presence of conflicting demands. The role ambiguity measures consisted of 5 items shich referred to the lack of feedback on one's skills and the lack of information about one's tasks. Overload, the quantity of work a person has to do, was measured with a 12-item scale. Future uncertainty (4 items) referred to the lack of certainty the person has about the stability of the organization he is working in. Responsibility (4 items) measures one's responsibility for persons.

Four indices of general *psychological strain* were employed, a 4-item measure of irritation, a 4-item measure of depression, a 3-item measure of anxiety, and a 4-item measure of threat.

There were two measures of *behavioural strain:* smoking (use of cigarettes) and drinking.

Five indices of *health problems* were used, a 5-item measure of heart complaints, a 9-item scale of general somatic complaints, and further on (a) systolic blood-pressure (SBP), (b) diastolic blood-pressure (DBP) and (c) level of cholesterol. These last three indices were examined by the medical staff of the Organizational Health Bureau.

Type A behaviour was measured with the Jenkins Activity Survey (Jenkins et al., 1974), a 36-item measure, translated and validated in the Netherlands by Appels (Verhagen et al., 1980).

Analysis

In our analysis we used a moderated regression method, that was also employed in our study about social support (Winnubst et al., 1982).

In this method, the multiple correlation between the predicted variable on the one hand and the predictors on the other, is determined twice: the first time with an interaction term, the second time without one. If there is an aggraving effect, the multiple correlation must increase significantly when the interaction term is included as a predictor (Zedeck, 1971; Arnold, 1982).

The equation will be as follows:

$$\hat{Y} = a + b_1 X + b_2 A + b_3 (X - c_1) (A - c_2),$$

where X = the stressor (or strain), A = Type A behaviour and $\hat{Y}$ = predicted strain (or health). The constants c_1 and c_2 are chosen in such a way that the interaction term $(X - c_1) (A - c_2)$ is independent of X and A. If these weights would not be included, the interaction term would be X.A: the simple product of X and A. In this case, the correlation between X.A on the one hand and X and A on the other, would be so large that the correlation matrix would be almost singular, making the estimation of the weights b_1, b_2 and b_3 very unprecise. The constants c_1 and c_2 are calculated by determining the regression of X.A on X and A

$$XA = c_2 X + c_1 A + \hat{xa}, \text{ where}$$
$$\hat{xa} = (X - c_1) (A - c_2) - c_1 c_2.$$

$\hat{xa}$ is the residual interaction term, left after substraction of the main effects X and A. The testing in the moderated regression method is a conservative one. In their studies about social support Pinneau (1975), House and Wells (1970), LaRocco et al. (1980) and Winnubst et al. (1982) therefore chose the significance leven p > .10 as minimally acceptable. In this we will follow these authors.

RESULTS

Main effects

In contrast with Caplan et al. (1975) we see in our study a whole series

184

of important main effects of Type A behaviour on stressors, strains and
health variables. The main effects of Type A behaviour on stressors are
nearly all strong and highly significant, except in the case of role
ambiguity: Type A behaviour is highly correlated with role overload and
responsibility. The direct relationships between Type A behaviour and
the psychological strains as threat, irritation and anxiety are also
highly significant. The relation with the behavioural strain is weak.
Correlations between Type A on the one hand and smoking, blood-pressure
and level of cholesterol on the other are zero of near zero. However,
the correlations between Type A behaviour, heart and general health
complaints are rather high.

	role confl.	role amb.	role overl.	respons.	fut.uncert.
Type A behaviour	.20 **	.06 *	.42 **	.25 **	-.07 **

** p < .01
* p < .05

Table 1. Correlations between Type A behaviour and stressors

	threat	irritation	depression	anxiety	smoking	drinking
Type A behaviour	.33 **	.42 **	.14 **	.32 **	-.02	.10 **

** p < .01

Table 2. Correlations between Type A behaviour and psychological and
behavioural strains

	heart	gen. health	SBP	DBP	Cholesterol	absent
Type A behaviour	.22 **	.31 **	-.03	.02	.00	-.01

** p < .01

Table 3. Correlations between Type A behaviour and health strains

The hypotheses 1, 2 and 3 about the main effects can be accepted,
except for role ambiguity, smoking, and the two physiological parameters.

When we confine our interest to main effects we see a Type A oriented person with more responsibility, higher workload, more irritated, anxious, and threatened, and with more frequent health and heart complaints. Now we will look at the interaction effects and see whether the picture will survive our prolonged analysis.

Interaction findings

The moderated regression analysis of the hypotheses about the aggravating effects of Type A behaviour in the stressor-strain relationships yields interesting results. Most impressive is Table 4 which summarizes the interactions between Type A behaviour and stressors in predicting strain. The number of significant interactions (11 of 30 or about 37%) is very high as compared to LaRocco et al. (1980), and Winnubst et al. (1982), which analysed the interaction effects of social support. The results are much better than might occur by chance.

	threat	irritation	depression	anxiety	smoking	drinkin
Role conflict	1%	1%		1%		
Role ambiguity	1%	1%		1%		
Role overload		10%				
Responsibility						
Fut. uncertainty	1%	1%	1%	1%		

a. Numbers in each cell represent significance levels (p <) for interaction effects. Empty cells indicate that interaction effects were
   not significant.

**Table 4. Interaction of stressors x Type A behaviour with psychological
and behavioural strains**

Table 4 shows that Type A behaviour is the connecting variable between role conflict, role ambiguity and future uncertainty on the one hand, and strains like threat and irritation on the other. Some effects can be seen on the anxiety and depression variables too. There is not any significant interaction effect on smoking and drinking. Intriguing is the total lack of interaction effects between role overload and

responsibility on the one hand and strains on the other for the Type A
behaviour variable. Role overload and a heavy responsibility are
higher for Type A's as can be seen in Table 1. This does not lead to
strains for Type A's nor for Type B's. This leads one to the conclusion
that A's accept their loaded job and high responsibility. Strains are
linked, for Type A's only, with complexities and conflict-emanating
aspects of the role or with uncertainty about holding the job in the
future but not with workload responsibility.

	heart	gen. health	SBP	DBP	cholesterol
Role conflict	10%	10%			
Role ambiguity					
Role overload	1%	10%	5%	10%	
Responsibility					
Fut. uncertainty	1%	1%	(1%)	(1%)	

a. Numbers in each cell represent significance levels ($p <$) for interaction effects. Empty cells indicate that interaction effects were
   not significant.
b. Parentheses indicate a reversal; i.e. the interaction effect reduced
   the relationship.

Table 5. Interaction of stressors x Type A behaviour with health strains

Not as clear are the results in Table 5. The number of significant
interactions is relatively high and again much more than might occur
by chance (10 of 25 or about 40%). Several number, however, are on the
10% level of significance and there are some reversals. Interesting is
the finding that Type A behaviour has an aggravating effect on heart
complaints and systolic blood-pressure in the case of high role overload.
Hypothesis 5 can be accepted only for this relationship.

Table 6 shows many aggravating effects of Type A behaviour in the
relationships between psychological strains on the one hand and health
strains on the other. The number of significant interactions is rather
high but most of them are concentrated in the relationships just mentioned (11 of 30 or about 37%). The conclusion must be that Type A

behaviour exacerbates the relationship between psychological strains as
threat, irritation, depression and anxiety on the one hand and health
and heart complaints on the other. Another finding is that smoking is
connected with high blood-pressure only for A's, not for Type B's.

	heart	gen. health	SBP	DBP	cholesterol
Threat	1%	1%			
Irritation	1%	5%			
Depression	1%	1%			
Anxiety	1%	1%			
Smoking			5%		
Drinking					

a. Numbers in each cell represent significance level (p <) for interaction effects. Empty cells indicate that interaction effects were
   not significant.

Table 6. Interaction of psychological and behavioural strains x Type A
         behaviour with health strains

DISCUSSION

In a recent and comprehensive review op Type A behaviour Matthews (1982)
made the following critical remark: "The lack of emphasis that has been
placed on the study of intervening processes has also impeded progress
in understanding the psychological natur of Type A" (p. 317). Our findings provide clear evidence for the moderating effects of Type A behaviour on the relationships between work stressors and psychological
strains and we hope to have gained some progress.

    Several authors (Caplan et al., 1975; Reiche, 1982) studied the
moderating effects of Type A behaviour in the Michigan model of stress.
However, they used the Sales Type A scale which has been criticized by
several authors (Chesney & Rosenman, 1980; Matteson & Ivancevich, 1980;
Cooper et al., 1981; Matthews, 1982). They consider the Sales Type A
scale to be a measure of work commitment that has nothing to do with
cardiovascular disease. In this light it is not surprising that Caplan
et al. (1975) and Reiche (1982) did find only a few main effects and not
any interaction effect of interest.

Using the Jenkins Activity Survey in our research we found important *main* effects. Type A behaviour is correlated with the stressors work load and responsibility, with the psychological strains irritation, anxiety and threat and with health strains. This picture is not new: Type A's (i.e. people showing Type A behaviour) have been described vigorous achievement strivers, fastly irritated and concerned very much with their health. Main effects on behavioural strains as smoking and drinking and on physiological strains as blood-pressure and cholesterol are absent. According to the literature (Dembroski et al., 1978) systolic blood-pressure exhibits elevations for A's only during the performance of difficult tasks. In our research blood-pressure was measured outside the work situation.

Noteworthy and new indeed, are the *interaction* effects that we found. Our study shows a complex but understandable pattern of these effects. Especially the stressors role conflict, role ambiguity and future uncertainty are connected with aggravating effects of Type A behaviour and are correlated, only for A's, with strains like irritation, anxiety and threat. Remarkable is the finding that the stressors role overload and responsibility are not correlated, for A's, with any psychological strain. Apparently Type A's are hectic people who accept a heavy workload without complaining. However, psychological problems are real for them, but for A's these problems are especially connected with conflict-emanating aspects of the role or with uncertainty about holding the job in the future. We may conclude that the intricacies of the role, not the workload itself are troublesome for Type A's.

Uncertainty, ambiguity and conflict are therefore the common denominators behind the psychological problems of Type A's. Cross-sectional data do not allow for causal conclusions but still the findings are intriguing. Glass (1977) describes how Type A behaviour reflects a specific way of coping with stressful aspects of the environment. A's try to control stressful events: for them uncontrollability is highly undesirable. When Type A's are threatened by a loss of control, they react by accelerating their efforts. Failure in this respect leads to giving up and feelings of helplessness. The uncertainty, ambiguity and conflict we found in our research as the common denominator behind the psychological problems of Type A's might be connected to uncontrollability

and helplessness. Matthews (1982) says: "The uncontrollability approach
suggests that Type A's are engaged in a chronic struggle to control
aspects of their environments that appear likely to harm them physically and psychologically" (p. 312). In our moderated regression analysis
we have shown that the Type A behavioural style is an aggravating link
between unclear and uncontrollable environmental aspects in which the
Type A person is submerged in on the one hand, and his psychological
problems on the other hand. He seems to be engaged in a never ending
spiral of causes and effects: the uncontrollability of the situation
triggers his reactions and his anxious reactions worsen his situation.

Another interesting difference between A's and B's in the stressor-
strain relationship is that Type A's with a high role overload react
significanly more with heart complaints and high blood-pressure. They
do not complain psychologically about their heavy workload but react
with physiological strains. We interpret these results as evidence
for a tendency of Type A's to somaticize their psychological strains.
Is there any ground, however, for the hypothesis that the tendency of
A's to repress their psychological complaints, is paid back with heart
complaints and high blood-pressure?

With regard to future uncertainty A's react as compared to B's with
significantly more heart and general health complaints. We can see that
A's react hypochondriacally to the possible loss of work, more than
their calm Type'B colleagues. And this is in line with what we know
about the work ethic of Type A. It is not clear for us however, why
they react on the possible job loss with a lower blood-pressure as
compared to B's.

Another series of aggravating effects can be seen in the relationship between psychological strains on the one hand and health complaints
on the other hand. Type A's that score high on threat, irritation, depression and anxiety show significantly more heart and general health
problems as compared to B's that score high on those psychological
strains. Thus, there is an interesting difference between A's and B's:
the behaviour of Type A's effectuates a connection between psychological
and somatic complaints. Again it is not clear what comes first: the
psychological or the somatic aspects. A possible point of criticism
could be that the domains of these kind of complaints have vague borders.

In summary, the conditioning effects of Type A behaviour are generally confirmed, as far as the variables are concerned that have to do with subjective experience: the psychological strains and the self-reported health strains. The less subjective variables e.g. the behavioural strains and objective health measures, show much less relations. We should be cautious therefore, because results could have been caused by 'within scale covariance'.

The very strong correlation between Type A behaviour and the psychological dimension of irritation, points to anger and subsequent aggression. When A's are thwarted in their work fever by ambiguity and conflict, or when are just creating the conflict by their workaholism, they get angry. As active copers they try to regain control over the situation. By not succeeding they feel helpless. It could be possible that A's feel chronically unsafe in their work and they are in a constant but unhealthy struggle, with a bad outcome on the long range. In a recent article Irvine et al. (1982) reported about the highly significant correlation between The JAS score and Eysenck's Neuroticism scale and they conclude: "Rather than regarding the Type A individual as somehow a cultural hero, we may perhaps better understand him as an anxious wretch who is incapable of keeping up with the demands that life and employment make of him" (p. 188). We agree with their conclusion that additional evaluation of anxiety factors in the Type A behaviour pattern is necessary to understand the psychological components of stress-related diseases.

This chapter has shown some of the first results corss-sectionally of a longitudinal study. Eventually 2.400 persons will be followed over five years in time, with three points of measurement. In the near future we will be able to refine our research by splitting the sample into social class, occupation age group, and so on. In the first analysis concerning the moderating aspects of Type A behaviour based on the Jenkins Activity Survey, we found encouraging results. Type A behaviour is related to pathology and has important and interesting relations with the work situation. With all the constraints of field research psychology in mind we can state that the study of Type A behaviour outside the laboratory or the clinical setting is rather promising.

REFERENCES

Arnold, H.J., Moderator variables: A clarification of conceptual, analytic, and psychometric issues. Organizational Behavior and Human Performance, 1982, 29, 143-174.

Buell, J.C. & R.S. Eliot, Psychosocial and behavioral influences in the pathogenesis of acquired cardiovascular disease. American Heart Journal, 1980, 100 (5), 723-740.

Caplan, R.D., S. Cobb, J.R.P. French, R.V. Harrison & S.R. Pinneau, Job demands and worker health. U.S. Department of Health, Education and Welfare, Publication no. (NIOSH) 75-160, 1975.

Chesney, M.A. & R.H. Rosenman, Type A Behaviour in the Work Setting. In: C.L. Cooper & R. Payne (Eds.), Current Concerns in Occupational stress. New York: Wiley, 1980.

Cooper, T., T. Detre & S.M. Weiss, Coronary-prone behavior and coronary heart disease: A critical review. Circulation, 1981, 63, 1199-1215.

Dembroski, T.M., S.M. Weiss & J.L. Shields (Eds.), Coronary-prone behavior. New York: Springer Verlag, 1978.

Ekehammer, B., Interactionism in personality from a historical perspective. Psychological Bulletin, 1974, 81, 1026-1048.

French, J.R.P. & R.D. Caplan, Organizational stress and individual strain. In: A. Marrow (Ed.), The failure of success. New York: AMACOM, 1972.

Friedman, M. & R.H. Rosenman, Type A behavior and your heart. Greenwich, Conn.: Fawcett, 1974.

Glass, D.C., Behaviour patterns, stress, and coronary disease. Toronto: Wiley, 1977.

House, J.S. & J.A. Wells, Reducing occupational stress; proceedings of a conference. In: A. Mclean, G. Black & M. Colligan (Eds.), Occupational stress, social support and health. U.S. Department of Health, Education and Welfare, HEW (NIOSH), Publication No. 78-140, 1978.

Howard, J.H., D.A. Cunningham & P.A. Rechnitzer, Work patterns associated with Type A behavior: A managerial population. Human Relations, 1977, 30 (9), 825-836.

Irvine, J., R.C. Lyle & R. Allon, Type A personality as psychopathology: personality correlates and an abreviated scoring system. Journal of Psychosomatic Research, 1982, 26 (2), 183-189.

Jenkins, C.D., R.H. Rosenman & M. Friedman, Development of an objective psychological test for the determination of the coronary-prone behavior pattern in employed men. Journal of Chronic diseases, 1967, 20, 371-379.

Jenkins, C.D., R.H. Rosenman & S.J. Zyzanski, Prediction of clinical coronary heart disease by a test for coronary-prone behavior pattern. New England Journal of Medicine, 1974, 290, 1271-1275.

Kahn. R.L., D.M. Wolfe, R.P. Quin, J.D. Snoek & R.A. Rosenthal, Organizational stress. New York: Wiley, 1964.

Kleber, R.J., J.A.M. Winnubst & Ch.J. de Wolff, Stress Research Group Nijmegen: working program. Nijmegen: Psychological Laboratory, University of Nijmegen, 1980.

LaRocco, J.M., J.S. House & J.R.P. French, Social support, occupational stress, and health. Journal of Health and Social Behavior, 1980, 21, 202-218.

Matteson, M.T. & M.T. Ivancevich, The coronary-prone behavior pattern: A review and appraisal. Social Science and Medicine, 1980, 14a, 337-351.

Matthews, K., Psychological perspectives on the Type A behavior pattern. Psychological Bulletin, 1982, 91 (2), 293-323.

McGrath, J.E. (Ed.), Social and Psychological factors in stress. New York: Holt, Rinehart & Winston, 1970.

Mettlin, C., Occupational careers and the prevention of coronary-prone behavior. Social Science and Medicine, 1976, 10, 367-372.

Mietinnen, D.S., Risk indicators for coronary heart disease. Heart Bulletin, 1973, 4 (3), 64-70.

Pinneau, S.R., Effects of social support on psychological and physiological stress. Unpublished doctoral dissertation. Ann Arbor: University of Michigan, 1975.

Reiche, H.M.J.K.I., Stress aan het werk. Lisse: Swets & Zeitlinger, 1982.

Rosenman, R.H., R.J. Brand, C.D. Jenkins, M. Friedman, R. Strauss & M. Wurm, Coronary heart disease in the Western Collaborative Group Study: final follow-up experience of 8½ years. Journal American of the Medical Association, 1975, 233, 872-877.

Rosenman, R.H., M. Friedman, R. Strauss, C.D. Jenkins, S.J. Zyzanski & M. Wurm, Coronary heart disease in the Western Collaborative Group Study: a follow-up experience of 4½ years. Journal of Chronic Diseases, 1970, 23, 173-190.

Van Bastelaer, A. & W. van Beers, Organisatiestress en de personeel- funktionaris. Lisse: Swets & Zeitlinger, 1982.

Van Dijkhuizen, N., From stressors to strains. Research into their interrelationships. Lisse: Swets & Zeitlinger, 1980.

Verhagen, F., C. Nass, A. Appels, A. van Bastelaer & J.A.M. Winnubst, A cross-validation of the A/B typology in the Netherlands. Psychotherapy and Psychosomatics, 1980, 34 (2-3), 178-186.

Winnubst, J.A.M., F.H.G. Marcelissen & R.J. Kleber, Effects of social support in the stressor-strain relationship: A Dutch sample. Social Science and Medicine, 1982, 16 (4), 475-482.

Zedeck, S., Problems with the use of moderator variables. Psychological Bulletin, 1971, 76, 295-310.

* This study is part of a large-scale longitudinal project organized by Ch. de Wolff, J. Winnubst, A. Leuftink, F. Sturmans, F. Marcelissen and A. van Bastelaer. Funding for this project was provided by a research grant from the Prevention Fund and from the Catholic Univer- sity of Nijmegen, the Netherlands. We thank R.J. Kleber for his com- ments on a previous draft.

IV
INDUSTRIAL RELATIONS

12. PATTERNS OF PARTICIPATION AND INFLUENCE IN FOUR EUROPEAN COUNTRIES

J.H.T.H. Andriessen & P.J.D. Drenth

INTRODUCTION

In this chapter some research findings from an international comparative study on industrial democracy in industrialized countries will be presented.* The original study has been carried out in 11 European countries plus Israel and was reported by the IDE-International Research Group (IDE, 1981). In this study findings on the differences in the *de jure* industrial democracy systems are related to the differences in the *de facto* participatory behaviour in organizations. For the present discussion some results with respect to the four countries Belgium, Great Britain, the Federal Republic of Germany and the Netherlands have been selected.

BACKGROUND OF THE STUDY

The research study was inspired by practical needs of policy makers and managers on national and international levels in the field of industrial democracy. It is generally assumed that attempt to introduce or to improve formal regulations and legislation with respect to industrial democracy will have behavioural effects indeed. The discussion of this issue however lacked for the most part empirical evidence about the

---

* The Dutch part of this research project was financially supported by the Netherlands Organization for the Advancement of Pure Research. The Dutch team consisted of Dr. J.H. Erik Andriessen, Prof.dr. Pieter D.J. Drenth and Prof.dr. Cor J. Lammers.

actual consequences of the various systems of industrial democracy.
Hardly any systematic cross cultural research data on behavioural consequences of the various participatory systems had been carried out and
the insights were based mainly on personal experience, case histories
and preopinions.

The IDE-project has tried to provide some empirical support for a
better understanding of how different systems of participatory management function in reality. In a way, the European scene with its many
different formal systems of industrial democracy formed an almost natural
experimental field in which the effects on the various systems could
be compared and analysed.

It has taken quite some time to develop the original idea (discussed
in a first meeting in 1973) into a substantial project. Most of the
data collection took place in 1977 and 1978. Some 30 social scientists
from 18 research institutes have been involved in the project. Each
participating country has produced a national report and the international comparative study was reported in two volumes (IDE, 1981a;
IDE, 1981b).

OBJECTIVE AND MODEL

The main objective of the study was to provide knowledge and insight in
the question of how different models of participatory management systems
function in reality in industrial organizations in various European
countries.

This main question was divided into four subquestions, which can be
illustrated by the (interrelations between) the boxes in the model as
presented in Figure 1.

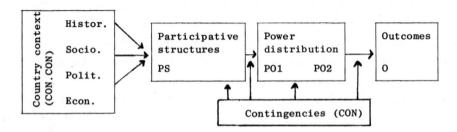

Figure 1. Hypothetical model of variable interactions

198

(1) How do the *de jure* participation systems (PS) influence the *de facto* organizational power distributions (PO). The concept of power distribution relates to the relative weight which various groups or levels in the organization (bargaining groups) bring to bear on influencing the outcome of decisions (PS → PO).

(2) What are the outcomes and consequences of participation, both *de jure* and *de facto*, in terms of organizations and people involved (PS/PO → O).

(3) What is the role and influence of a number of contingency factors either as (co)predictor or as moderator with respect to the above mentioned relationships. In other words, what other factors influence PO and O, and under which conditions does PS influence PO, or PS/PO influence O (CON →).

(4) Is it possible to explain the different findings in the various European countries in terms of a number of historical, socio-political and economic data in each of the countries under study (CON.CON. →).

Emphasis in this study has been put on decision-making. Unlike some other studies on distribution of influence in organizations (e.g. the 'control graph', Tannenbaum, 1968) in which general questions are asked as to the perceived influence of various bargaining groups, a deliberate selection of decisions has been made in order to make possible an analysis of the distribution of power and influence over particular decisions or groups of decisions. As is indicated in Figure 2 the

| | | Content of decisions | | |
		Work/social conditions	Personnel	Economic aspects
Time perspective	Short-term	Task assignment Personal equipment Working conditions Working hours Holidays	Training courses Transfers	
	Medium-term	Work study Wage levels	Dismissals Hiring procedures New department head Appointment own supervisor	Reorganization
	Long-term			Investment New product

Figure 2. Decision-set paradigm

decisions selected show a variation in terms of content (Work/Social conditions, Personnel, Economic aspects) and time perspective (Short term, Medium term, Long term).

The core question of this study is concerned with differences in participation and influence between the different hierarchical levels and other relevant groups or institutions within or outside the company.

For the definition of the "groups" the following characterizations have been used:

A - Workers, white- and blue-collar, without supervisory functions.

B - First-line supervisors - foremen - (lowest level with supervisory functions).

C - Middle managers: according to establishment usage; all hierarchical levels above B and below D (including staff members at comparable levels).

D - Top management: according to establishment usage; all persons considered to belong to the top management of the establishment.

E - Level above the plant: control or supervisory groups, managerial bodies (e.g. conglomerate management), shareholders, or owners.

F - Permanent representative bodies at the establishment level, no matter of what origin: Works' Councils, Workers' Councils, union representative bodies, and union representatives like shop stewards.

G - Bodies/institutions outside the company - external groups - (not necessarily outside the establishment): unions, banks, community councils, regional planning councils, etc.

MEASUREMENT

A variety of instruments have been developed to measure the concepts represented in the boxes in the model. In this chapter we will not discuss all of them, but confine ourselves to those which have been used in the comparison of the four countries for this particular purpose. For detailed information the reader is referred to the original publication.

200

De Jure Participation (PS)

The *de jure* participation describes the formal framework of participation in organizations. It should refer to formal written down operative rules and regulations for the involvement of various parties in decision-making.

Two questions have been answered regarding the *de jure* participation.

In the first place: "What is the amount of formal participation for each of the bargaining groups" (called the *Mode* of PS). The following six point scale was used to indicate the mode of involvement:

1. No regulations.
2. Information (unspecified) must be given to the group.
3. Information ex ante must be given to the group (i.e. before the decision is made).
4. Consultation of the group is obligatory (i.e. group must always be consulted prior to the decision taken).
5. Joint decision making with the group (i.e. group has the power of veto and must give its approval).
6. Group itself has the final say.

The *de jure* participation information can be coded by organization as in the PS-matrix represented in Figure 3. In countries where there is very little variance over organizations, since the *de jure* participation is determined mainly by national law, the organization PS-matrix looks pretty much like the country PS-matrix.

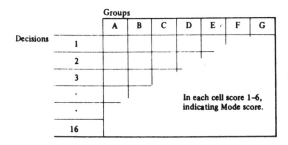

Figure 3. *De jure* participation-matrix

201

The second question referred to the basis for the extent of formal participation (Base). Various possibilities have been distinguished, to be grouped into three clusters: National or local laws, Bargaining contracts and Managerial policies laid down in formal regulations and procedures.

De Facto Participation (PO)

The actual participation in decision making of the various bargaining groups has been measured by two types of instruments.

In the first place a rating of influence on a five point Likert type scale ranging from 'no influence' to 'very much influence' (PO1). This rating was done by key-respondents who had a central role in the organizations and can be considered as experts. The ratings were averaged in case there were more than one key-respondent. This rating of influence, again, resulted in a matrix (PO1 information matrix, see Figure 4) indicating the influence distribution per organization over the various bargaining groups.

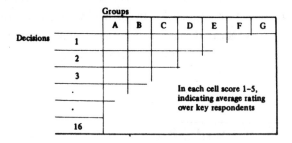

Figure 4. Influence-matrix

In the second place a rating of involvement by a sample of respondents from each organization (PO2). Each respondent was asked to indicate the extent to which he perceived himself to be involved in the several decisions. For this purpose the six options of the PS scale were adapted to:

202

1. I am not involved at all.
2. I am informed about the matter beforehand.
3. I can give my opinion.
4. My opinion is taken into account.
5. I take part in the decision-making with equal weight.
6. I decide on my own.

In the *Outcome* box a number of instruments have been developed so as to measure satisfaction with participation, satisfaction with work, organizational climate, rating of consequences of direct and indirect participation, absenteeism, turnover and the like.

Two groups of data have been collected in the *Contingency* category. Data referring to the personal background of the respondent (education, sex, type of job, unionization and the like), and data referring to company characteristics, such as technology, organizational structure, personnel structure and financial/economic position.

SAMPLE

A minimum of nine companies in each country were studied, chosen according to size (small, medium, large) and technology (metal low skill, metal high skill, service). More companies could be included if the national teams were to find this feasible. All together 134 organizations were included in the study, involving nearly 1000 key-respondents, and almost 8000 individual respondents.

RESULTS

In this chapter we will focus our attention primarily on the relationship between *de jure* participation and *de facto* participation in the organizations studied. This focus implies that only data at the organizational level will be presented. Individual level analysis of involvement (PO2), opinions, expectations and attitudes (O) will, consequently, not be included, although the report of the IDE-project devoted quite some attention to these issues.

This presentation of results is divided in three parts.

First, a few findings on *de jure* participation will be discussed. The main differences between countries as far as the formal rules and regulations for participation of the various groups in organizations are concerned will be shown.

Secondly, data on the distribution of *actual* power and influence are presented.

And thirdly, relationships between *de jure* and *de facto* participation will be analysed.

Also the role of other possible determinants of the actual influence distribution in organizations will be given some attention. These determinants include characteristics of the organizational structure, technology and the personnel structure.

Formal rules and regulations

The formal rules and regulations concerning involvement in decision-making can be based on national laws, collective bargaining agreements, and various management regulations. It appears that countries differ to quite an extent as far as these bases are concerned. Restricting ourselves to the four countries of interest in this chapter we find that in the Federal Republic of Germany, the Netherlands and Great Britain the rules for participation are to be found primarily in national laws (e.g. the Works' Council Law, etc.) while in Belgium the majority of rules concerning (prescribed) involvement are based upon management regulations. However, when the countries are compared as to the number of decisions for which there is, in one way or the other, a formal rule concerning involvement (the scope of *de jure* participation), the picture is quite different (see Figure 5).

Figure 5 shows that in Germany and the Netherlands the extent of formal involvement of organizational groups in decision-making is very large. In Belgium there is somewhat less formal regulation, but particularly in Great Britain only few formal rules and little regulation concerning the participation in decision-making is found.

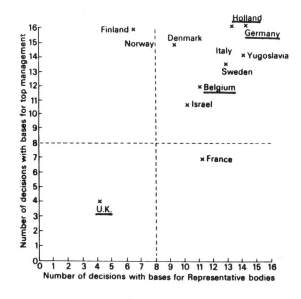

Figure 5. *De Jure* Participation for top management and representative
bodies

As was described earlier for each of the seven identified groups
(A to G) the level of *de jure* participation in each of the 16 decisions
was established. By averaging these PS-scores over the 16 decisions and
over the organizations per country a mean *de jure* participation score
for each of the seven groups was calculated for each country. If these
seven scores are combined, they provide a kind of 'prescribed control
graph'. The graphs of our four countries are presented in Figure 6.
Two different patterns seem to emerge. In the first place a so called
'Hierarchical Two Peak Pattern' in a.o. the Netherlands and Germany,
and a *'Low Profile Pattern'* in Belgium and the United Kingdom. It may
be informative to add that two additional patterns were identified in
the IDE study: A *'Hierarchical One Peak Pattern'* (in France, Norway and
Sweden, where topmanagement (level D) and the level above the companies
(level E) have the most formal power) and the *'Representative Peak
Pattern'* found only in Yugoslavia where the representative body (Workers
Council, level F) has the highest level of prescribed involvement.

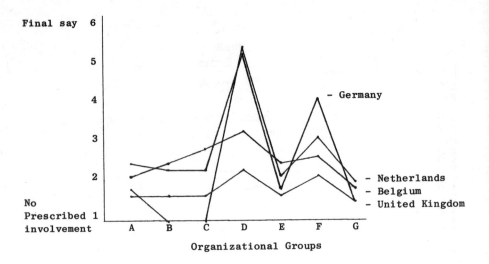

Figure 6. Patterns of modes (formal participation)

These four patterns indicate four basic systems of formalized schemes for democratization in organizations. Of course countries which have the same basic pattern can and will be different, to some extent, as far as the details of the industrial democracy system goes. Moreover, being comparable in terms of the *de jure* involvement distribution does not necessarily imply that the distribution of actual influence of the various groups is also similar.

De facto participation

As was indicated the PO-scores were based on the judgement of key-persons in the companies. Averaging the scores over decisions and organizations resulted again in a mean influence score for each group in each country. The IDE-report contains a discussion on the pros and cons of this way of averaging scores. The majority of the analyses in the IDE-project, however, were done with the separate scores per decision or per subset of decisions (short term, medium term and long term decisions).

A combination of the mean influence score for each group provides an actual influence graph per country. The graphs for the four countries

Belgium, Great Britain, Germany and the Netherlands are presented in
Figure 7.

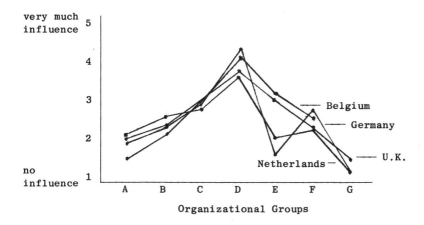

Figure 7. Distribution of influence

The similarities between the four countries is striking, the more
since the corresponding PS-graphs were not quite similar. Apparently
for Belgium and the United Kingdom the PS-based 'Low Profile Pattern'
does not prevent the actual influence distribution to be as one-peaked
as in the other countries. Moreover the relatively high PS-level for
the representative body (the Works' Council) in the Netherlands is not
reflected in a high corresponding PO-level. A more detailed comparison
of *de jure* participation (PS) and *de facto* participation (PO) is
subject of the next section.

De jure and de facto participation

In each country it is possible to compare the formally prescribed involvement with the actual influence of each group in the organizations.
In this chapter this analysis is mainly done for level F (representative
bodies). As an example we start with the data for the Netherlands
(Figure 8).

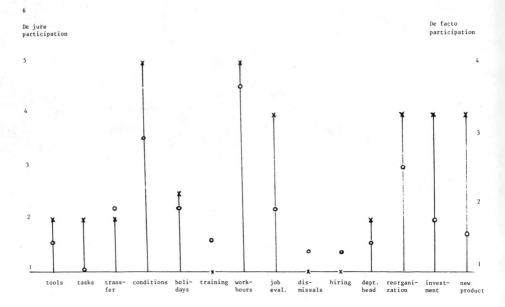

Figure 8. De jure and de facto participation of dutch workscouncils

N.B.: X = de jure   O = de facto

From the data in Figure 8 it can be seen that the influence of the Works' Council tends to be higher on those decisions for which its prescribed involvement is also relatively high. Exceptions are the two strategic, long term decisions on the right side of the figure.

A comparison of the mean PS- and PO-scores of level F in all the countries again yields a positive relationship (Figure 9). Of course the absolute levels are not directly comparable. But the differences between countries in PS-scores, are reasonably matched by comparable differences in PO-scores. This relationship is further reflected in the correlation coefficient between PS- and PO-scores (of level F) over all 140 organizations: $r = .55$.

A similar relationship is found between PS-PO scores for level A (workers): $r = .44$. For the other organizational levels the PS- and PO-

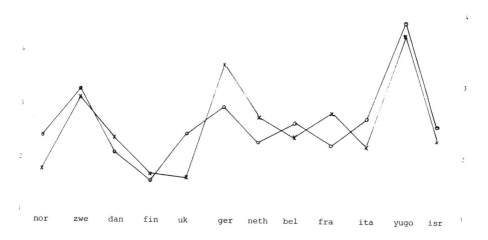

de jure
participation

de facto
participation

nor   zwe   dan   fin   uk   ger   neth   bel   fra   ita   yugo   isr

Figure 9. De jure and de facto participation of representative bodies
X = de jure participation   O = de facto participation

scores do not correlate. For supervisory and middle management levels
the actual influence is apparently not determined by the formal rules
concerning involvement in decision-making. This is not surprising in
view of the fact that the lower and middle management levels derive
their power mainly through delegation by topmanagement and not through
legally prescribed rules. It appears therefore that particularly the
influence of workers and representative bodies is supported by the formal regulations about their involvement in decision-making.

However, the correlations are not perfect, and other factors might
be important as well. One may think of factors such as skill level,
production process, organizational structure, etc. In the IDE-study
quite a few of these characteristics were measured and related to the
influence distributions (Table 1).

209

Contextual variables	Influence (PO1a)									Levels		
	Workers (A)			Top management (D)			Representative body (F)			A	D	F
	ST[b]	MT	LT	ST	MT	LT	ST	MT	LT	Σ	Σ	Σ
Formal independence of enterprise						.26	−.24	−.17				−.19
Market domination of enterprise		−.19*			−.27		.21				.20	.16
Political instability							−.17	−.16	−.18			−.19
Sector	.27					−.27	.26					
Skill			.23				.19					.17
Automatization			−.22					−.22	−.17			−.19
Technological interdependence												
Product complexity		.18		.20						.22	.17	
Functional differentiation		.29	.25				.26	.26	.30			.33
Vertical span												
Formalization					−.24	−.30					−.23	
Span of top management		−.16										
Intensity of control												
Stability of work force			−.19					−.17				
Male domination												
Mobilization	.19	.45	.42	−.20	−.30	−.19	.35	.33	.50	.33	−.27	.43
Evaluation of success												
Growth of enterprise												
Log size												
Multiple R	.396	.613	.617	.529	.501	.585	.558	.531	.631	.479	.554	.606
Adjusted R²	.006	.05	.26	.14	.10	.21	.17	.14	.28	.08	.16	.24
Σ = all decisions, influence of respective level	.96	3,11	3,17	2,01	1,78	2,69	2,33	2,02	3,42	1,54	2,17	3,00
P	.50	.000	.000	.01	.04	.001	.004	.01	.000	.08	.007	.000

[a]Values in the table are standardized beta coefficients with p < .07
[b]ST = short-term decisions, MT = medium-term decisions, LT = long-term decisions.

Table 1. Multiple regressions; dimensions of Influence are regressed by contextual variables[a]

Of all the contingency variables only a few have a substantial relationship with the various influence levels. The variable which is consistently related to the PO-scores of workers, of top management and particularly of representative bodies is the mobilization index, a measure of the degree of unionization in the company.

Taking the findings presented in this chapter together, it can be concluded that industrial democracy does not seem to be primarily structurally, technically or economically conditioned. The main conditional variables appear to be related to the socio-legal or socio-political environment of an organization. In other words, industrial democracy seems to be rather voluntaristic than reïficative in nature.

REFERENCES

IDE International Research Group, Industrial democracy in Europe.
   Oxford: Oxford University Press, 1981a.
IDE International Research Group, European industrial relations.
   Oxford: Oxford University Press, 1981b.
Tannenbaum, A.S., Control in organizations. New York: McGraw Hill,
   1968.

13. WORKS' COUNCILS: THE DUTCH AND GERMAN CASE

A.M. Koopman-Iwema & D. Flechsenberger

INTRODUCTION

This chapter deals with a comparative study of the situation regarding the existence and the operation of Works' Councils in labour organizations in the Netherlands and the Federal Republic of Germany.

First, attention is given to the main similarities and dissimmilarities between these Councils, deriving from the laws in both countries, followed by a presentation of some empirical data. By means of these data the hypothesis is tested whether some major differences between the Dutch and the German situation can be explained from the different historical background of the Works' Councils in both countries.

WORKS' COUNCILS IN THE NETHERLANDS AND THE FEDERAL REPUBLIC OF GERMANY

Most labour organizations in the Netherlands and the Federal Republic of Germany are obliged by law to establish a Works' Council. By means of this Council representatives of the work force (blue and white collar) participate in decision-making on the company level. With respect to the history and the discretionary power of the Works' Councils there are similarities as well as differences between the German 'Betriebsrat' and the Dutch 'Ondernemingsraad'.

A short historical outline may contribute towards a fuller understanding of one of the essential differences between the German and the Dutch participative bodies.

The Federal Republic of Germany

The institutionalization of 'Fabrikausschüsse' (plant Committees) had been demanded in as early as 1848 by the first German National Convention (Frankfurter Nationalversammlung; see Brigl-Mathias, 1926), but it was only in 1920 that these demands resulted in a first comprehensive legal regulation, the 'Betriebsrätegesetz' (Works' Councils Act).

There are of course earlier examples of plant committees in single plants, which were, however, mostly tied to patriarchical conceptions of the employers. E.g. from 1905 onward there were committees in the mining industry with very limited competences.

The Law of 1920 must be seen in relation to the growing revolutionary Soviet movement after the end of World War I. The soviet councils

"... had been elected directly by the employees, being permanently under their control. At any time they could be withdrawn. So they seemed to be more closely tied to the plant affairs as well as more democratic than the old highly bureaucratic organizations of the party and the unions" (Von Oertzen, 1963, 40).

The German unions, mainly oriented towards a policy of social reforms, were afraid that the extension of basis-oriented Soviet movements might reduce their influence within the plants. As a result of the cooperation of the unions with the employers (Dybowski-Johannson, 1980), in 1920 a law was enacted, containing two principles, which later formed the basis for the regulations of 1952 and 1972. Firstly, hegemony of the unions in the Works' Councils could only be secured if direct anti-capitalistic orientations of the Works' Councils were abandoned. Secondly, Works' Councils were obliged to cooperate with the plant management in a peaceful and harmonious manner:

"The Works' Councils were conceided the co-decision right only in the areas of social affairs, the passing of official regulations, the making of work regulations and guidelines for labour agreements and payment regulations. On the other hand the co-decision rights of Works' Councils were substantially restricted concerning engagements and releases whereas in economic affairs they were conceided only an information and consulting right" (Dybowski-Johannson, 1980).

After World War II, the political constellation was different in various respects. At least partly because of the close cooperation

between the large industry and the 'National Socialists', after 1945
there was a solid ground for a policy directed towards the limitation
of the potential power resulting from capital rights. Such considerations even appeared in the programs of the christian conservative parties, as, for example, the demand for socialization of basic industries
in the 'Ahlener Programm' of the Christian Democrats in 1948. Concerning
the unions this lead to comprehensive demands for a reconstruction of
Germany along socialistic lines. With respect to representative committees in the enterprises this demand meant elaborated decision rights
for the Works' Council in all managerial decision areas (Dybowski-
Johannson, 1980).

The Law of 1952, however, did not meet these demands and in some
respects it even fell short of the regulations of 1920. One of the main
reasons was the restrictive attitude of the Allied Forces toward democratization initiatives in the economic sphere (Brock, 1976). This made the re-
establishment of the old economic system possible, built up upon the
idea of free enterprises. Conservatives successfully impeded the extension of decision rights for the employees, whereas the demands of the
unions for far-reaching rights of Works' Councils together with a comprehensive re-organization of the plant constitution and the constitution of the economy as a whole remained unattainable.

Nevertheless - despite its codified orientation towards the idea of
social partnership - the unions considered the Works' Council as an
instrument to pursue labour interests. This is even reflected in a
comment of a former President of the Federal Labour Court:

> "The Works' Council has been built up mainly to moderate and
> partly to eliminate the subordination stemming from the work
> relation, i.e. as a representation of the interests of the
> employees" (Hueck-Nipperdey, 1976).

The same holds for the amendment of the Works' Constitution Act in 1972.
Following the pressure of the unions, the rights of the Works' Councils
concerning social and personnel affairs were extended and - although
to a less degree - in genuine co-decision rights (veto-rights, necessity for consent).

Summing up, the German Works' Council movement has been closely tied

to the Trade Union Movement and was always considered by the unions as
an instrument to put through interest of the employees.

The Netherlands

In the Netherlands the development has been different (Koopman-Iwema,
1980). The first Works' Council Law was not enacted until 1950. This
Law reflected the ideas of cooperation and reconstruction that dominated social and economic life in the Netherlands after World War II.

   The primary task of the Works' Council was to contribute towards
the good functioning of the firm. The fact that a member of the plant
management of the entrepreneur himself acted as the chairman of the Council, illustrates the harmonistic perspective of the Dutch Works' Councils. The autonomous position of the emppployer, however, was not
touched at all. Competences of the Dutch Works' Council were limited
only to certain social marginal affairs like e.g. the plant saving
regulations.

   In the Netherlands as well as in the FRG there were discussions in
the nineteen-sixties about the extension of the rights of the Works'
Councils. The idea of common interests of employers and employees was
replaced by conceptions about conflicting interests between these
societal groups. This development resulted in an amendment of the Dutch
Law in 1971. By this amendment the Works' Council was given a dual
duty: on the one hand (as in the 1950 Law) to act as a consultative
body between the employer and the employees "in the interest of a good
functioning of the firm in all its goals as a whole" and on the other
hand to be an institution representing the interests of the employees
in the plant. The rights of the Works' Council were extended concerning
information rights in the economic sphere and consulting rights in
social affairs.

   After 1971, the Socialists unions persisted in stressing the importance of the independent position of the Works' Councils, i.e. as a
body representing labour interests only. As long as there was no basic
change in the economic order they refused to take responsibility for
the plant policy, which remained to be one of the major duties of the

215

Works' Council as a consultative body, even after 1971. The Socialist unions wanted the Works' Council to control managerial decisions without being bound to the decision process itself.

The Christian unions in the Netherlands preferred a scheme according to which the Works' Council was to take part in the decision-making process and to cooperate with the employer. They flavoured the traditional way of composing the Works' Council of representatives of the employer *and* the employees, and only questioned the position of the employer as a chairman of the Council.

After a revision of the Law in 1979, the Dutch Works' Councils only consist of representatives of the employees. Nevertheless, its duty has remained a dual one: on the one hand it has to be an institution of representation of the interests of labour, serving, on the other hand, as a consultative body for the plant management as well (Koopman-Iwema, 1980).

Differences

A comparison between the Dutch and the German Works' Councils shows, that the decision-making competences are quite similar in both cases (Table 1).

In general, the German 'Betriebsverfassungsgesetz' is more detailed and its articles are more elaborated and specific as compared to the articles in the Dutch 'Wet op de Ondernemingsraden'. In the Dutch Law several regulations are mentioned in a global way leaving interpretation and application to the Works' Councils themselves (WOR, 1979).

Considering this, it is striking that in both countries competences of the Works' Councils in decision-making decrease the closer the topics are to the economic core spheres of the enterprise. The co-determinative and consultative rights of the labour force are most far-reaching regarding frame conditions in personnel affairs and social working conditions and the autonomous discretionary power of the capital owners are only marginally restricted by the Works' Council.

Table 1. Competences of the Works' Councils in the Netherlands and the Federal Republic of Germany, according to Law.

	The Netherlands	Federal Republic of Germany
A. CO-DECISION RIGHTS:	1. regulations of the working time	1. regulations of the working time
	2. making of vacation plans	2. making of vacation plans
	3. payment regulations	3. payment regulations
	4. regulations concerning accident prevention and health care	4. regulations concerning accident prevention and health care
	5. personnel training and development regulation	5. realization of personnel training programs; hiring/ firing of instructors
	6. regulations concerning the plant social work system	6. form, arrangement and administration of social institutions within the plant
	7. hiring-, firing- and pro- motion regulations	7. principles of personnel selection, hiring, trans- fer and firing
	8. principles of job evaluation	8. 'ad hoc' actions in personal affaires
	9. regulations concerning pensions, profit sharing and plant saving supports	9. dismissals
	10. formal regulations for a system of consultative meetings between super- visors and subordinates ('werkoverleg')	10. time, place and type of payment
	11. regulations how to handle complaints	11. regulation of the order of the plant
	12. regulations concerning the position of young employees	12. installation and appli- cation of technical ar- rangements to measure the employees' performance
		13. assignment of plant owned appartments
		14. principles of a proposal ('idea-box') system
		15. reduction of work load, caused by technical changes in working proce- dures or work places

	The Netherlands	Federal Republic of Germany
B. CONSULTATION RIGHTS:	1. hiring or dismissal of members of the plant management	1. planning on buildings, technical installations, working procedures, work methods and work places
	2. the plant management has to consult the Works' Council on the following topics:	2. personal planning and consequences with respect to personnel actions and professional training

	- selling of the plant; selling of shares
	  - buying or selling of shares of other firms
	  - cooperation with other firms
	  - lie downs
	  - restrictions or extensions of business scope
	  - change of the internal organizational structure
	  - change of plant location
	  - groupwise recruitment or renting of employees
	  - important investments
	  - taking larger credits
	  - conclusion and kind of consulting contracts
		3. establishment and equipment of plant institutions for professional training
		
		4. changes of plant proceedings which might cause essential disadvantages for the employees
		
		5. measures on safety and health

C. RIGHT TO GET INFORMATION FROM THE PLANT MANAGEMENT:	1. all relevant information and documents that are necessary for an ordinary execution of the Works' Councils' duties	1. early and comprehensive information and documents, that are necessary for the execution of the Works' Councils' duties
	2. at the beginning of each Works' Council period: information in written form about the legal constitution of the firm (e.g. name(s) of owner(s), shareholders, etc.)	2. hiring or other personal changes of members of the plant management
	3. twice a year the Works' Council has to be informed about the activities and results of the firm in the past period and the expectations for the future period	3. information about economic affairs (through the 'Wirtschaftausschuss')

The Netherlands	Federal Republic of Germany
4. once a year statistics should be presented to the Works' Council about the development and composition of the work force, the practiced social policy and the expectations for the future periode	4. the Works' Council can demand the announcement of work places within the plant.
5. annual balances of the past period and future budget plannings	
6. planned consulting contracts.	

A substantial difference between the Dutch and the German situation may be found in the procurement of information about economic affairs. In the Netherlands the Works' Council itself has to be informed directly whereas the German Works' Council is informed via the 'Wirtschaftsausschuss'. This is a body to be installed in plants with more than 100 employees, and in which at least one member of the Works' Council is represented. Its duty is to confer at least once a month with the plant management about economic affairs and consequently to inform the Works' Council about these consultations.

As a more essential difference it should be kept in mind that in Germany the Works' Council is understood in a *monistic* way (Chmielewicz & Imhoffen, 1977), i.e. as a representative body for the interests of the labour force, whereas in the Netherlands the Works's Council - due to its *dual* conception - can be seen as being tied to the management process in order to contribute to the solution of problems concerning both management and the employees (Koopman-Iwema, 1981).

This difference is of some importance if we try to assess differences in work-related attitudes between employees in the FRG and the Netherlands. The question is if divergent conceptions of the Works' Councils in both countries result in different attitudes of the employees? Employees in German plants might feel better represented by the Works' Council and therefore have a more positive attitude towards this

body as compared to the employees in Dutch plants, where the Works'
Council has to serve two - often antagonistic - interests. Therefore
our main research question is:

> Will the different conceptions of the Works' Council in the
> German and the Dutch law be reflected in different attitudes
> of the employees towards this representative body?

The following aspects will be considered in detail:

1. The influence of the Works' Council in both countries as perceived
   by the employees, as well as its access to information.

2. The contacts between the employees and their representatives in the
   Works' Council.

3. Several individual reactions of the employees, like e.g. their
   motivation and job satisfaction, as well as their view on organizational conflicts.

THE STUDY

As part of a broader international comparative research project in
five countries[*] a questionnaire was administered in 10 Germand and 10
Dutch plants to samples of at least 60 employees including the Works'
Council members. Among the respondents were about 40 rank-and-file
workers and 20 managers (from the first-line supervisors of the selected
production groups up to the plant top management). The data were collected from 1976 to 1978. Table 2 shows characteristics of the 10
German and Dutch plants included in the study.

---

[*] Data used in this article stem from the international research project 'Members participation in Industrial Organizations' (MPIO). Scien-
tists from five countries cooperated in this project: P. Clark (United
Kingdom); K. Bartolke, D. Flechsenberger (Federal Republic of Germany);
A.M. Koopman-Iwema, Hk. Thierry (The Netherlands); O. Leviatan, E.
Navon, M. Palgi, M. Rosner (Israel); F. Norrgren, S. Rubenowitz (Sweden).
D. Nightingale (Canada) and A.S. Tannenbaum (USA) shared in an earlier
phase of the study. The present authors are responsible for the con-
tent of this contribution. The study in Germany was funded by the
Minister für Wissenschaft und Forschung des Landes Nordrhein-Westfalen.
In the Netherlands financial support was obtained from the Dutch
Organization of Pure Research (ZWO).

	number of plants	
	Federal Republic of Germany	the Netherlands
branch . food	-	6
. chemical/pharmaceutical	4	-
. metal	4	3
. textile	2	1
size of the plants		
(number of employees) 100 - 200	3	2
200 - 300	4	2
300 - 400	2	2
400 - 500	1	-
600 - 700	-	2
> 700	-	2
forms of participation		
. Works' Council	7	4
. Works' Council, semiautonomous work groups	1	-
. Works' Council, job consultation (direct and indirect)	-	6
. Partnership Committee ('Partnerschaftsausschuss', i.e. joint council composed of an equal number of members of the plant management and departmentwise elected representatives of the employees)	1	-
. Semiautonomous work groups	1	-

Table 2. Some plant characteristics

In Table 3 demographic characteristics of the respondents involved are shown.

	Federal Republic of Germany	the Netherlands
A. Number of respondents		
managers	171	256
rank and file workers	374	481
worker representatives in Works' Council	56	109
B. % male		
managers	88	99
rank and file workers	54	93
worker representatives	77	97
C. Average age (years)		
managers	42,0	47,0
rank and file workers	35,4	36,2
worker representatives	38,1	41,0
D. Average seniority in the plant (years)		
managers	8,7	11,0
rank and file workers	4,6	7,5
worker representatives	9,7	12,8

Table 3. Demographic characteristics.
(The average level of education is not presented
due to the incomparability of the school system
in both countries.)

RESULTS

The influence of the Works' Council and its access to information

With respect to the influence of the Works' Councils concerning specific
decision topics, data were collected from the workers, the managerial
personnel and the worker representatives. The following Figure shows
the relevant German and Dutch data of the first two groups mentioned.
On the horizontal axis the different decision topics are depicted. The
vertical axis shows the amount of influence of the Works' Council, as
perceived by workers or managers.

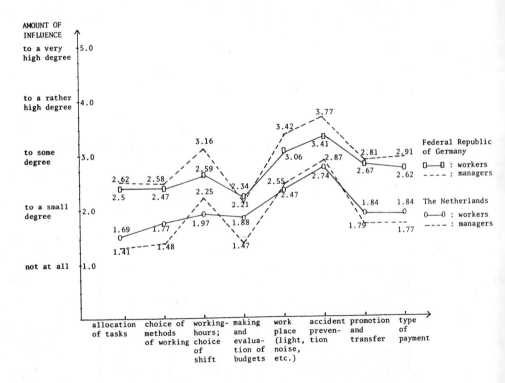

Figure 1. Influence of the Works' Council concerning several decision
topics, as perceived by workers and managers

According to the study, workers as well as their supervisors in Germany ascribe more influence to the Works' Council in all subjects of decision-making than their colleagues in the Netherlands. This result is statistically significant for each of the decision topics ($p < .05$; 2-tailed t-test). Possibly it is easier for the German Works' Councils 'to sell' decisions to their constituency which were realized, modified or blocked as a result of initiatives of the Works' Council. Following this interpretation the German employees do ascribe comparatively more influence to the Works' Council.

However, another interpretation might be given, relating to the fact that in some Dutch plants a system of direct participation on the shop floor level ('Werkoverleg') can be found in addition to the indirect way of participation by means of the Works' Council. This 'Werkoverleg' system might be relevant for the data presented for two reasons.

A more *objective* interpretation is that the Works' Council might loose power in decision-making potential as a consequence of the consultations via the 'Werkoverleg'-system. In plants with a 'Werkoverleg'-system the employees might prefer to regulate their affairs directly with their superiors, excluding the Works' Council. This could result in the perception of a comparatively lower level of influence for the Works' Council in the Netherlands.

An interpretation more oriented towards the *subjective* awareness of the employees assumes that the consultation process within the 'Werkoverleg'-meetings will intensify this awareness with regard to the several topics mentioned. As a consequence of the thereby increased expectation level, employees in plants with a 'Werkoverleg'-system might ascribe a lower degree of influence to the Council, in spite of an equal degree of 'objective' influence of the Works' Council in these plants and in plants without 'Werkoverleg'.

These assumptions could be tested by the data of our study. An indirect system of participation was found in six Dutch plants; direct participation via the 'Werkoverleg' existed only in four plants. If the assumptions concerning the 'Werkoverleg' should prove to be right, one might expect that the differences between the Dutch and the German plants will disappear if one compares only the Dutch plants *without* a

'Werkoverleg'-system with the German plants with indirect participation. For this purpose we computed, for all decision topics together, the average difference between the Dutch influence measures and the German scores. For all Dutch plants taken together this value is .68 for the group of the workers. This score reduces to .31 if one includes only the Dutch plants *without* the 'Werkoverleg'-system. This difference shows that the assumed change of the employees' perceptions concerning the Works' Council's influence due to the existence of 'Werkoverleg' finds some support. These data, however, do not provide an answer to the question as to whether this change is caused by a modified expectation level of the respondents or by a 'real' reduction of the influence of the Works' Council.

The above interpretation referred only to differences in the amount of influence of the Works' Council, not differentiating between decision topics. Figure 1 shows that in the Netherlands as well as in Germany the Works' Council was ascribed to have strongest influence on the decision topics 'accident prevention' and 'workplace (light, noise, air, etc.)'. These perceptions are in accordance with the formulations in the Laws in both countries, offering most co-determinative rights to the Works' Councils on aspects of the immediate work environment and work regulations. With regard to the decision topic 'making and evaluation of budgets', in both countries the Works' Council is perceived to have relatively small influence. This again reflects the legal regulations, offering in both countries only a right of information concerning economic affairs to the worker representatives in the Works' Council.

Nevertheless, there is a difference between the Dutch and the German situation. While in the Netherlands we find 'allocation of tasks' and 'choice of work methods' on a level comparable with 'making and evaluation of budgets', in Germany the influence of the Works' Council on budgets is absolutely minimal in comparison with all other decision topics mentioned.

Again the interpretation may be sought in the legal regulations. Presumably the limited information rights indirectly given to the Works' Council via the 'Wirtschaftsausschuss' (as in the German case) instead of directly to all Works' Council-members (as in the Netherlands) are reflected in the data. Also the general information on economic results, to be given twice a year to Dutch Works' Councils, may explain the higher amount of influence on economic matters ascribed to their Council by the Dutch respondents.

Some general data were gathered concerning the distribution of power and control in Dutch and German plants. Figure 2 shows - on the horizontal axis - hierarchical groups as existing in every plant: plant management, the supervisors and the workers as a group. The vertical axis indicates the amount of influence. By means of a 'Control-graph' the distribution of influence on plant affairs among the hierarchical level is illustrated, as perceived by the *workers* (Figure 2, continued line). The *desired* distribution of influence among the hierarchical groups is also given (dotted line). (A survey on studies applying the controle-graph method is given by Tannenbaum (1978). For criticism of control-graph methods see Gundelach & Tetzschner (1978).)

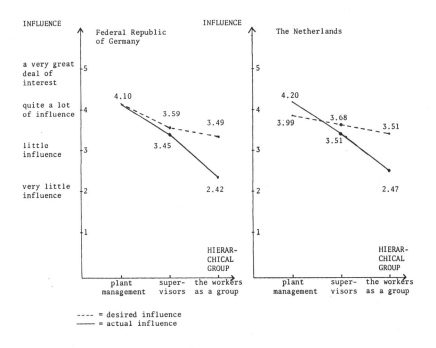

Figure 2. Control graph in German and Dutch plants (as perceived by workers)

The control-graphs show that the distribution of actual influence as perceived by the workers is very similar in both countries. The slopes of both graphs are almost identical. The graphs of the desired influence distribution, however, are different.

While in Germany the workers more or less agree with the amount of influence of the plant management (the actual and the desired score are identical), Dutch workers opt for a lesser degree of influence for plant management compared to the actual situation. The 'actual' and 'desired' influence scores for the other two groups ('supervisors' and 'workers as a group') are almost identical in Germany and the Netherlands. A comparison between both countries shows that the Dutch workers prefer a flatter distribution of control between the plant management and the other hierarchical groups.

The data on the desired amount of influence gathered from the Dutch workers as a tendency fit the concept of a fixed total amount of control, which means that like in a zero-sum-game, the increase of control of one group will coincide with the decrease of control of another group. In the German case, on the contrary, the desired total amount of control increases. This difference may be due to different cultural patterns in both countries: the workers' understanding of the actual distribution of influence within plants in Germany as well as their own perception of the desired situation seems to be more closely tied to hierarchical schemes of organization of work in Germany than in the Netherlands.

Nevertheless, two identical features may be observed in both countries: firstly, the workers prefer the distribution of influence to be less hierarchical, i.e. the differences in influence between the different hierarchical levels should be smaller and secondly, the workers as a group should have more influence.

Looking at the perceptions of actual and desired influence of the representatives in the Works' Councils, as perceived by the *representatives* themselves (Figure 3), another phenomenon may be observed: the representatives in Germany, although statistically not significant (t-test), rate their influence on plant affairs higher than their colleagues in the Netherlands. Their perceptions of the desired amount of control are also higher compared to their Dutch colleagues. In addition to this, the German representatives consider the gap between their actual and desired influence as being wider. Nevertheless, in both countries the representatives opt for much more influence than they actually have.

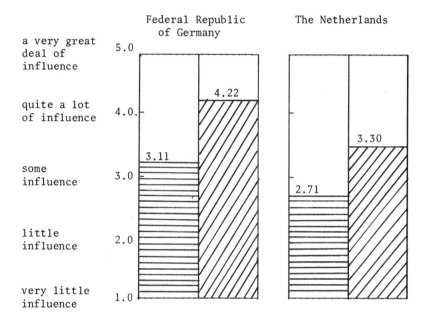

Figure 3. Influence of the Works' Council, as perceived by the Council members

These data are in accordance with the statements of the *workers* and the *supervisors* in both countries. In Germany these groups too, ascribe more actual and desired influence to the representatives in the Works' Council than their colleagues in the Netherlands (t-test; p = .001). Here again, the experience of having influence comes together with aspirations for even more influence.

Contacts between representatives and Works' Council members

In our study 'contacts between representatives and Works' Council members' are measured by means of two items: we asked Council members to estimate their perceived frequency of contacts with their constituency and parallel to this the organization members themselves were asked how often they get in touch with their representatives. The data are presented in Table 4.

frequency of contacts:	FEDERAL REPUBLIC OF GERMANY			THE NETHERLANDS		
	supervisors	workers	representatives	supervisors	workers	representatives
constituency → representatives	3.36	2.93	3.60	2.35	2.16	2.81
representatives → constituency	2.74	2.52	3.88	2.35	2.16	3.54

Table 4. Frequency and direction of contacts between the employees and their representatives in the Works' Council, as perceived by managers, workers and representatives in German and Dutch plants (1 = never, ..., 5 = very often)

There are two differences in the perceptions of German Council members as compared with their colleagues in the Netherlands: firstly, they perceive a higher frequency of communication between Works' Council members and the constituency, and secondly, the contacts are almost equally often initiated by the Works' Council members themselves as well as by their constituency.

From these data it may be concluded, that Works' Council members in Germany are on the one hand more keen to get in touch with the basis, and on the other hand that the German employees feel a stronger motivation to get in touch with their representatives than in the Netherlands. This again may be ascribed to the existence of the 'Werkoverleg'-system in four of the ten Dutch plants. In these plants the employees may possibly prefer to settle things by themselves than via their representatives in the Works' Council.

In both countries there is, however, a difference between the statements of the Works' Council members and those of the other employees:
the workers as well as the supervisors state a lower level of communicative relations with the Works' Council members than the Council members
report. Additionally the German respondents indicate that these contacts
are more often initiated by themselves than by the Works' Council members (Table 4, t-test; p = .00).

Concerning the *access* to information that is relevant for the Works'
Council members and for the operation of the Council, the Works' Council
members in Germany perceive that they more often get important information from the plant management than do their colleagues in the Netherlands (t-test; p = .00). The same applies to information they get from
their constituency (Table 5).

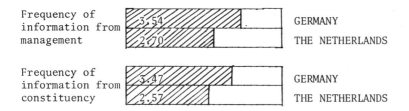

Table 5. Frequency of information for the Works' Council members,
as perceived by them (1 = never, ..., 5 = very often)

According to these data it is not surprising that the German Works'
Council members are more *satisfied* with their situation than the Dutch
worker representatives (t-test; p = .00). Consequently the attitudes
towards participation in decision-making in the Works' Councils are
more positively evaluated in Germany than in the Netherlands, following
the statements of all groups of respondents involved (t-test; p = .00).

Individual reactions and organizational effects

Finally, some data were analysed regarding the relationship between the
kind of representation of labour interests by the Works' Council in

both countries and some individual reactions and organizational effects, as described by the respondents.

We found that in the German plants - according to the statements of the workers and the Works' Council members - a larger amount of conflicts between the plant management and the workers was perceived than in the Netherlands (t-test; p = .00).

However, a positive significant relationship was found between the German scores on motivation and job satisfaction on the one hand and the amount of influence ascribed to the Works' Council on the other (Table 6).

	perceived influence of the Works' Council	
correlated with:	Germany	The Netherlands
motivation	r=.12 N=502 p=.004	r=-.07 N=774 p=.02
job satisfaction	r=.18 N=514 p=.001	r= .05 N=789 p=.09

Table 6. Correlations between perceived influence of the Works' Council and individual reactions like motivation and job satisfaction

CONCLUSION

From the data presented above, quite a clear picture may be drawn. The situation in German plants is - at least with regard to the data collected - different from the situation in Dutch plants. For various decision topics, workers, supervisors and Works' Council members ascribe more influence to the Works' Council in Germany than their Dutch counterparts.

One possible interpretation of this phenomenon is the different historical development of the Works' Councils in Germany (monistic representation of the interests of the employees) and in the Netherlands (dualistic representation of interests including those of the employees as well as those of the employer).

However, another interpretation also seems to be valid: the conception of participation in the Netherlands is different from the German model. While in German plants the Works' Council usually is the only institutionalized form of representation of labour interests, in the Netherlands there is a consultative system on the shop floor level in addition to this indirect form of participation on the plant level. This 'Werkoverleg' (job consultation) involves regular consultations between a superior and his group of subordinates on matters concerning the work and work environment. It seems plausible that dealing with social and personnel affairs on the shop floor level detracts Dutch employees from the Works' Council and from the representation of their interests by this Council.

REFERENCES

Brigl-Mathias, K., Das Betriebsräteproblem in der Weimarer Republik. Berlin/Leipzig: De Gruyter, 1926.

Brock, A. et al., Die Interessenvertretung der Arbeitnehmer im Betrieb. Köln: Europäische Verlagsanstalt, 1976.

Chmielewicz, K. & A.O. Inhoffen, Die Mitbestimmung nach dem Betriebsverfassungsgesetz 1972 aus organisatorischer Sicht. Die Betriebswirtschaft, 1977, 4, 591-613.

Dybowski-Johannson, G., Die Interessenvertretung durch den Betriebsrat. Frankfurt a. Main: Campus, 1980.

Gundelach, P. & H. Tetzschner, Measurement of Influence in Organizations - Critique of the Control-Graph-Method. Acta Sociologica,
   1978, 1, 49-63.

Hueck-Nipperdey, Lehrbuch des Arbeitsrechts. Frankfurt a. Main: Vahlen,
   1976.

Koopman-Iwema, A.M., Macht, motivatie, medezeggenschap. Assen: Van
   Gorcum, 1980.

Koopman-Iwema, A.M., Möglichkeiten zur Mitbestimmung des Betriebs-
   rates in deutschen und holländischen Betrieben. Dortmund: Bundes-
   kongress '81 Sektion Arbeits- und Betriebspsychologie im Berufsverband Deutscher Psychologen, 1981.

Oertzen, P. von, Die Probleme der wirtschaftlichen Neuordnung und der
   Mitbestimmung in der Revolution von 1918. Frankfurt a. Main:
   Europäische Verlagsanstalt, 1963.

Tannenbaum, A.S. & R.A. Cooke, Organizational control. A review of
   research employing the control graph method. In: C.J. Lammers &
   D. Hickson (Eds.), Organizations alike and unlike. London: Routledge
   & Kegan Paul, 1978.

Wet op de Ondernemingsraden, 1979.

14. ORGANIZATIONAL DESIGN AND TASK STRUCTURE AS PRECONDITIONS FOR JOB CONSULTATION

H. Kuipers, C.A.J.M. Aarts, P.M. Bachgus & J. Praagman

INTRODUCTION

In the last decades in The Netherlands much experience has been gained
with job consultation (or: 'Werkoverleg'). Drenth and Koopman (1982)
define job consultation as follows:
- it is a system of regular and formalized consultation,
- between a superior and his subordinates as a group,
- aimed at participation in and influence upon decision-making,
- especially with respect to their own work situation.

At first the expectations of job consultation were pitched high. Job
consultation was considered as:
- a contribution to industrial democracy;
- a means of personal growth and development, and
- a means to stimulate productivity.
Corresponding with these goals three different theoretical approaches
to participation can be distinguished: an ideological, a psychological
and a productivity approach (Dachler & Wilpert, 1978).

Two ideological streams are: democratic and socialistic theory.
According to these theories participation is a social value in itself.
It is expected to contribute respectively to a free and democratic
society and to the economic liberation of workers.

Psychological theories (e.g. McGregor, 1960; Argyris, 1964) state
that higher order needs like self-actualization can be satisfied through
participation.

The productivity approach seeks "an instrumental understanding of human beings and their capacities" and "people are considered to be manipulated toward maximum output through appropriate social technologies" (Dachler & Wilpert, 1978).

In the second half of the seventies it became apparent that the expectations had been put too high with regard to the effects of participation through job consultation. Nevertheless: job consultation is still widely practised, not only in production organizations, but also in non-profit organizations like government agencies and universities. Thus: the question why the original expectations are only partly realized is very actual, especially since the Work Environment Act came into force.

In our opinion the central problem in theory and practice of job consultation is that the mentioned approaches pay little attention to preconditions in the work itself and in the organizational design, i.e.
- the ideological approach confines itself to political preconditions and constraints in society and to formal power and ownership relationships within the organization as a whole;
- the psychological approach, indeed, points out the constraints of Tayloristic principles. However, a serious limitation of these theories with respect to participation is that they are far from specific about the precise role and the particular characteristics of participatory arrangements in relation to task structure and organization designs. Therefore these theories only have limited value for the *design* of form and content of job consultation;
- the productivity approach focuses on the improvement of commitment to the decisions in which participation is allowed. In addition, participants will obtain more accurate information about the issues concerned. This will lead to increased productivity.

However, these effects can only be expected to the extent that:
- involvement and information are important determinants of productivity;
- participation via job consultation is a means to foster commitment and to give participants the required information;
- the right issues are selected for participation.

This, again, depends on the kind of work and the design of the organization. A productivity approach which is not based upon the relationship between form and content of job consultation on the one hand and the task structure and the organization design on the other hand is reduced to manipulative 'tricks'.

FUNCTIONS OF JOB CONSULTATION

From a sociotechnical point of view job consultation is viewed primarily as a potential contribution to an efficient and flexible running of the production process and to an optimal design of the task- and production structure. The fact that open sociotechnical systems, like work-units, are capable of equifinality - i.e. that they are capable to make choices in an uncertain, sometimes turbulent environment in order to reach their goals - is the cornerstone of this approach. Job consultation is one of the means to make these choices.

The viability of this means is dependent upon its usefulness. That leads to the question of what exactly can be the potential usefulness of job consultation in the context of work and organization. Under which task conditions is job consultation required and under which organizational conditions is job consultation possible?

There is no simple answer to this question. Therefore, we will have a look at the potential functions of job consultation from four different angles:
1. Short term (small scope) or long term (broad scope) functions.
2. Stability or innovation functions.
3. Coordination or support functions.
4. Functions in different areas of decision-making.

Short term or long term functions

Short term job consultation focuses on detailed decision-making and evaluation concerning a restricted planning period (one or more weeks). Short term problems concerning working conditions, workflow, production structure, and the like are discussed.

Long term job consultation focuses on global planning and evaluation in the long run (from one to several years). More strategic questions concerning product, process or structure are discussed. Whether short term resp. long term consultation is usefull (and viable) depends on different factors. Let us give an example. Workers usually have detailed information about uncertainties in the production flow and bottle necks in the production structure. If these uncertainties and bottle necks require short term problem solving and regular adjustments of planning and coordination, there is a need for short term job consultation. E.g.: a team of mutually dependent operators in a plant with frequent troubles in the production flow.

Long term job consultation is required in work-units if long term policy decisions cannot be disconnected from the work itself because the members of a work-unit 'make' policy in their daily work. This is the case for instance in research units working on long term projects, in sales departments which enter into long term contracts or in design departments for product innovation. The expertness and commitment of members of such units is of vital importance for long term policy-making.

Stability or innovation functions

The aim of job consultation may be either stability or change and innovation. 'Werkoverleg' as it is mostly practized in Holland emphasizes the stability function. In the Japanese Quality Circles innovation of the production-process is emphasized.

Planning the work flow, allocating tasks, solving ad hoc troubles, reducing variances and uncertainties are self-maintaining activities, in which job consultation potentially plays an important role, if the information about these uncertainties enters the organization on the level of the subordinates. Thus, the usefulness of stability-focused job consultation depends on the degree of uncertainty, variety and mutual dependency in the task itself.

Task designs, renewal of the production structure, technical optimization, product innovation, and quality or quantity improvements are forms of innovation and change. Many of these changes come from outside the work-unit. The Quality Circles prove that under certain conditions change and innovation may come from the work-unit itself.

One of these conditions is the true receptivity of management to inno-
vations from the bottom. An innovative, problem solving contribution of
workers is useful in market conditions which require that work-units
excel in refined and flexible work methods and in high quality products.
The specific information of the workers on potential improvements plays
an important role.

Coordination or support functions

Job consultation may be focused either on mutual coordination of the
work of members with (different) interdependent contributions or on
mutual support of members with equal contributions.

Consultation aiming at coordination is particularly required in
product-oriented units with different mutually dependent specialists
or a high degree of uncertainty in the work flow and production structure. This may be the case in relatively autonomous work-units, producing relatively complex group-products. It may particularly be the
case if staff and support functions, like detailed planning and daily
maintenance, are integrated in these autonomous groups (Van Assen,
1978).

Consultation aiming at mutual support is required in functionally
organized units. Members of such units can help each other to maintain
an acceptable professional level or to cope with stress. This may be
required if individual tasks are characterized by professional or
emotional uncertainties and need permanent mutual learning and counseling. For instance the highly skilled work in design or research
departments may require mutual professional support. A team of nurses
in a psychiatric clinic or a team of warders in a prison may require
mutual emotional support.

Functions in different areas

Job consultation may be relevant for different areas of decision, like
for instance:
- the work flow and production structure (regulations);
- the organization of the work-unit itself (governance);

- the decisions which are independent of work flow, production-structure or work-units (freedom);
- the quantity and quality of goals.

It holds for these different fields of decision-making that only if the characteristics of the task-structure require consultation and only if the organization design offers latitude for participative decision-making, job consultation is a good device.

JOB CONSULTATION: A MODEL

The basic hypothesis which will be tested in this section is, that organization design and task-structure are important determinants of the influence members of work-units can exert on decision-making via job consultation. These determinants have both a direct effect on the influence of job consultation groups as well as an indirect effect via 'organizational climate', 'group relations' and 'motivation on skill'. Figure 1 shows the conceptual model which will be further elucidated.

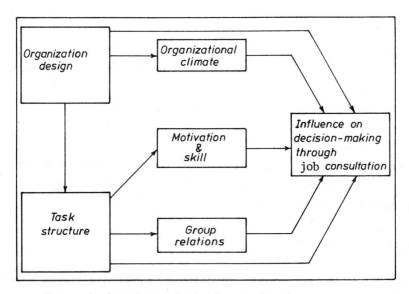

Figure 1. Causal model of job consultation

ELABORATION OF THE MODEL AND DESIGN OF THE STUDY

The study was carried out in the central service departments of
Eindhoven University of Technology. Within these departments about
1.000 people are working in about 80 work-units (Aarts, 1982).

In 1980 the university board decided to introduce a system of job
consultation in the work-units in the service departments. In 1981 the
study was carried out to evaluate and to stimulate job consultation in
these work-units.

Each individual employee was asked to fill out a multiple choice
questionnaire. Each department head and work-unit-leader was interviewed
individually to gain additional information. Pilot research was carried
out in two work-units of Tilburg University and one work-unit of Delft
University of Technology. In the next two sections we will discuss the
different variables in our model and their operationalization in this
study.

Dependent variable

Our 'dependent' variable is the influence of the members of a work-unit
in 22 areas of decision-making through job consultation. The 22 items
were selected on the basis of a content analysis of the minutes of job
consultation sessions. They were divided in 4 areas:
- working conditions (e.g. safety, physical working conditions);
- work performance (e.g. planning, budgetting, choice of work methods);
- organization and personnel policy (e.g. job and performance evaluation);
- work goals.
For each of the 22 items, the respondents scored the degree of influence in decision-making (varying from 'authoritarian decision-making
by the leader' via 'consultation' to 'joint decision-making by the
work-unit').

The effects of organizational design

In this study organizational design was operationalized as the latitude

of decision-making of a work-unit in four different areas:
- self-regulation; decisions which are directly related to the work itself, about coordination, allocation, and boundary maintenance;
- self-governance of the unit; these decisions bear upon the internal organization of work-units;
- independence decisions; these decisions may be made by members of a unit, unless specific organizational or technological constraints prevent them from doing so;
- goal decisions; decisions about quantity and quality of goals.

The first three variables are derived from Susman (1976). These four variables are measured via the structured interview with the leaders of the work-units (16 questions).

Direct effects

Decentralization or the resulting latitude of decisions on the level of the work-unit is of primary importance for the possibility to make decisions, amongst others in the context of job consultation.

Self-regulation decision-making is an integral part of the daily work. These decisions are intrinsic to the production process itself. Possibly needed consultation during production is not the same as the formal periodical job consultation. Therefore we predict that self-regulation has no direct effect. It may have an effect via task structure. The other three decentralization variables are supposed to have direct effects, because short term or long term decision-making and consultation in these areas are extrinsic to the daily production process.

Via organizational climate

Three aspects of organizational climate are considered:
- participation climate;
- admission to information;
- tendency to bureaucratic behaviour.

We predict that decentralization in the four areas stimulates an open, participative, non-bureaucratic atmosphere. And thereby, it stimulates

240

the influence on decision-making through job consultation. The different aspects of organizational climate are measured by 9 questions in the general questionnaire.

Via task-structure

Decentralization in the four areas, but particularly self-regulation, means 'injection of uncertainty' and 'injection of mutual dependence' in the work-unit, because the work-unit obtains more (collective) responsibilities. On the other hand, decentralization, and the resulting decision latitude, are not the only organizational variables which affect task structure. Van Assen (1980), for instance, stated that production-units with integrated support and staff functions have more enriched group tasks than functionally organized departments without support and staff functions. Change in the direction of production-units with integrated support and staff functions leads, again, to 'injection of uncertainty and mutual dependence'.

The effects of task structure

Task structure is operationalized by four variables:
- conversion uncertainty: the uncertainty about the transformation process itself;
- boundary transaction uncertainty: the uncertainty about the moment and place where materials, supplies, requests for production, etc. will cross the work group boundary;
- variety of products, services and conversion activities;
- technically required cooperation between the members of a unit.
The variables are derived from Susman (1976) and measured with 11 questions in the structured interview with the leaders.

Direct effects

The first three variables are chosen because uncertainty and variety in the work itself require decision-making and uncertainty reduction in order to cope with these uncertainties and complexities.

241

Technically required cooperation puts demands upon mutual coordination and thereby will strengthen the need for job consultation. In general, uncertainty, variability, and technically required cooperation, lead to more job consultation issues like planning problems, ad hoc troubles, production bottlenecks, task distribution and coordination problems, quality control, task redesign, process innovation and so on.

Via group relations

Three aspects of group relations are considered:
- the internal power structure;
- the relations between superior and subordinates;
- the relations between co-workers.
We predict that these group relations are partly determined by the task variables. Above all technically required cooperation is supposed to stimulate a team spirit with equalization of power and good vertical and horizontal relations. And group relations, in turn, affect job consultation influence. These three variables are measured by 7 questions in the general questionnaire.

Via motivation and skill

Our general hypothesis is that a positive relationship exists between job consultation requirement and the motivation to participate.
Further we suppose that the requirements of mutual coordination, collective decision-making and so on, will give the participants the necessary social skill. Thus, uncertainty, variety and required cooperation are supposed to promote the development of job consultation through motivation and skill. These variables are measured by 7 questions in the general questionnaire. Figure 2 shows the elaborated model.

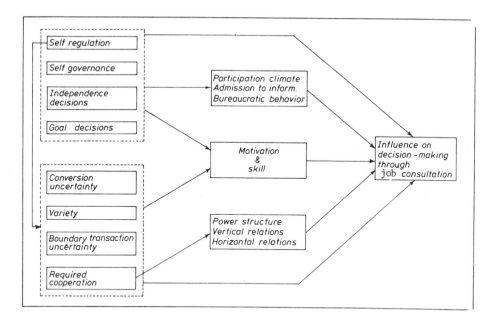

Figure 2. Operationalization of the variables and predicted relationships
in the model

RESULTS

From the total number of 80 work-units 67 participated in the investigation. The other units were too small (less than 4 members). In this
study, the units of analysis are groups. Individual scores were sum-
mated to group scores. If less than sixty percent of the members of a
work-unit answered a specific question, the group score for that question was considered as missing.

31 Work-units showed no missing data at all. Because of the central
role played by the correlations in our analysis, the correlation matrix,
based on these 31 units was compared to two other matrices:
- the matrix based on pairwise deletion;
- the estimate of the correlation matrix according to Beale and Little
  (1975).

No substantial differences between these three matrices could be shown. Therefore, it was decided to carry out all further analyses on the 31 units.

Factor analyses and construction of scales

First we wanted to answer the question if the a priori variables in our model were 'empirically based'. Between the items of the a priori variables intercorrelations and internal consistency reliability coefficients were computed.

Principal component analyses were carried out on the items of
- decision latitude;
- task structure;
- the dependent variable.

Decision latitude

On the matrix of intercorrelations between the 16 decision latitude items a principal component analysis was carried out. On the basis of the curve of eigenvalues the factor solution with two factors was chosen. The two factors accounted for 42.2% of variance (eigenvalues 3.76 and 2.98 respectively).

The two factors correspond with the a priori variables 'self-regulation' and 'self-government' respectively. Therefore, we decided to use the unweighted sum of items with the highest loadings on each of these two factors to measure these variables. The internal consistency reliability of these scales: self-regulation $rtt = 0.85$ and self-government $rtt = 0.80$. 'Decisions of independence' and 'goal decisions' did not appear as independent factors, and were excluded from further analysis.

Task structure

The 11 task structure items were intercorrelated and factoranalyzed in the same way. The three factors solution accounting for 64.9% of the variance was preferred.

Factor I is a combination of the variables 'conversion uncertainty' and 'variety'.

Factor II corresponds with 'required cooperation'.

Factor III may be interpreted as 'work pressure'. This variable does not fit in our original model (see Discussion).

Boundary transaction uncertainty did not appear as an independent factor. The unweighted sum of the scores on the items with the highest loadings on factor I is taken as a measure of 'conversion uncertainty' and 'variety'. The internal consistency of this variable is rtt = 0.70. In the same way the sum of the scores on the items with high loadings on factor II is taken as a measure of 'required cooperation' (rtt = 0.89).

Organizational climate, group relations and motivation and skill

The variables 'organizational climate', 'group relations', and 'motivation and skill' are measured by the unweighted sum of the scores on the concerning items. The internal consistency reliability coefficients are 0.86, 0.85 and 0.90 respectively.

Influence on decision-making through job consultation

The 22 items of this dependent variable were intercorrelated and factoranalyzed. The one factor solution was chosen for interpretation (eigenvalue 9.28, accounting for 42.2% of the variance). This factor was measured by the unweighted sum of the scores on the 22 items.

On the basis of the data reduction analyses the theoretical model was modified according to figure 3.

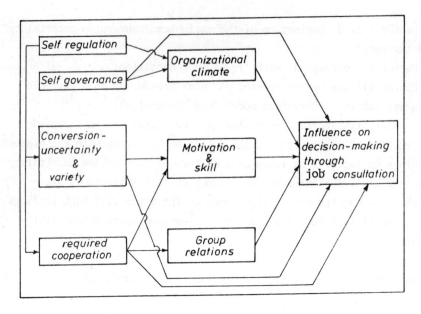

Figure 3. Modification of the model based on data reduction analysis

Test of the causal relationships of the model

As a first step in testing the hypothesized relationships a step-wise multiple regression of the 'dependent' variable on the 'independent' variables was carried out. In Table 1 the intercorrelations between the variables in the model are presented.

No	Variable	1	2	3	4	5	6	7	8
1	Influence in decision-making.	1.00							
2	Required cooperation	-.29	1.00						
3	Conversion uncertainty	.27	.02	1.00					
4	Self-regulation	.20	-.03	.36	1.00				
5	Self governance	.46	-.34	.01	.12	1.00			
6	Group relations	.46	-.50	.03	-.00	.51	1.00		
7	Organizational climate	.43	-.37	-.09	-.13	.57	.55	1.00	
8	Motivation and skil	.37	-.35	.06	-.10	.12	.65	.45	1.00

Table 1. Intercorrelations between variables in the model

In Table 2 the results of the regression analysis are presented. The 'independent' variables are presented in column 1, in order of insertion in the regression equation. Column 2 shows the zero-order correlations of each 'independent' variable with the 'dependent' variable. In the columns 3, 4 and 5 above the dotted line the standard regression coefficients are presented for each step in the regression analysis. Under the dotted line the partial correlations with the dependent variable, controlling for the effects of the variables already in the equation, are shown.

	"Independent" variable	zero-order correlation with "dependent" variable	step 1	step 2	step 3
1	Self-governance (Sg)	.46	.46	.42	.42
2	Motivation and skil (Mosk)	.37	.36	.32	.31
3	Conversion uncertainty (Cu)	.27	.30	.30	.25
4	Self-regulation (Sr)	.20	.16	.22	.13
5	Organizational climate (Oc)	.43	.23	.07	.13
6	Group relations (Gr)	.46	.29	.07	.07
7	Required cooperation (Rc)	-.29	-.16	-.05	-.07
multiple correlation			•46	•56	•61

Table 2. Step-wise multiple regression

From Table 2 one can see that there is a marked decline in the partial correlations of Organizational Climate (OC), Group Relations (GR) and Required Cooperation (RC) in step 1 and step 2. This suggests that there are alternative models which are statistically equivalent.

Four other regression analyses were carried out. In each of the first three of these, one of the three predictor variables included in the first multiple regression model was left out. In the fourth analysis all three predictor variables were left out. The results of these regression analyses are summarized in Table 3.

From Table 3 it can be concluded that the multiple R's of the alternative models differ only slightly from the multiple R of the model in Table 2.

No	Suppressed variable	Inserted variable	Multiple R
1	Conversion uncertainty (Cu)	Sg, Mosk, Sr	.59
2	Motivation and skil (Mosk)	Sg, Cu, Gr	.59
3	Self-governance (Sg)	Gr, Cu, Oc	.58
4	Cu. Mosk. Sg.	Gr, Oc, Sr	.56

Table 3. Alternative regression models

The choice between different models is based upon two considerations:
1. The chosen model should account for no less variance than the alternatives.
2. The chosen model should represent the theoretical model if possible. Actually, the theoretical model consists of two different parts: one part with the decision latitude variables as independent variables and one part in which the task-structure variables are the independent variables. To test the specific implications of the model, with exclusion of interfering effects of interrelations *between* the variables of both parts, analyses on these different parts of the model were carried out.

In Table 4 the partial correlations of the task-structure variables with the dependent variable 'Influence in decision-making' are presented.

No	Variable	Variable partialled out			zero order corr.
		group relations	motivation/ skill	both	
1	Required cooperation (Rc)	–08	–19	–08	–29
2	Conversion uncertainty (Cu)	.28	.26	.28	.27

Table 4. Partial correlations of task-structure variables
with 'Influence in decision-making'

From Table 4 it is concluded that there is a direct relationship between 'conversion uncertainty' and 'influence' and an indirect relationship (via 'group relations') between 'required cooperation' and 'influence'

In Table 5 the partial correlations of the decision latitude variables with 'influence' are presented.

No	Variable	Variable partialled out organizational climate (Oc)	zero order correlation
1	Self-governance (Sg)	.30	.46
2	Self-regulation (Sr)	.29	.20

Table 5. Partial correlations of decision latitude variables
with 'Influence in decision-making'

From Table 5 it is concluded that there are *direct* relationships
between the two predictor variables and the dependent variable. Combination of these results leads to the choice of the second model in
Table 3. This model is presented in Figure 4.

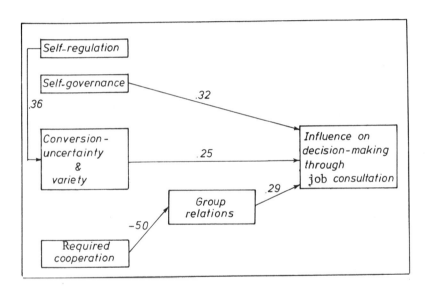

Figure 4. Regression model: Test of the theoretically predicted
relations. The coefficients are standard regression
coefficients

Comparison of the model with the theoretical model leads to the following conclusions. Two of the three predicted direct relationships with the
dependent variable are confirmed. 'Self-governance' and 'conversion uncertainty' (+ 'variety') are direct predictors. Only one of the five
predicted indirect relationships is confirmed: 'required cooperation' via

'group relations'. The predicted relationships between 'self-regulation' and 'conversion uncertainty' is also confirmed.

DISCUSSION

Being correlational, this study has its limitations in testing causal relationships. With this in mind, two important conclusions can be drawn from the results of the analyses.

1. The basic hypothesis of the study is essentially confirmed. Task structure and organization design are preconditions for job consultation. That is: actual influence in decision-making via job consultation depends on task-structure and decision latitude.

2. 'Relational' variables like 'motivation and skill', 'group relations' and 'organizational climate' have no direct independent effect. The zero-order correlations of these variables with the 'dependent' variable disappear completely when controlling for the structural variables.

A practical implication of the results is that interventions like team-building, improvement of climate or improvement of motivation and skill are insufficient to promote influence on decision-making through job consultation. From an ideological point of view this means that not only political and formal power conditions have to be changed to reach the ideal of participation. A psychological approach to participation should be specific about the motivating characteristics of participatory arrangements depending on task and organization variables. The productivity approach should pay more attention to the question if and exactly how job consultation stimulates a productive and flexible functioning of the organization.

In the beginning of this chapter the potential functions of job consultation were discussed. It was concluded, that uncertainty and variety, mutual dependency (functional, emotional or professional) and need for innovation and change, are important preconditions of job consultation. Another important precondition is the latitude to cope with uncertainty and variety. The model was for the greater part based upon these general conclusions. The aim of this study was to investigate the impact of some vital preconditions. However, we are aware of the fact that sometimes the relationships between task and organization on the one hand and job consultation on the other hand are more complicated. For instance, there may be discrepancies between the (subjectively experienced) interests of the participants and the goals of the organization, because:

- consultation on innovation and rationalization may lead to reduction of the number of jobs;
- mutual coordination of tasks may reduce individual freedom of subordinates;
- consultation may negatively affect the experienced control and power of the superior.

Technically required cooperation as an intrinsic part of the production process gives the individual members a broad view on the functioning of their work-unit (Van Assen, 1980). Thus, there is a viable basis for job consultation about problems concerning cooperation and coordination. One of our predictions is that technically required cooperation stimulates job consultation. Nevertheless, it is not sure that members of such units always feel a strong need for formal periodical job consultation. A lot of problems may be discussed in the daily interactions. For units without self-regulation latitude, job consultation may have counterbalancing functions.

De Sitter (1981), for instance, states that 'work pressure' stimulates the need for job consultation if the workers have no decision latitude in their daily work. In this study actually one of the factors of the principal components analysis was interpreted as 'work pressure'. This factor did not fit in our model and 'work pressure' was an ad hoc interpretation. Therefore it was left out. Still it is interesting to test the counterbalance hypotheses in an explorative way.

The results of a regression analysis including the ad hoc variable 'work pressure' are more or less in agreement with this hypothesis: 'work pressure' appears to be an independent predictor of job consultation and correlates (weakly) negatively with self-regulation. This short conclusion leads to the conclusion that more research is needed to get a more complete picture of the sometimes complex and seemingly paradoxal relationship between task, organization and job consultation.

REFERENCES

Aarts, C.A.J.M., Evaluatie van het werkoverleg binnen de diensten van de Technische Hogeschool Eindhoven. T.H.E., Afd. Bedrijfskunde, 1982.

Argyris, C., Integrating the individual and the organization. New York: Wiley, 1964.

Assen, A. van, Organisatie-ontwerp, een analyse model voor werkoverleg en werkstructurering. In: Assen, A. van, F. den Hertog & P. Koopman (Eds.), Organiseren met een menselijke maat. Alphen a/d Rijn: Samson, 1980.

Beale, E.M.L. & R.J.A. Little, Missing values in multivariable analysis. Journal Royal Stat. Soc. B., 1975, 30, 129-145.

Dachler, H. & B. Wilpert, Conceptual dimensions and boundaries of participation in organizations; a critical evaluation. Admin. Sci. Quart., 1978, 23, 1-29.

Drenth, P.J.D. & P.L. Koopman, Experiences with 'werkoverleg' in the Netherlands; implications for quality circles. General Management, 198:

McGregor, D.M., The human side of Enterprise. New York: McGraw-Hill, 1960.

Sitter, L.U. de, Op weg naar nieuwe fabrieken en kantoren. Deventer: Kluwer, 1981.

Susman, G.I., Autonomy at work, a socio-technical analysis of participative management. Praeger Publishers, 1976.

V
ORGANIZATIONAL NATURE AND CHANGE

15. CLIMATE AND CULTURE

R. Nauta

INTRODUCTION

Climate and atmosphere are sometimes used as concepts to characterize
and summarize the psychological meaning of differences between organizations, with respect to geographical location, interior decoration, customers and personnel, goods and services, history and future orientation.
All these specific attributes of the organization contribute to a global, molar impression - the feel of the work place. Churches and pubs,
schools and universities, multinationals and the grocery on the corner,
each has its own atmosphere.

Although the concept of climate is meant to characterize organizations, the observer is always present at the background. His perceptions
of specific situations are translated into an impression of the total
climate. This confoundedness of person and situation leads to a certain
ambiguity in the use of the term climate. Hence theoretical and method-
ical questions rise with respect to level and unit of analysis as well
as personal and organizational determinants and effects of climate perceptions.

A less psychologically oriented concept like culture might possibly
give a less equivocal representation of quality and style of the organization. When one uses the word culture to denote the specific style
of the organization, emphasis is put on the meaning and communicative
aspects of organizational relationships, procedures and artifacts. More
so than climate, it seems obvious that organizational culture is not

just the product of an individual's interpretation of what is going on. Culture refers to an outside, external, intersubjective reality, which might be the collective result of many individual actions, interactions and interpretations and, in turn, also influences these actions and perceptions. Pettigrew describes culture as the system of publicly and collectively subscribed meanings operating for a given group at a given time (Pettigrew, 1979, p. 74). Cultural elements like symbols, language, rituals and myths, ideologies and vocabularies direct attention toward the mobilization of consciousness and purpose, the codification of meaning, the emergence of normative patterns, the rise and fall of systems of leadership and strategies of legitimization. It is through such processes that cultures evolve, and in turn, act as a determinant or constraint on further attempts to handle issues of purpose, integration and commitment (Pettigrew, 1979, p. 576-577).

In this chapter it will be suggested that the link between climate and culture might be found in (a typology of) motivated behaviour patterns. By watching motivation and behaviour in a certain way, these patterns can be regarded on the one hand as a reflection of the collective culture of the organization and on the other hand as representing a particular individual perspective and personal experience of the organization.

First a brief analysis will be given of the appropriateness and relevance of the climate concept for describing differences between and within organizations. In discussing a recent research project on organizational climate, behaviour and motivation, it will be suggested that climate perceptions are related to the development and support of a professional identity, while the structure of the relations between behaviour and motivation (behaviour patterns) can be understood as representing sub-cultural differences within the organization. At the end some remarks will be made about the symbolic analysis of organizational life.

Organizational climate and psychological climate

In order to analyse the influence of environmental differences on individual behaviour in a psychologically consistent way, emphasis should
be laid on the perception of the environment (Campbell et al., 1970;
Indik, 1965). Perceptions of the organizational environment are referred to as perceptions of the climate of the organization (Schneider,
1975; James & Jones, 1974). The totality of these perceptions is sometimes described with the term *organizational climate*, especially when
the object of these perceptions is stressed; sometimes as *psychological
climate*, when there is a focus on the person who perceives and in his
perception tries to structure and order the environmental stimuli and
impressions (Mischel, 1977; Jones & James, 1979).

The ambiguity deriving from this subject-object determination of
climate perceptions is most effectively described by Woodman and King
(1978, p. 818): "phenomenologically, climate is external to the individual, yet cognitively the climate is internal to the extent that
it is effected by individual perceptions." The perceptual-cognitive
character of climate perceptions implies that there does not need to
exist agreement between different observers with regard to the nature
of the situation, nor that these perceptions accurately reflect the
factual situation. On the other hand, climate is reality-based and thus
capable of being shared in the sense that observers or participants
may agree upon the climate of an organization or group, although this
consensus may be constrained, as already suggested, by individual differences (cf. Woodman & King, 1978, p. 818).

When organizational characteristics are perceived and when these
perceptions are shared by different observers the term organizational
climate might be used and distinguished from psychological climate
which refers to a person's idiosyncratic, multidimensional, descrip-
tive model of the organization (Gavin & Howe, 1975).

Substantive references of climate perceptions

There is also some disagreement about the substantive reference of climate perceptions. Three different approaches to this issue can be distinguished.

Organizational perspective

Some researchers stress the importance of the organizational relevance of climate perceptions. James and his co-workers (James et al., 1977; 1979) refer to those environmental aspects which characterize different levels in the organization - task, job, workgroup, department - in analyzing its climate. Others, e.g. Pennings (1982) have argued that design variables of the organization - like quality of communication between levels, social interaction with local environment, customer orientation, or personnel mix - are the main contributors to differences in style between organizations. Therefore these attributes should be considered as ingredients or determinants of the climate of the organization. In a review of the literature on organizational climate Heller et al. (1982) conclude that process variables like number of performance reviews per year, professional autonomy or support appear to have a stronger relationship with the perceived work environment than structural variables (cf. Lawler et al., 1974), of which size seems to indicate the more consistent relationship with various climate dimensions (Payne & Pugh, 1976). In their own research they explain the absence of a strong relationship between subjective and objective measures of organizational climate post-hoc by suggesting the importance of such social variables as the attributes of the leader.

Managerial perspective

In a second approach it is assumed that those who possess power within an environment determine environmental variation. In this line of thinking, Litwin and Stringer (1968) emphasize aspects of leadership behaviour which create different motivation patterns in otherwise comparable, artificial, organizations, and Schneider and Bartlett (1968) ask

managers to describe their behaviours and attitudes in order to determine the degree of support characterizing the agency's climate. Woodman
and Kingman (1982) explain the disagreement between different hierarchical levels as an artefact of the way climate is measured. The conceptual nature of most climate instruments is more in line with managerial thinking than with experiences at the shop floor.

Psychological perspective

In the third approach the psychological relevance of the environment
for the participant is at the centre of interest. In the tradition of
research done by Stern and Murray (1938), stressing the relevance of
person-environment fit, the environment is described in terms of a
priori notions about personality structure (Pace & Stern, 1958; cf.
Cohen & Scaife, 1973; Pervin, 1967, 1968; Pervin & Rubin, 1967). Self
and environment are described in mutually relevant, commensurate terms
like: warm, friendly, open, aggressive, etc. (Graham, 1976).

In a more indirect way the subjective relevance of organizational
climate is based on the way in which environmental features are structured, interpreted and conceptualized into a psychologically meaningful whole. Meglino (1976), in discussing the relationship between climate and performance, suggests that the evaluation dimension of climate
perception is the most important one in explaining seemingly contradictory results. Job performance can be viewed as an interaction effect of
the degree to which climate is evaluative, and task competence (cf.
Joyce et al., 1982). Evaluation enhances behaviour that is well learned,
but interferes with behaviour which is poorly learned. While the degree
of evaluation is properly a perceptual dimension of organizational climate, it relates to a number of organizational or sub-unit factors
which are relatively enduring (e.g. closeness of supervision, presence
of deadlines, competition among employees, etc.) (Meglino, 1976, p. 60).
He suggests that in many instruments used to measure climate, certain
items or factors (reward orientation, support, consideration, warmth -
Campbell et al., 1970), relate to perceived evaluation. The behavioural
effects of different motivational climates in the Litwin and Stringer
(1968) study might also be described as an interaction effects of high

259

task competence (easy tasks) and a high (achievement oriented) or low (affiliation oriented) level of evaluation. Constructing or conceptualizing more molar and unitary interpretations of the organizational environment helps to a better understanding of its psychological meaning and behavioural importance.

EDUCATION AND 'MOTIVATIONAL CLIMATE'

The preceding paragraph showed the conceptual and methodological problems in research on collective phenomena like style and climate, with the individual as unit of analysis. The concept of psychological climate must be understood as a reductionistic solution to these problems. It views psychological climate as something which exists within the boundaries of individual experience.

   In this paragraph a research project will be briefly discussed in which climate perceptions appeared to support the development of a particular identity. Some motivationally distinct behaviour patterns of individuals were found, which could be interpreted as reflecting differences between subcultures within a technical universiy. In this way an organizationally relevant characterization of the university environment was reached.

A study of student motivation and behaviour

In this research project 280 students of a university of technology in the Netherlands participated. They belonged to two different departments (physics and engineering) and were more or less advanced on their route to the master's degree. The departments differed in the emphasis laid on either a pure or an applied research orientation. Graduates of these departments worked either in research or managerial jobs. According to current opinion on the campus, both departments had quite a different culture and atmosphere.

   By answering a questionnaire students provided information on the amount of time they spent, during an average week, on each of several categories of activities (studies, culture, politics, sports, religion, social contacts, etc.), on the degree to which they expected that engaging in such an activity would help or hinder to attain each of several outcomes (instrumentally), and information on the valence they attributed to these 12 outcomes. The outcomes could be divided, theoretically and empirically, into four sets: scientific (e.g. being able to follow new developments in my field of specialization), professional (e.g. being able to solve technical problems in a practical manner), personal (e.g. getting insight in my capabilities and shortcomings), societal (e.g. to contribute to the development of our society). The format of these questions was derived from an expectancy-valence model of motivation (Nauta, 1982, reports this study in detail).

Given the importance of outcome valences in this motivation model, it seemed correct to assume that the dominant values of the organizations might influence the relation between motivation and the time spent on an activity (cf. Pritchard & Karasick, 1973). When there is agreemnt between individual and organization in the values attributed to certain outcomes, students will be stimulated and rewarded for behaviour that is consistent with these outcomes. The value aspect of the motivational climate was measured by asking respondents to describe how their peers and the academic staff would value these different outcomes.

In discussing the results, the ambigious meaning of climate perceptions is illustrated. More than representing an external reality, they seem to be used to legitimize and justify 'deviant' motivation and behaviour patterns.

Psychological climate and student identity

The motivation for *study activities* stem from the expectation that they will lead to personal and societal outcomes. This result is surprising when one expects study activities to be motivated primarily by the instrumentality and/or valence of scientific and professional outcomes. It becomes understandable when one assumes that if a 'programmed', average time expenditure on education is guaranteed, by the institution, to lead to scientific and professional outcomes, more or less time spent on study activities is dependent on a student's motivation in relation to the personal and societal utility of his studies.

The motivational climate supports the individual pattern of motivation:

the higher one's peers and the academic staff are perceived to value personal and societal outcomes, and the higher the consensus with regard to these outcomes, the more time students will spend on study activities. Alternatively, one can argue that students attribute to their peers a higher outcome valence, in order to legitimize the time spent on study activities in the pursuit of these personal and societal outcomes. In this case climate perceptions may also function to reinforce identity.

An individual's identity may not only be reinforced by emphasizing congruence with his peers, but also by stressing differences in motivation and behaviour. E.g. students motivated by the perceived scientific instrumentality of their studies view themselves as different from their peers. More than their fellow students they seem to value scientific understanding and knowledge. Based on an impression of what is normal behaviour within the organization's culture, combined with an understanding of their own 'deviant' motivation, they attribute a different, opposite, value pattern to their peers. In doing so, climate perceptions, i.e. the outcome valences attributed to peers and faculty, emphasize the exceptional behaviour pattern exhibited by the students in question given the dominant culture at the university.

In relation to the passive and active involvement in *cultural activities*, a parallel process of contrasting the motivational climate with one's own values and behaviour takes place. It was found that in general the higher the perceived personal relevance of cultural activities and the lower the values attributed to professional outcomes, the more time is spent on this type of activities. However, students who spend more time on culture, tend to disagree with their peers over the value of professional outcomes. This might be interpreted in terms of an attributed contrast between one's own and other's identity, based on the experience of a deviant experienced involvement in the cultural sphere. "Because most students spend far less time on cultural affairs than I do myself, they must be different from me. And probably, given my own value priorities, be more practical and professional oriented."

These results illustrate the psychologically complex nature of the perceptual/attributional effects involved in processes of rationalization and justification of behaviour (cf. Salancik & Pfeffer, 1978). But they do not seem to offer any conclusive or consistent characterization of the relevant organizational environment.

ORGANIZATIONAL CULTURE AND PATTERNS OF MOTIVATED BEHAVIOUR

The results discussed in the preceding paragraph illustrate the subjective, psychological meaning of climate perceptions. In analyzing behaviour patterns and their motivational base, a more objective but still psychologically meaningful way to describe the quality of the environment and the style of the organization, was found. Goodenough, as cited by Dougherty and Fernandez (1982, p. 413), emphasizes the cognitive aspects of culture: whatever it is one must know or believe in order to operate in a manner acceptable to other members of (his) culture and to do so in any role accepted by them for themselves. Particularly interesting in this definition of culture is the link which is suggested between systems of thought and behaviour which normatively characterizes a group or organization. Normative in this respect refers to the distribution and frequency of certain activities. As such, the analysis of the dimensions on which motivation and behaviour can be related and ordered, and the analysis of the relative importance of certain behaviour patterns, illuminate the cultural meaning of the organization by showing how certain interaction patterns are explained and justified. It is clear that these patterns and dimensions are collective characteristics, not individual projections or attributes. The difference between the individual and collective level might suggest a relevant distinction between the climate and culture interpretations of organizational quality and style.

Dimensions and patterns

The question of how and why students distribute time over different categories of activity, may be seen a problem of motivated choice. The problem is a special one. Choice is not between mutually exclusive alternatives, but relates to the relative degree of time spent on each of several categories of activities. Choice, in other words is not a matter of either/or but an issue of more or less. This choice problem can be analysed, between subjects, with the help of canonical correlation and discriminant analysis. The first method analyses empirical patterns of time expenditure and motivation, the latter one can be used to answer the question how motivational variables (beliefs and values) contribute to the discrimination of several, formally distinct, behaviour patterns. Both methods show, of course, a convergence of results (see appendix 1 and 2).

When the expenditure of time on the different categories is standardized, a comparison of the relative importance of different behaviour patterns is made possible. Logically, three different, molar patterns can be constructed (Table 1). A pattern labeled study (S) characterizes those students who spend relatively more time on study than on politics or culture - i.e. their standard-score for studies is higher. Politics (P) characterizes those students who spend relatively more time on politics than on their studies or on cultural activities. And in a similar way, culture (C) defines those students who spend, relatively speaking, most of their time on cultural affairs. Through discriminant and canonical analysis these patterns can be discriminated and related to motivational variables.

Name	Main characteristics	N
Study	study > pol - study > cult	124
Politics	pol > study - pol > cult	76
Culture	cult > study - cult > pol	76

Table 1. Patterns of relative time distribution.

Two dimensions seem to explain the relations between behaviour and motivation. On the first dimension *study* activities are contrasted with *cultural* affairs. This reflects that some students spend more time on their studies at the cost of time spent on culture, while others spend more time on culture at the cost of time spent on their studies. This choice is a motivated one and dependent on the valence of professional

and scientific outcomes, on beliefs about the attainability of personal
and societal outcomes and on the importance that one's fellow-students
seem to attach to the activities in question. For students who spend
much time on study activities (and, consequently, a very small amount
of time on cultural activities) scientific and professional outcomes
are very important. They believe also that study activities (and not
cultural activities) will help to attain personal and societal outcomes,
and that their fellow-students attach more importance to study than to
culture. On the other side there are students who spend more time on
cultural activities at the cost of study-related effort, because they
think that particularly these cultural activities will lead to personal
and societal outcomes, that their fellow-students attach no great importance to study activities, and for whom scientific and professional
outcomes are relatively unimportant.

A second dimension, relating specific elements of motivation and behaviour, illustrates a behaviour pattern characterized by the relative
amount of time spent on *political* activities as explained by the belief
in the instrumentality of political activities and the valence of personal and societal outcomes.

These patterns may be seen a characteristic of the organization. The
way in which students work and live on the campus of this technical university, can be described in a meaningful manner by the quality and
degree of their relative interest in study or culture and their involvement in political affairs.

Typology

The dimensions on which different behaviour patterns were discriminated,
can also be used to construct a typology of student orientations and
educational involvement. Such a typology can be viewed as a psychological
interpretation of organizational culture and subculture. In many
business-firms and multinationals, the culture of the organization is
personified in the opinions, attitudes, beliefs and behaviours of its
personnel. That makes it possible to speak of a 'Shell-man' and distinguish such a person from a 'Philips-man'. For workers in other

organizations, only a professional or institutional reference seems relevant - the teacher, the doctor, the worker in a social welfare organization. The fact that there is no organizational base for their stereotype of work involvement, might be interpreted as a relative dominance of professional and institutional cultures over organizational ones.

The two dimensions along which motivated behaviour patterns were discriminated, allow for four extreme student-types. In Figure 1 the relevant quadrants are shown.

Figure 1. Typology of student orientations and educational involvement

Activity		politically		
		active		not active
more time spent on	study	1 X		2 0
	culture	3 ▢		4 +

Valences		contribution to society		
		important		not important
contribution important to science and		1 X		2 0
profession not important		3 ▢		4 +

Instrumentality		political activities		
		instrumental		not instrumental
personal and study societal outcomes		1 X		2 0
attained through culture		3 ▢		4 +

1 X = Manager - Generalist   3 ▢ = Alternative activist

2 0 = Engineer - Specialist   4 + = Cultural connoisseur

Quadrant 1 pictures the student who is active in politics and spends a lot of time on his studies as well. Both educational and political activities are perceived as instrumental, especially so for personal and societal outcomes. Scientific and professional outcomes are important. The student characterized by these beliefs and behaviours could be described as the potential *manager-generalist*.

Quadrant 2 pictures a student who is primarily interested in his studies. He values scientific and professional outcomes, and thinks that his studies are instrumental for personal development and prepare him for his future contribution to society. This student is the prototype of the *engineer-specialist*.

Quadrant 3 shows the student who is rather out of place in this technical university. He is relatively more interested in cultural activities than in his studies, he is politically active too, he does not value scientific and professional outcomes very much, but he is convinced of the utility of political involvement and the personal and societal instrumentality of his cultural interests. This student might be called the *alternative activist*.

Quadrant 4 shows a behaviour pattern dominated by culture (at the cost of study) and a rejection of political involvement. The student characterized by this pattern might be labelled the *cultural connoisseur*.

These types can be paired along the diagonals of the matrix: Manager versus connoisseur and specialist versus activist. The most representative student type seems to be the (potential) manager. The man who likes the organize and run a business-firm. The engineer is representing the more professional orientation within the university, the staff specialist. The activist is interested in all things but his studies, he is actively pursuing personal development and not primarily a professional training. The cultural connoisseur has restricted his activities and interests to the cultural sphere of life. He enjoys the pleasures of this involvement in cultural events and activities, and bears the burden of his study only because it is the necessary condition for his presence at this campus.

Given the absolute and relative amount of time spend on activities (cf. Table 1), it could be argued that the manager represents the dominant student culture in this university, the alternative activist and engineer-specialist represent different and opposite subcultures, while the cultural connoisseur seems to belong to the counter-culture of this university.

CONCLUSION

To conclude that climate is perceptual and subjective and culture is behavioural and collective, would summarize quite succintly the discussion in the preceding paragraphs. The previous analysis is only an illustration of the attempt to define culture in terms of empirically constructed, motivated behaviour patterns. A complexer picture might have resulted from involving more activities, beliefs and attitudes in the analysis. Still, the analysis seems to represent some reality in this organization as it can be explained from structural arrangements and historical developments. Introducing a typology to emphasize the psychological meaning of organizational cultures and - subcultures, might open a perspective to a broader analysis of culture. Not only cognitive elements, but also symbolic elements, should be incorporated in such an approach. The analysis of stories, language, myths, rituals and ceremonies characterizing a particular (sub)culture represents the growing interest in the symbolic meaning of organizations (Dandridge, Mitroff & Joyce, 1980; Pettigrew, 1979; Kanter & Stein, 1979).

As a symbolic meaning system the culture of the organization provides a social identity for its members (Louis, 1980a). In the socialization process new-comers make sense of themselves and their environment through a personalized version of the local cultural frame-of-reference or interpretation scheme (Louis, 1980b, p. 2). Analysis of socialization processes therefore may lead to a better understanding of the cultural milieu of the organization, its style and psychological quality.

REFERENCES

Campbell, J.P., M.D. Dunnette, E.E. Lawler & K.E. Weick, Managerial behavior, performance and effectiveness. New York: Mc Graw-Hill, 1970.

Cohen, L. & R. Scaife, Self-environment similarity and satisfaction in a college of education. Human Relations, 1973, 26, 89-99.

Dandridge, Th.C., J. Mitroff & W.F. Joyce, Organizational symbolism, a topic to expand organizational analysis. Academy of Management Review, 1980, 5, 77-82.

Dougherty, J.W.D. & J.W. Fernandez, Introduction special issue on Cognition and Symbolism. American Ethnologist, 1981, 8, 413-421.

Gavin, J.F. & J.G. Howe, Psychological climate: some theoretical and empirical considerations. Behavioral Science, 1975, 20, 228-240.

Georgopoulos, B.S., Normative structure variables and organizational behavior. Human Relations, 1965, 10, 155-169.

Graham, W.K., Commensurate characterizations of persons, groups, and organizations: development of the Trait Ascription Questionnaire. Human Relations, 1976, 29, 607-622.

Guion, R.M., A note on organizational climate. Organizational behavior and Human Performance, 1973, 9, 120-125.

Heller, R.M., S.J. Guastello & M. Aderman, Convergent and discriminant validity of psychological and objective indices of organizational climate. Psychological Reports, 1982.

Hellriegel, D. & J.W. Slocum, Organizational climate: measures, research and contingencies. Academy of Management Journal, 1974, 17, 255-280.

Indik, B.P., Organization size and member participation. Human Relations, 1965, 18, 339-350.

James, L.R. & A.P. Jones, Organizational climate: a review of theory and research. Psychological Bulletin, 1974, 81, 1096-1112.

James, L.R., A. Hartman, M.W. Stebbins & A.P. Jones, Relationship between psychological climate and a VIE model for work motivation. Personnel Psychology, 1977, 30, 229-254.

James, L.R., M.J. Gent, J.J. Hater & K.E. Goray, Correlates of psychological influence: an illustration of the psychological climate approach to work environment perceptions. Personnel Psychology, 1979, 32, 563-538.

Jones, A.P. & L.R. James, Psychological climate: dimensions and relationships of individual and aggregated work environment perceptions. Organizational Behavior and Human Performance, 1979, 23, 201-250.

Joyce, W., J.W. Slocum & M.A. Van Glinow, Person-situation interaction: competing models of fit. Journal of Occupational Psychology, 1982, 3, 265-280.

Kanter, R.M. & B.A. Stein (Eds.), Organizational life. New York: Basic Books, 1979.

Lawler, E.E., D.T. Hall & G.R. Oldham, Organization climate: relationship to organizational structure, process and performance. Organizational Behavior and Human Performance, 1974, 11, 139-155.

Litwin, G.H., Organizational climate and practices questionnaire. Boston: Forum Corp., 1974.

Litwin, G.H. & R.H. Stringer, Motivation and organizational climate. Boston: Harvard University, 1969.

Louis, M.R., Culture in organizations - toward an explication of cultural phenomena in organizations and an understanding of the role of culture in organizational socialization. Monterey, Naval Postgraduate School, 1980.

Louis, M.R., Surprise and sense-making: what newcomers experience in entering unfamiliar organizational settings. Administrative Science Quarterly, 1980, 25, 226-251.

Meglino, B.M., Theoretical synthesis of job performance and the evaluative dimension of organizational climate: a social psychological perspective. Academy of Management Review, 1976, 1, 58-65.

Murray, H.A., Explorations in personality. New York: Oxford University Press, 1938.

Nauta, R., Motivatie en gedrag. Assen: Van Gorcum, 1982.

Pace, C.R. & G.C. Stern, An approach to the measurement of psychological characteristics of college environments. Journal of Educational Psychology, 1958, 49, 269-277.

Payne, R.L. & D.S. Pugh, Organizational structure and climate. In: M.D. Dunnette (Ed.), Handbook of industrial and organizational psychology. Chicago: Rand McNally, 1976, 1125-1174.

Pennings, J.M., Organizational climate, a methodological note. New York: Graduate School of Business, Colombia University, 1982.

Pervin, L.A., Satisfaction and perceived self-environment similarity: a semantic differential study of student-college interaction. Journal of Personality and Social Psychology, 1967, 35, 623-634.

Pervin, L.A., Performance and satisfaction as a function of individual-environment fit. Psychological Bulletin, 1968, 69, 56-58.

Pervin, L.A. & D.B. Rubin, Student dissatisfaction with college and the college dropout: a transactional approach. Journal of Social Psychology, 1967, 72, 285-295.

Pettigrew, A.M., On studying organizational cultures. Administrative Science Quarterly, 1979, 24, 570-581.

Pritchard, R.D. & B.W. Karasick, The effects of organizational climate on managerial job performance and satisfaction. Organizational Behavior and Human Performance, 1973, 9, 126-146.

Salancik, G.R. & J. Pfeffer, A social information approach to job attitudes and task design. Administrative Science Quarterly, 1978, 23, 224-253.

Schneider, B., Organizational climates: an essay. Personnel Psychology, 1975, 28, 447-479.

Schneider, B. & C.J. Bartlett, Individual differences and organizational climate. I. The research plan and questionnaire development. Personnel Psychology, 1968, 21, 323-333.

Schneider, B. & C.J. Bartlett, Individual differences and organizational climate by multitrait, mulirater matrix. Personnel Psychology, 1970, 23, 493-512.

Schneider, B. & D.T. Hall, Toward specifying the concept of work climate: a study of roman-catholic diocese priests. Journal of Applied Psychology, 1972, 56, 447-455.

Woodman, R.W. & D.C. King, Organizational climate: science or folklore. Academy of Management Review, 1978, 3, 816-826.

Distribution of time among study, politics and culture and motivational determinants: canonical analysis.

CANONICAL ANALYSIS				
Canonical correlation	$.471^{xxx}$		$.418^{xx}$	
Eigenvalue	.222		.175	
Redundancy: $R^2_{c.p.(2)}$		.14		

VARIANCE MATRIX[1]				
CRITERIUM CARIABLES	CRITERIUM VARIATES		PREDICTOR VARIATES	
Z_{study}	.37	.01	.08	.00
$Z_{politics}$	.01	.98	.00	.17
$Z_{culture}$	.74	.00	.17	.00
$R^2_{c.p.(2)} = \sum_{k=1}^{2} \sum_{j=1}^{3} L^2_{jk}/3) =$	.08		.06	

PREDICTOR VARIABLES	CRITERIUM VARIATES		PREDICTOR VARIATES	
OUTCOME VALENCES				
SCIENCE	.01	.00	.07	.00
PROFESSION	.03	.00	.12	.00
PERSON	.00	.01	.00	.06
SOCIETY	.00	.03	.00	.19
INSTRUMENTALITY STUDY				
SCIENCE	.00	.00	.01	.00
PROFESSION	.01	.01	.04	.05
PERSON	.06	.00	.26	.00
SOCIETY	.04	.01	.20	.05
INSTRUMENTALITY POLITICS				
SCIENCE	.00	.04	.02	.23
PROFESSION	.00	.04	.01	.20
PERSON	.00	.08	.02	.46
SOCIETY	.01	.09	.03	.53
INSTRUMENTALITY CULTURE				
SCIENCE	.00	.01	.00	.04
PROFESSION	.01	.00	.04	.01
PERSON	.07	.00	.31	.00
SOCIETY	.03	.00	.14	.02

PREDICTOR VARIABLES	CRITERIUM VARIATES		PREDICTOR VARIATES	
NORMS STUDY				
STUDENTS	.01	.00	.04	.02
FACULTY	.00	*.00*	.01	.01
NORMS POLITICS				
STUDENTS	*.01*	.01	*.05*	.04
FACULTY	*.04*	.00	.00	*.01*
NORMS CULTURE				
STUDENTS	*.02*	.00	*.10*	*.00*
FACULTY	.00	*.00*	.00	*.00*
n=276 xx: p < .01 xxx: p < .001				

1) Loadings in the variance matrix are squared correlations between a
variable and a variate. Loadings with a negative sign in the structure matrix are cursified.

APPENDIX 2

Distribution of time among study, politics and culture and motivational
determinants: discriminant analysis.

DISCRIMINANT ANALYSIS							
Discriminant function	Eigenvalue	Canonical correlation	Discriminant function	Wilks lambda	Chi^2	df	p
I.	.182	.393	1-2	.730	82.45	44	.000
II.	.158	.369	2	.863	38.53	21	.011

STRUCTURE MATRIX		
Variables	Discriminant Functions	
	I	II
OUTCOME VALENCES		
SCIENCE	.357	-.001
PROFESSION	.404	.112
PERSON	-.010	.123
SOCIETY	.008	.437
INSTRUMENTALITY STUDY		
SCIENCE	.180	.028
PROFESSION	.305	.010
PERSON	.366	.148
SOCIETY	.366	-.095
INSTRUMENTALITY POLITICS		
SCIENCE	-.112	.366
PROFESSION	-.079	.323
PERSON	-.298	.499
SOCIETY	-.273	.682
INSTRUMENTALITY CULTURE		
SCIENCE	-.133	.152
PROFESSION	-.246	.008
PERSON	-.446	-.029
SOCIETY	-.405	-.078
NORMS STUDY		
STUDENTS	.355	.217
FACULTY	-.149	-.024
NORMS POLITICS		
STUDENTS	-.058	-.123
FACULTY	-.076	-.032
NORMS CULTURE		
STUDENTS	-.165	-.071
FACULTY	.047	-.363

APPENDIX 3

Primary patterns of time distribution:
group centroids in the discriminant space.

Primary pattern	Discriminant functions	
	I	II
STUDY (S)	.418	-.200
POLITICS (P)	-.079	.637
CULTURE (C)	-.603	-.310

16. ORGANIZATIONAL DEVELOPMENT IN PSYCHIATRIC HOSPITALS: SOME EXPERIENCES AND CONSIDERATIONS

INTRODUCTION

This contribution draws upon some of the theoretical ideas and results obtained during a series of organizational change studies in several Welsh hospitals. These studies began in 1975 with the following objectives:

1. to identify aspects of their work, and the way it was organised, which ward nursing staff regarded as unsatisfactory;

2. to advise and assist such organizational changes as might improve matters;

3. to evaluate the impact of these changes.

The research orientation towards our first objective had clearly to be as detached and objective as possible. But it should lead to inferences about work attitudes and job satisfaction that were firmly anchored to the nurses' own experiences and views, as well as to their behaviour. It soon became apparent that in order to interpret the data credibly, we would also have to enquire into the nature of the 'nursing function' and 'patient care', as perceived by nurses. Nor could we avoid considerations of organizational effectiveness when trying to assess the importance of attitudes and satisfaction.

Our second and third objectives were to be reached through an 'action research' approach. Here our role would be a collaborative and 'interventionist' one, helping to implement and sustain the process of organizational change as well as monitoring its impact. Any success would depend upon nurses being persuaded of a need for change and being sufficiently well motivated to sustain any agreed ways of meeting that need.

At this point in time, the National Health Service in Britain was struggling to implement a profound re-organization of its administrative and professional management structures, at all levels. A particularly important innovation was the setting-up of a new grading structure for State Registered Nurses (i.e. the fully qualified ones), whose direct control over their own professional work and careers was to be more firmly established than hitherto. Morale in the hospital service was uncomfortably low, especially among psychiatric nurses. Not only was there the stress of coping with a re-definition of roles, but public interest in and criticism of the quality of patient care was growing. It was around that time, for example, that Ethical Committees (with lay members as well as professional) were set up in each hospital to act as watch-dogs over research and practice affecting the interests of patients. Adverse effects of these various pressures showed up in the high wastage rate for student nurses in training (about 1 in 5 at one psychiatric hospital in the local Area Health Authority), and in the very first overt expressions of militant action by hospital staff, designed to remedy what many of them saw as unsatisfactory pay and conditions.

This, then, was the organizational climate in which our research team began to operate. The research programme discussed here went on until 1980. Detailed accounts of most of it have already been reported (Wallis & Cope, 1980a, 1980b; Cope & Cox, 1980; Cope, 1981). In this chapter I shall concentrate on the methodological and theoretical aspects of our work in two psychiatric hospitals, each with just over 400 beds, one situated at the edge of a city and the other in a relatively remote rural location. Senior nursus suggested that our studies should focus on the Psychogeriatric Wards, four in the one hospital, and two in the other. In British hospitals, most of the day-to-day nursing care for psycho-geriatric patients is in the hands of untrained Nursing Assistants, supervised by qualified (i.e. Registered Mental) Nurses.

METHOD

Our initial concern was to examine work content and the assignment of roles and responsibilities at ward level. Detailed enquiries about pay had been expressly excluded from our terms of reference. We were also warned to tread carefully with respect to enquiries about satisfaction with professional supervision. Since a 'task and role' orientation towards data-collection was implied, the conceptual framework adopted was broadly as in Figure 1. It incorporates the well-known 'socio-technical' principle of interacting organizational relationships, adding to it the equally important psychological component. Their quality of working life (QWL), as perceived by nurses, was expected to supplement what could be inferred from their expression of job satisfaction.

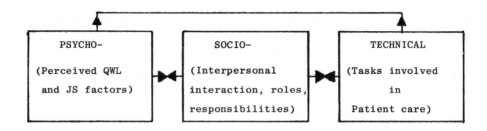

Initial Conceptual Framework For
Study of Psychogeriatric Unit

Figure 1. Psycho-socio-technical system of patient care

The working model has implications for empirical data collection. Social and technical factors can be inferred directly from observation of behaviour and working conditions, and from hospital records or other documents. But less 'objective' methods are needed to elicit just how staff are perceiving and construing their day-to-day experience of the organization in which they work.

In the event, our systems approach led us to employ a number of different methods of data collection from each hospital. They amounted to the following:

a. *participant observation:* two members of the research team spent up to eight weeks working as Nursing Assistants; this proved to be not only informative for data collection purposes, but was a necessary

condition of gaining adequate credibility and acceptability from the
nursing and other hospital staff;

b. *interviews:* both open-ended and structured; and repeated with certain key individuals;

c. *questionnaires:* a brief extract from one questionnaire designed for
the first hospital is shown below;

d. *group discussions;*

e. *collection of critical incidents;*

f. *experimental introduction of special ward programmes,* where these
had lapsed or not been tried, e.g. reality-orientation therapy;
regular nursing and medical assessments of patients; personalised
clothing for patients;

g. *activity sampling* of nursing functions;

h. *documentary evidence.*

A distinctive, and perhaps controversial, feature of the project was
its action research mode. We were in fact obliged under the terms of
our research sponsorship to operate through an action research method.
Looking back over the five years work, it now seems inevitable that
any effective and lasting organizational change programme can only come
about through the joint client-researcher collaboration which action
research entails. However, our experience confirms that the action
researcher's role can be extremely stressful. It can confront him from
time to time with acute interpersonal sensitivities and ethical uncertainties related to personal responsibility, identification of problems,
and being direcly involved in organization development. He has somehow
to reconcile the customary research functions of data collection,
analysis, and interpretations, with the consultant change-agent's
function of helping to initiate, implement, and evaluate changes.

This is how satisfied I feel with:

	very satisfied	satisfied	neither satisfied nor dissatisfied	dissatisfied	very dissatisfied
The variety in my work					
The amount of recognition given for doing a good job					
The general status given to psychiatric nursing by the community					
The freedom to usually work without too much supervision					
The extent to which my skills and abilities are used					
Doing work that is of direct benefit to other people					
Having the chance sometimes to do different parts of my job in my own way					
The general interest of the work itself					
The help I get for my job from people working elsewhere in the hospital					
The general physical conditions and appearance of the ward					
The responsibility attached to my job					
The clinical facilities and equipment in the ward					
The non-clinical facilities and equipment in the ward					
The way my hours of work are arranged					
The way my work is generally organised					
The sense of achievement I get from my job					
The adequacy of the in-service training I have received					
The amount of consultation we get before decisions are made which affect us					
The feeling I have that patients really need me					
The help I generally get for my work from other staff on the ward					
The pay compared to other workers in the hospital					
The pay compared to other workers outside the hospital					

SOME RESULTS: NURSES' ATTITUDES AND BEHAVIOUR

No more than a few general comments can be offered on the very extensive and detailed data from this research programme, since our objective here is rather to present a model of how 'process' variables appear to operate when an organizational change occurs. This model has been drawn up after reflecting on the empirical data from both hospitals, particularly in the light of differences between them.

The overall situation in both units of psychogeriatric wards was broadly as follows. Nursing staff from Assistant to Senior Nursing Officer (managerial) levels expressed high general satisfaction with their jobs, coupled with a very wide range of specific sources of great dissatisfaction and frustration. They were strongly motivated, it appeared, by the total dependence of patients upon them - yet were prevented, they claimed, from spending enough time with their patients. They enjoyed their status as 'caring' people. But their best efforts to provide optimal, or even just-acceptable care, were constantly being undermined by inadequate resources, administrative incompetence, ineffective and 'distant' psychiatric medical control, and so on. This was the general impression emerging from interviews, questionnaires, and group discussions.

We encountered great difficulty, however, in trying to unravel this general pattern, which indeed was complicated by quite wide individual differences in expressed motivation and satisfaction. First, it didn't square at all closely with the corresponding behavioural data that we recorded from the same nurses in their wards; especially so in the first, urban, hospital. Secondly, but in this case only in the urban setting, it didn't square at all closely with their behaviour and attitudes after a number of experimental interventions had been introduced - with their agreement - specifically to remedy or remove the very sources of dissatisfaction which they had identified. Thirdly, there appeared in the early stages to be an uncomfortable incompatibility between the two principal objectives of our whole action research programme i.e. to assist the organization to improve patient care, and at the same time enable the staff to achieve higher motivation and satisfaction in their work.

This third problem could be interpreted as a kind of cognitive dissonance between the hospital management's desire for more self-supporting, independent, outcomes for patients (leading to quicker turnover and less long-stay patients), and the nursing staff's desire to maximise the satisfaction they get from having patients wholly dependent on them. This dissonance, of which staff appeared to be at least faintly aware, was accommodated by the useful mechanism of asserting that no changes in ward organization, therapeutic interventions, staff participation in control of material resources, or indeed virtually anything different at all, were possible in a hospital like theirs!

A fourth problem, common to both hospitals when we first studied them, was a disturbing lack of clearly perceived and agreed objectives appertaining to the social and psychological aspects of patient care. Without specific objectives of this kind to aim at, nurses felt under no pressure to behave in ways which would give as much priority to remedial and therapeutic, as to physical and custodial, care. Indeed it was only when in the rural hospital, we were able to devise ways of allowing nurses to perceive for themselves that there were weaknesses to be remedied, and realistic nursing objectives to set for themselves, that they stopped being resistant to change.

Three general *conclusions* from the research programme are apposite to the theoretical model of organizational behaviour which follows. First, a person's expressed view of his work motives and sources of job satisfaction, even though subjectively felt, may not square at all closely with his behaviour, even when opportunities for consistency are there. Secondly, individuals vary quite widely in their pattern of expressed 'wants' in a work situation, so that aggregated data may be unhelpful when applied to small groups. Thirdly, the most difficult practical issue to be faced by an organizational change agent is not the identification of objectives, behaviours, and organizational characteristics, which ought to be changed. Instead, it is an inherent resistance to change of any kind, because of the 'dynamic stability' which seems to be a key characteristic of work organizations.

In an earlier report we suggested a theoretical model to account for the motivated behaviour of individuals engaged in organised work activities (Wallis & Cope, 1977; Cope, 1981). Based on expectancy and equity theory, and incorporating the notion of discrepancy between job-related desires and perceived rewards as a motivating agency, this model also postulates a 'balance' mechanism which serves to minimize the extent of discrepancy. It is as though individuals set the level of their aspirations about what they want from their job, to an appraisal of what experience leads them to believe they can realistically expect. The relevance of this model of an individual's motivated work behaviour is that it leads, *inter alia*, to the prediction that for most people, and for most of the time, we should expect only a *small* discrepancy between what they hope to gain from working and what they perceive as their actual rewards. Hence they will show little inclination to work harder or differently, and will experience high levels of overall job satisfaction even though reporting specific items for complaint. This is just the outcome revealed in our hospital studies.

Now let us turn to the level of operation of the organization itself. At this level the behaviour of individuals has to be aggregated. The organization can be represented, as in the *static model* of Figure 2, as a stable system operating to optimize costs and benefits, inputs and outputs, objectives and outcomes. Just as the individual worker is usually in a state of dynamic equilibrium with respect to his own wants, performance, rewards, and satisfaction, so too is there normally a state of equilibrium between the organization and its constituent individual workers. The example of a Psychogeriatric Unit illustrates this state of affairs very well. The organization makes demands upon individual nurses, and groups of them, which are responded to in terms of matching performance. Arising from this aggregated performance (though not, unfortunately, always in direct relationship to it) the organization provides rewards which individuals perceive as more or less matching their balanced job-related wants. There is, as Schein (1965) has put it, an implicit psychological contract between individuals and the organization.

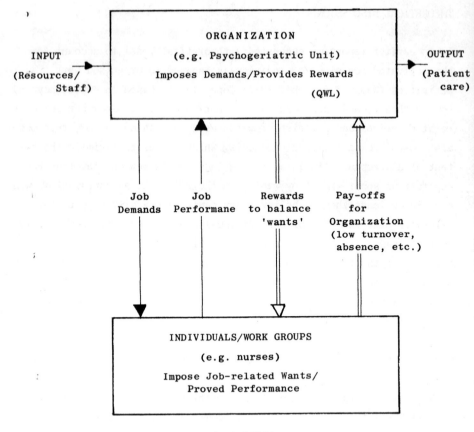

Figure 2. Model of organizational stability

If there is indeed a satisfactory economic relationship between organizational input and output - the latter being an admittedly difficult one to quantify in our example - then we may assume a period of stability in the organization. At such times the costs represented by pay-offs received by individuals are balanced by the organization's benefits, the latter in the shape of aggregate job performance. From the perspective of individuals, the demands imposed upon them are balanced by the pay and other perceived rewards which they get through performing adequately.

We now have another reinforcement of the circumstances encountered in our fieldwork i.e. that organizations are normally in a stable state of internal equilibrium from which it is difficult to shake them from within. Unless its Input (of material resources and staff) were to be substantially increased, it is difficult to see how our Psychogeriatric Unit could increase or improve its Output of patient care. Yet in times of financial and economic stringency like the present, organizational changes and development towards improvements and gains in output or productivity, are constantly being urged from *within* the organization's existing resources. How then can such organizational changes be induced in the face of natural forces encouraging stability at both individual and organizational levels?

To account for the relative success of organizational changes which were eventually established in the rural Welsh psychiatric hospital (Cope & Cox, 1980), as contrasted with the lack of success when analogous changes were introduced earlier in the urban hospital, we have devised a further, *dynamic model* of how the process of change may be initiated and sustained. Figure 3 illustrates it.

Let us suppose that the organization is, as hitherto, a Psychogeriatric Hospital Unit and the individuals staffing it are nurses. The normal state of affairs is shown as Level 1. It represents a dynamic equilibrium, like that shown in the Figure. The total *pay-offs* to the members of staff as individuals, and to the Unit as an organization, are perceived as being in trim. We hall argue that these pay-offs for individuals are the sum total of constituent elements (including pay, interesting work activities, good working conditions, and so forth) of what those individuals perceive as a satisfactory quality of working life (QWL). For the organization, the pay-off is conceived of as aggregated staff performance amounting to an acceptable output assessed in terms of patient care. The dynamic flavour of this 'normal' state is represented by the oscillating line around average performance at Level 1.

The model assumes that minor fluctuations in the average Level 1 performance occur, without leading on to a significant change, whenever (for example) small increases or decreases in organizational *demand* take place. Perhaps an additional patient above the usual ward capacity has to be temporarily cared for without a staff increment. Positive phases of these fluctuations reflect what are likely to be positive responses from the staff, in the form of more effort and

285

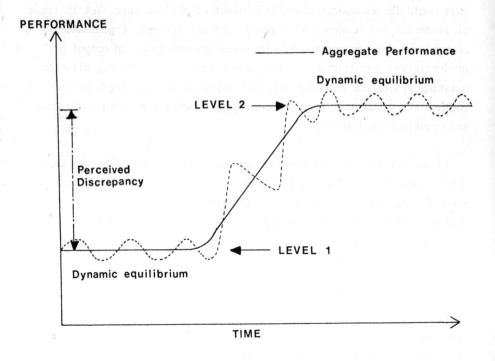

Figure 3. Dynamic model of organizational change

therefore higher 'output'. If this extra demand is quickly relaxed, or indeed if it is continued without a commensurate gain in perceived rewards, then performance will fall away again. However, if the staff as a whole should begin to let their performance slip below Level 1, without an acceptable reason, then before long some form of organizational sanction - withholding of certain rewards, privileges or benefits - is likely to be imposed. Provided such withheld rewards are indeed valued by the staff, the latter's lapse is likely soon to be made good again. All this can be represented as the normal state of dynamic equilibrium both for individuals and for the organization as a whole.

Now suppose that a significantly different level of performance -

Level 2, say - is urged upon the organization. Using the example of the Psychogeriatric Unit, we may envisage this new Level 2 to be a higher standard of patient care, which the hospital must achieve *not* by pumping in fresh resources (e.g. offering more pay), but through internal job re-design and organizational improvements, to be accompanied by some form of additional valued benefits for staff. How can the stability be broken, a change induced, and a new stable performance attained at Level 2?

The model requires that a strong and sustained perturbation upwards must occur. Just as a downward shift would follow if there were a sharp curtailment of rewards below the amount perceived by staff as an equitable return for Level 1 performance - so there must be a direct association between any sharp increase of organizational demand, and an increase of *perceived* benefits for staff as an adequate pay-off for their responding positively. Only if these *added*, valued, benefits go on rising, as rising demands are met, will a sustained change of performance up to a Level 2 eventually be achieved.

An important qualification, as we know from our later fieldwork, is that the initial 'positive' perturbation is most likely - perhaps only likely - to occur when both staff and management in the organization have themselves identified and conceded that Level 2 is a more desirable state than Level 1. In other words, they must all have become aware of a discrepancy between Levels 1 and 2 which is, by general agreement, both undesirable and capable of being reduced. This procedure is analogous to the vital 'unfreezing' process with Lewin (1947) argued so long ago was a prerequisite to organizational change. If there is a temporary, perhaps unintended, lag between the attainment of a breakaway from Level 1 and the anticipated rewards appropriate to it, there will be a temporary check in the rise of performance, or even a decline, until an equitable 'exchange' is perceived to have caught up. Eventually, as the model implies, a new state of dynamic equilibrium at Level 2 will be in force.

CONCLUSIONS

For the past two decades at least, studies of how workers react to
organizational change and development have provided a fertile growth
area for our subject. A respectable corpus of research-based knowledge
and practical experience is now available to us. However, apart from
some relatively recent exceptions (Boekholdt & Kanters, 1978; Wall &
Lischeron, 1977) nearly all our empirical data on work motivation,
job satisfaction, and organizational variables affecting performance
and attitudes have been gathered in industrial or commercial work
environments. Theories of organizational behaviour, and prescriptions
for effective organizational development, are firmly implanted in these
environments (e.g. Hackman & Oldham, 1975; Van Assen & Wester, 1980).

We should not assume too readily that such knowledge and experience
can be applied directly to an organization like a hospital. As 'caring'
institutions, hospitals are characterized by a quite different working
ethos from that encountered in productive industrial and marketing
companies. They exist to provide a public (sometimes also a private)
service, not a material product. To an economist, their 'widgets' are
intangible. The criterion of excellence or success for hospitals is the
quality of service they deliver to patients. Difficult though this
criterion may be to assess, it cannot sensibly be replaced by industrial
criteria like 'productivity' or 'output'. For although hospitals have
to be managed within prescribed financial limits, they are not usually
profit-making organizations.

The circumstances of employment and the characteristics of jobs
differ also. Security of employment is distinctly higher for most
hospital employees than for most industrial workers. Financial incentives
to improve output and performance play little, if any, part in the
health services. And whereas so much of industrial work has traditionally
been repetitive, short-cycle, and de-skilled, these are not the hall-
marks of nursing, medical, and other professional jobs in hospitals.
(Even though the work of Nursing Assistants is, by definition, sub-
professional and undemanding of sophisticated skills and knowledge, it
is at least varied in nature and implies a considerable degree of res-
onsibility for the welfare of patients.)

Despite the differences, there are no reasonable grounds for believing that the processes underlying organizational behaviour and organizational change in hospitals are fundamentally different from those operating in other organized work environments. It is hoped that the process models described here, of organizational stability and change respectively, may be shown by further empirical study in hospitals and elsewhere to have some generality and potential for further refinement. In the meantime, we would argue that our own research data suggest these contentions, implicit in the modeling:

1. Any work organization can be envisaged as a kind of 'mini-economy', even under conditions where financial incentives and the profit motive are virtually inadmissible. It operates normally in a state of dynamic equilibrium between counter-balancing forces of inputs and outputs, costs and benefits, effort and rewards, which are aggregated across the behaviours of individuals.

2. These normal relationships between motivating (or demand) characteristics and performance (or output) ones are stable and indeed difficult to disturb. Since this is the case for individual employees, it is equally so for the aggregated behaviour which we observe at an organizational level. If a disturbance - an 'improvement' or other change in organizational output - is required, then there are definite preconditions which have to be met before the change can take off and be sustained.

REFERENCES

Boekholdt, M.G. & H.W. Kanters, Team nursing in a general hospital: Theory, results and limitations. Journal of Occupational Psychology, 1978, 51, 4, 315-326.

Cope, D., Organizational development and action research in hospitals. Epping, Essex: Gower Press, 1981.

Cope, D. & S. Cox, Organizational development in a psychiatric hospital: creating desirable changes. Journal of Advanced Nursing, 1980, 5, 371-380.

Davis, L. & A.B. Cherns, The Quality of Working Life. 2 Vols. Glencoe, Ill.: Free Press, 1975.

Hackman, J.R. & G.R. Oldham, Development of the job diagnostic survey. Journal of Applied Psychology, 1975, 60, 159-170.

Lewin, K., Frontiers in group dynamics. Humand Relations, 1947, 1, 5-41.

Schein, E.H., Organizational Psychology. Englewood Cliffs: Prentice Hall, 1965.

Van Assen, A. & P. Wester, Designing meaningful jobs: A comparative analysis of organizational design practices. In: Duncan, K.D., M.M. Gruneberg & D. Wallis (Eds.), Changes in working Life. London: Wiley, 1980.

Wall, T.D. & J.A. Lischeron, Attitudes towards participation and satisfaction among nurses. In: Worker participation. A critique of the literature and some fresh evidence. London: McGraw-Hill, 1977.

Wallis, D. & D. Cope, Job satisfaction among professional workers: Discussion of a project, some theories, and a model. Occasional Paper No. 5, Department of Applied Psychology, UWIST, Cardiff, 1977.

Wallis, D. & D. Cope, Job satisfaction and organizational change in hospitals: Final Report on the Nursing Staff Project in Wales. UWIST, Cardiff and the Work Research Unit, London, 1980a.

Wallis, D. & D. Cope, Pay-off conditions for organizational change in the hospital service. In: Duncan, K.D., M.M. Gruneberg & D. Wallis (Eds.), Changes in working Life. London: Wiley, 1980b.

THE AUTHORS

C.A.J.M. Aarts is research assistent at Eindhoven University of Technology.
Address: Department of Industrial Engineering and Management Science,
Den Dolech 2, 5612 AZ Eindhoven, The Netherlands.

J.H.T.H. Andriessen is senior researcher at the Institute of Social
Research in Tilburg.
Address: Hogeschoollaan 225, 5037 GC Tilburg, The Netherlands.

A.M.L. van Bastelaer is senior statistician at the Dutch Central Bureau
of Statistics in Heerlen.
Address: P.O. Box 4481, 6401 CZ Heerlen, The Netherlands.

P.M. Bagchus is professor of social psychology of organizations at
Eindhoven University of Technology.
Address: Department of Industrial Engineering and Management Science,
Den Dolech 2, 5612 AZ Eindhoven, The Netherlands.

R. Claes is senior researcher at the State University of Ghent.
Address: Laboratory of Socio-psychology of Organizations, Louis
Pasteurlaan 2, 9000 Ghent, Belgium.

P. Coetsier is professor of applied psychology at the State University
of Ghent.
Address: Laboratory of Socio-psychology of Organizations, Louis
Pasteurlaan 2, 9000 Ghent, Belgium.

291

P.J.D. Drenth is professor of work and organizational psychology at
the Free University of Amsterdam.
Address: De Boelelaan 1081, 1081 HV Amsterdam, The Netherlands.

D. Flechsenberger is staff member at the Department of Business
Administration of the University of Wuppertal.
Address: Gausstrasse 20, 5600 Wuppertal-1, Federal Republic of
Germany.

H.-U. Hohner is research fellow at the Max Planck Institute for Human
Development and Education in Berlin.
Address: Lenteallee 94, 1000 Berlin 33.

L.A. ten Horn is senior staff member at the Department of Philosophy
and Social Sciences at Delft University of Technology.
Address: Kanaalweg 2b, 2628 EB Delft, The Netherlands.

H.-L. Horney is professor of industrial psychology at the Advanced Mining
School in Bochum.
Address: Hernerstrasse 45, 4630 Bochum 1, Federal Republic of
Germany.

A.M. Koopman-Iwema is senior staff member at the Department of Psychology at the Catholic University of Nijmegen.
Address: Montessorilaan 3, 6525 CG Nijmegen, The Netherlands.

R.N. van der Kooij is senior researcher at the Dutch Railway Company N.V.
Address: Postbox 2025, 3500 HA Utrecht, The Netherlands.

H. Kuipers is senior staff member at Eindhoven University of Technology.
Address: Department of Industrial Engineering and Management
Science, Den Dolech 2, 5612 AZ Eindhoven, The Netherlands.

L. Lagrou is professor of community psychology at the Catholic University
of Leuven.
Address: Psychological Institute, Tiensestraat 102, 3000 Leuven,
Belgium.

A.E. Leuftink is former director of the Regional Occupational Health
Service 'Oost-Gelderland' in Doetinchem.
Address: Gezellenlaan 12, 7005 AZ Doetinchem, The Netherlands.

A. Maasen is chef de service-adjoint at the Division of Social Affairs of the Société Générale de Banque.
Address: 3 Warandeberg, 1000 Bruxelles, Belgium.

F.H.G. Marcelissen is junior researcher at the Department of Psychology at the Catholic University of Nijmegen.
Address: Montessorilaan 3, 6525 CG Nijmegen, The Netherlands.

R. Nauta is senior staff member at the Department of Psychology at the State University of Groningen.
Address: Rode Weeshuisstraat 8, 9712 ET Groningen, The Netherlands.

J.B. Naylor is principal lecturer of business policy at the Department of Business Studies of Liverpool Polytechnic.
Address: 98 Mount Pleasant, Liverpool L3 5UZ, United Kingdom.

J. Praagman is staff member at Eindhoven University of Technology.
Address: Department of Industrial Engineering and Management Science, Den Dolech 2, 5612 AZ Eindhoven, The Netherlands.

J. van Rensbergen is staff member at the Center for Community Psychology at the Catholic University of Leuven.
Address: Psychological Institute, Tiensestraat 102, 3000 Leuven, Belgium.

R.A. Roe is professor of work and organizational psychology at Delft University of Technology.
Address: Department of Philosophy and Social Sciences, Kanaalweg 2b, 2628 EB Delft, The Netherlands.

A. Ruiz Quintanilla is senior researcher at the Institute for Psychology at the Technical University of Berlin.
Address: Dovestrasse 1, 1000 Berlin 10.

R. Selis is personnel director at Raychem N.V.
Address: Diestsesteenweg 692, 3200 Kessel-Lo, Belgium.

B. Senior is senior lecturer of industrial relations and organizational psychology at the Department of Business Studies of Liverpool Polytechnic.
Address: 98 Mount Pleasant, Liverpool L3 5UZ, United Kingdom.

S. Shimmin is professor of behaviour in organizations at the University of Lancaster.
Address: School of Management and Organization Sciences, Bailrigg, Lancaster LA1 4YX, United Kingdom.

D. Wallis is professor of applied psychology at the University of Wales' Institute of Science and Technology.
Address: Department of Applied Psychology, Llwyn-y Grant, Penylan, Cardiff, CF3 7UX, United Kingdom.

B. Wilpert is professor of psychology at the Technical University of Berlin.
Address: Institute for Psychology, Dovestrasse 1, 1000 Berlin 10.

J.A.M. Winnubst is senior staff member at the Department of Psychology at the Catholic University of Nijmegen.
Address: Montessorilaan 3, 6525 CG Nijmegen, The Netherlands.

H. de Witte is staff member at the Institute for Community Psychology át the Catholic University of Leuven.
Address: Psychological Institute, Tiensestraat 102, 3000 Leuven, Belgium.

Ch.J. de Wolff is professor of work and organizational psychology at the Catholic University of Nijmegen.
Address: Montessorilaan 3, 6525 CG Nijmegen, The Netherlands.